The Unruly Woman

Thomas Schatz, editor **Texas Film Studies Series**

The Unruly Woman

*Gender and the
Genres of Laughter*

BY KATHLEEN ROWE

 University of Texas Press, Austin

Copyright © 1995
by the University
of Texas Press

All rights reserved
Printed in the
United States of America
First edition, 1995

Requests for permission to reproduce material from this
work should be sent to Permissions, University of Texas
Press, Box 7819, Austin, TX 78713-7819.

ⓧ The paper used in this publication meets the minimum
requirements of American National Standard for Informa-
tion Sciences—Permanence of Paper for Printed Library
Materials, ANSI Z39.48-1984.

Library of Congress Cataloging-in-Publication Data

Rowe, Kathleen, date
    The unruly woman : gender and the genres of laughter /
Kathleen Rowe.
        p.   cm.—(Texas film studies series)
        Includes bibliographical references (p.   ) and
        index.
        ISBN 0-292-79072-4.—ISBN 0-292-77069-3 (pbk.)
        1. Women in motion pictures.   2. Feminism and mo-
tion pictures.   3. Comedy films—History and criticism.
4. Women in television.   5. Television comedies.   I. Title.
II. Series.
PN1995.9.W6R65   1995
791.43′652042—dc20   94-13656

To my parents, **Mary Devine Karlyn**
and **Al Karlyn**

ontents

cknowledgments

Grants from the University of Oregon Center for the Study of Women in Society supported my research for this book in its early stages and enabled me to present sections of it at Society for Cinema Studies conferences. Material from Chapter 2 appeared in "Roseanne: Unruly Woman as Domestic Goddess," *Screen* 31.4 (1990): 408–419. Material from other parts of the book also appears in "Comedy, Melodrama and Gender: Theorizing the Genres of Laughter" in *Classical Hollywood Comedy,* edited by Henry Jenkins and Kristine Karnick, Routledge, 1994; and "Masculinity and Melodrama in Post-Classical Romantic Comedy," in *Me Jane: Masculinity, Movies and Women,* edited by Pat Kirkham and Janet Thumim, Lawrence & Wishart, 1994.

Many teachers, friends, and others have generously and graciously contributed to this book.

I wish to thank Roseanne Arnold for the work she does in popular culture and for the opportunity to talk with her about it. I would also like to thank Annie Leibovitz, and Jeffrey Smith at Contact Press Images Inc., for the photograph that appears on the cover. This photograph originally appeared on the cover of the December 1990 (Vol. 53, No. 12) issue of *Vanity Fair*. Women Make Movies, Inc., provided me with copies of videotapes to study.

Frankie Westbrook at the University of Texas Press saw this project as a book from the outset, and on her retirement Betsy Williams took it to completion. Thomas Schatz has been a meticulous and superb editor. I would also like to thank Patricia Erens for her helpful suggestions. Thanks as well to Carolyn Cates Wylie, and especially to Mandy Woods for her careful editing.

Patricia Mellencamp and Dana Polan gave me timely encouragement. I am also grateful for the friendship and intellectual encouragement of Jacqueline Bobo, Chuck Kleinhans, Nanci LaVelle, Randall McGowen, Roy Metcalf, Tres Pyle, Bill Willingham, and Claudia Yukman. Bill Cadbury provided me with an inspiring introduction to film studies, and I thank him for his unstinting support. Thanks also to Linda Kintz, whose advice and good cheer have seen me through critical moments. Julia Lesage has contributed generously and significantly to my work from the beginning.

Most of all, I wish to thank Ellen Seiter. She first turned my attention to Roseanne Arnold, and her unerring instincts and advice, her commitment, and her warm affection have made all the difference. She has guided this book from its inception and left her imprint on every page.

My parents, Mary and Al Karlyn, have given sustenance of every kind. I thank them for teaching me the value of the comic perspective and, most of all, for their confidence and love. My daughters, Elizabeth, Miranda, and Helen, inspire and sustain me every day with their tender support and with the immense rewards of watching them grow into adulthood.

Finally, I thank George, who has been steadfast at my side in this as well as in every other endeavor I have cared the most about, for the better part of my life.

ntroduction
Feminist Film Theory
and the Question
of Laughter

*Isn't laughter the first form of liberation from a
secular oppression?* Isn't the phallic tantamount
to the seriousness of meaning? *Perhaps woman,
and the sexual relation, transcend it "first" in
laughter?*

—LUCE IRIGARAY
(*THIS SEX WHICH IS NOT ONE* 163)

*Perhaps women, white and of color, are upping the
ante, redirecting the terms of vision and spectacle
in stories and theories which dance on opposite
shores without the fatal end of patriarchy.*

—PATRICIA MELLENCAMP (*INDISCRETIONS:
AVANT-GARDE FILM, VIDEO & FEMINISM* 129)

Toward the end of the Dutch film *A Question
of Silence* (1982), directed by Marleen Gorris, a
group of women—three of them on trial for
murder—break into contagious, uncontrol-

lable laughter. Their laughter is explosive and irresistible. It breaks boundaries, filling the void left by their refusal to speak, or bear witness, in the language of their oppressors. It is both terrible and wonderful, expressing anger at the injustice and illogic of the law and forging a bond among women who up to that point shared nothing but their gender and their silence. When the women begin to laugh (and they are all "very ordinary, very normal," as one puzzled character describes them), they transform themselves into a spectacle that is incomprehensible and frightening to the men in the film. Their laughter, as they march out of the trial-turned-farce, hints at the collective power of women to shatter the symbolic authority of the patriarchy.[1]

A *Question of Silence*, part of an emerging canon of feminist films, tells the story of the brutal, spontaneous, and seemingly inexplicable murder of a male dress-shop owner by three women previously unknown to each other.[2] Its real drama, however, concerns Janine, the psychiatrist who is assigned to investigate the murder and who, as she doggedly pursues the "why" of the killing, awakens to a feminist consciousness. Janine's husband is a lawyer, and their marriage represents the symbolic union of the two discourses that seek to know and contain the women—psychology and the law. Neither is adequate to the task; the case slips beyond their boundaries. And although the systems underlying these discourses ultimately prevail over the lives of these women, their laughter—beginning with the old, fat, and raucous Ann, and finally sweeping into its embrace the cool and cerebral Janine—bears the seeds of revolution. The film's final shot shows a glimpse of utopia written on Janine's face, framed in a close-up, as she expectantly turns from her impatient husband to the unknown women on the steps of the courthouse. This turn suggests the power of their unspoken solidarity to transcend the symbolic order or language of patriarchy, which, like the graffiti framing them on the courthouse walls, continues to impinge on them.

While the laughing women are indeed very ordinary, they are also more than ordinary. Their crime, their silence, and finally their laughter color them with the demonic or the grotesque. In her essay "Female Grotesques: Carnival and Theory," Mary Russo observes a telling omission from Mikhail Bakhtin's discussion of a sculpture of senile, pregnant hags to explain his concept of the grotesque (219). "The old hags are laughing," Bakhtin notes (*Rabelais and His World* 24). Yet he does not ask why. Like the women in the courthouse, the laughing hags violate the age-old sanction women learn against "making a spectacle of themselves," usually by "inappropriate" exposure of their bodies in public places. What, Russo asks, is the meaning of their laughter? What does it have in common with the laughter in *A Question of Silence*, which, like the grotesque, contains both life and death, enacting the destruction that necessarily precedes the birth of a new order and creating the solidarity on which such an order must be built? I suspect that understanding this laughter—and the unruly women who have laughed in such ways, or have wanted to—might help loosen the bitter hold of those social and cultural structures that for centuries have attempted to repress it.[3]

Consider two other examples of female spectacle making, this time from contemporary U.S. culture:

• In numerous movies and appearances on television, the glamorous Muppet Miss Piggy preens coyly and coos in a throaty falsetto to her beau, Kermit the Frog, whom she overpowers with her size and affection. She also delivers devastating karate chops to anyone who gets in her way. Beloved by many, she is described on a national newscast after the death of her creator, Jim Henson, as "a study in self-centeredness."

• Roseanne Arnold, the 200-plus-pound star of the number one show on prime-time television, screeches the national anthem at a San Diego Padres baseball game, grabs her crotch, spits on the ground, then makes an obscene gesture to outraged fans booing from the stands. By the end of the day, the comedian, already notorious for her Rabelaisian persona and her angry, outspoken views, has been reprimanded by the President of the United States and has received threats on her life.

While these two examples may appear to have little in common with each other, or with the scene from *A Question of Silence*, a closer look suggests that they all share a kind of transgressiveness and ambivalence associated with the social and literary traditions of carnival, or what might be called the "genres of laughter."[4] Each shows women who make spectacles of themselves as vulnerable to ridicule and trivialization—but also as vaguely demonic or threatening. Arnold in particular, despite being made the object of derisive laughter, especially in the early years of her career, has conveyed a clear sense that comedy is not a framework that has been imposed on her, but a tone, a set of conventions, and a voice she has chosen for herself and, indeed, given a distinct inflection of her own. In her hands, laughter is a powerful means of self-definition and a weapon for feminist appropriation.

This book investigates the power of female grotesques and female laughter to challenge the social and symbolic systems that would keep women in their place. More often, the conventions of both popular culture and high art represent women as objects rather than subjects of laughter.

But because as women we cannot simply reject these conventions and invent new "untainted" ones in their place, we must learn the languages we inherit, with their inescapable contradictions, before transforming and redirecting them toward our own ends. *The Unruly Woman* takes a step in that direction by examining the conventions that govern gender and comedy—or rather, as I will later explain, the spectacle-making unruly woman and the comedic genres of laughter.

 Purity and Danger

If it is curious why Bakhtin never raised the question of laughter in relation to the grotesque hags, it is perhaps even more curious why feminism, until recently, has largely avoided it as well—especially feminist film theory, which has played a major role in opening up the connections between female subjectivity and spectacle. To judge from much influential scholarly work in two areas of study—comedy and the carnivalesque on the one hand, and feminist theory and criticism on the other—it would seem that women and the genres of laughter have had little to do with one another. While theorists such as Bakhtin and Northrop Frye have readily acknowledged the importance of sex to comedic forms, they have had little to say about gender. The same is true in film studies, where until recently major research on comedy has proceeded with minimal attention, if any, to feminist theory. At the same time, with a few important exceptions, feminists working in film, television, and cultural theory have been drawn more to melodrama than to comedy.[5] Before turning to comedy myself, I would like to consider some consequences of that neglect.

In the late 1980s, many feminist film theorists began to note an "ennui" that was "haunting" the project of feminist film criticism and arising from the unresolved issue of female spectatorship (Bergstrom and Doane 15).[6] This ennui, I believe, is tied to the long-standing hold of melodrama on the female imagination. For many women, the social contradictions of gender have been played out most compellingly in artistic forms centered on their victimization and tears rather than on their resistance and laughter: the domestic novel, the Gothic novel, the women's weepy film, the television soap opera, the made-for-TV movie. Founded on the bedrock of women's suffering, feminist film criticism has made powerful, if uneasy, use of a Lacanian-based psychoanalysis which, like melodrama, takes as its given women's identification with loss. Psychoanalysis, with its feminization of hysteria, derives in part from Western culture's fascination with the notion of "women and madness," and despite its many variations it constructs woman as castrated man, outside subjectivity, agency, and the symbolic. The Euro-American enthusiasm for psychoanalysis is, of course, not universally shared. Yet in the absence of a more persuasive account of subjectivity and desire, psychoanalysis has enabled feminists to explain the workings of the cinematic apparatus in objectifying the female body and denying the female spectator any gaze—any subjectivity or desire—of her own.

As a result, texts which might suggest an alternative view of female subjectivity have not received the scrutiny they might. I am referring in particular to those which position women as subjects of a laughter that expresses anger, resistance, solidarity, and joy—or those which show women using in disruptive, challenging ways the spectacle already invested in them as objects of a masculine gaze. The genres of laughter have long proven elusive and difficult to theorize in humanist and other forms of literary and cultural criticism. Yet that is no reason for feminists not to investigate these genres for what they might teach us, not only about the construction of gender within repressive social and symbolic structures, but also about how those structures might be changed. Such a project, I believe, wouldn't deny the attractions of melodrama but would examine melodrama in relation to other genres, such as comedy. Nor would it deny the insights of psychoanalysis, but would use them with an ever-vigilant awareness of their historical determination. Feminist film theory will not readily dispel the ennui that now troubles it without engaging itself as fully in women's laughter as it has in their tears, and without expanding its scope beyond the familiar terrain of melodrama and television soap opera to a wider range of cultural texts and the models of subjectivity they might suggest.

One such model derives from the notions of parody or masquerade. Using anthropologist Mary Douglas's apt terms, Mary Russo describes women's cultural politics as having traditionally included strategies of purity ("radical negation, silence, withdrawal, and invisibility") and danger ("feminine performance, imposture, and masquerade").[7] I would like to suggest that melodrama depicts strategies of purity, while comedy, with its exaggerations, hyperbole, and assault on the rational, depicts those of danger. *A Question of Silence* moves from one to the other, working its way from the melodrama of the "silence around Christine" (*De Stilte Rond Christina M.,* the film's Dutch title) into the comedic excess of laughter.

In the last pages of her study of the woman's film, *The Desire to Desire*, Mary Ann Doane makes a similar but more tentative move when she argues that the "tropes of femininity" which melodrama valorizes—the waiting, suffering, self-sacrifice—need to be made to appear "*fantastic, literally incredible*" (180).[8] This can happen, she suggests, through a kind of mimicry or masquerade, a parodic performance of the feminine that "makes visible" what is supposed to remain concealed: the artifice of femininity, the gap between an impossible role and the woman playing it. Although early work on masquerade viewed it within the context of psychoanalysis—as a disguise, lure, or other sign of women's lack—Doane argues that its assertion of a "radical distance between the woman and her 'own' fully feminized gestures" also points in other directions (*The Desire to Desire* 182).[9] Because this distance does not depend on an internal masculine standard, it circumvents the issue of fetishism that has dominated discussions of gendered spectatorship and implies a different model of subjectivity.

Doane, however, backs away from the implications of her argument. The time has come to move beyond melodrama toward fantasy as a site of "textual intervention," she writes, but while an obvious site of fantasy and masquerade is comedy, she hesitates to invoke laughter, seeing it structured, like spectatorship, at women's expense. Applying Freud's analysis of the dirty joke to a 1948 photograph by Robert Doisneau ("Un Regard Oblique"), she demonstrates in her essay "Film and Masquerade: Theorizing the Female Spectator" how the figure of a woman serves as both object of a male gaze and butt of a male joke.[10] Seen in this way, the cinematic apparatus and the joke share a parallel tripartite structure in which women can engage only through a masochistic identification with the female victim or a transvestite identification with the male agents. Doane asserts that any critical, feminist response can come only *after* an initial complicit one. Current feminism is under great pressure, she grants, "to find pleasure, the pressure to laugh, the pressure to not feel excluded from the textual field of a dominant mass culture" ("Masquerade Reconsidered" 52). Yet she warns that we must be wary of that pressure. For women, nonmasochistic, nontransvestite laughter apparently belongs only to the future.

While courageously confronting the myth of the humorless feminist and correctly urging caution about the risks of easy laughter, Doane is perhaps too cautious herself. Risks, in fact, are needed to move beyond the impasse she describes. One of those risks concerns those strategies of danger, including masquerade. Masquerade has much in common with irony as it has traditionally been understood in literary and film studies. However, while irony is often used to affirm the cultural superiority of those who "get it" over those who don't, masquerade creates a "bottom-up" distinction based on shared recognition within a subcultural group. As a form of self-representation, masquerade retains the distance necessary for critique, but a distance that is Brechtian and politicized, created by the subject between herself and various forms of representation available to her. Roseanne Arnold, for example, fashioned her Domestic Goddess persona out of clichés in U.S. culture about the fat, noisy, and vulgar working-class housewife in order to make those clichés both visible and positive. Because she so convincingly conveys her own control over that performance, it succeeds as masquerade.

Another strategy of danger, and one closely related to laughter, concerns anger. To deny women active participation in the mechanisms of the joke as well as in those of spectatorship is to replicate our culture's historical denial of women's anger as an available and legitimate response to the injustices they experience. As Tania Modleski suggests, a woman can simultaneously identify with the victim of a sexist joke and apprehend her victimization; she may "get" the joke and get angry (*The Women Who Knew Too Much* 27). Anger is what motivates the women in *A Question of Silence*; once they recognize that they have been set up as butts of what might be seen as a monstrous joke, they respond *not* with masochism or with transvestite identification with their oppressors, but with action, anger, and jokes of their own, and indeed it is anger which underlies the laughter that shakes the courthouse. This anger simply cannot be contained within the psychoanalytic framework the therapist Janine struggles to impose on it. As Modleski notes, anger remains the most unacceptable of emotions for women and is as yet largely unincorporated into feminist film theory.

Since Freud, few people question laughter's entanglements with aggression. Both spring from the unconscious, and both are, to varying degrees, taboo for women. The notion of "angry young women films" like the "angry young men" films popular in the 1950s and 1960s has itself been laughable, at least until *Thelma and Louise*, Ridley Scott's 1991 take on the buddy movie/road movie, shocked, moved, and polarized audiences on the issue of women's violence against men. Women's anger more often remains unspoken, as Julia Lesage writes, repressed beneath "all of women's depression—all our compulsive smiling, ego-tending, and sacrifice; all our psychosomatic illness, and all our passivity" ("Women's Rage" 421). Because women lack acceptable aesthetic or social structures through which to express or even "think" anger, it rarely erupts into the violence or transgressive laughter of *A Question of Silence* or *Thelma and Louise*. In melodrama and film noir, for example, women's anger appears as insanity or perversity, including grotesque images of lesbianism. Even art by women has rarely contained direct expressions of women's rage. What's needed are "self-conscious, collectively supported, and politically clear articulations of our anger and rage," in Lesage's words—articulations that cannot be made in the mode of "nice girls" ("Women's Rage" 420, 427). That is, women must be willing to offend and to be offensive, to look beyond the doomed suffering women of melodrama and the evil ones of film noir.

I would like to suggest that those structures for expressing women's anger do exist—in the genres of laughter, and, at least in rudimentary form, in the structure of narrative itself. The case for narrative as a means toward social transformation has been made by theorists as divergent as Fredric Jameson, Susan Suleiman, and Teresa de Lauretis, and many feminists have recently advocated a return to narrative after the skepticism of earlier years. In her 1985 essay "Changes: Thoughts on Myth, Narrative and Historical Experience," Laura Mulvey revises the position she held in her most influential essay "Visual Pleasure and Narrative Cinema" (1975), shifting her emphasis *from* visual pleasure, and the structures of vision that are the focus of Doane's work, to narrative form.

As Mulvey suggests, narrative's potential lies not in the static resolution of conflict with which it invariably ends, but in the upheaval and change before that resolution, where binary oppositions dissolve into process and events are linked in time. Here narrative gives representation to the struggle for change and to collective but unspoken conflicts with the rule of law. In such moments, narrative represents a state which anthropologist Victor Turner has described as "liminal," or associated with transitions, margins, and thresholds: "For every major social formation," he writes, "there is a dominant mode of public liminality, the subjunctive space/time that is the counterstroke to its pragmatic indicative texture" (34–35). In other words, all societies carve out spaces or times that exist on the edge of normal activities and that are marked by contradiction and ambiguity. Often dramatic or performative, they allow a society to comment on itself through experimentation and play. Liminality is never a permanent state but exists in relation to dominant or "indicative" time. While the Oedipal paradigm posits a similar period of instability and transformative potential in the subject's passage through the Oedipal complex, the concept of liminality reaches more effectively into the social as well.[11] Thus it has much in common with Bakhtin's notion of the carnivalesque.

 "The Laugh of the Medusa"

All narrative forms contain the potential to represent transformation and change, but it is the genres of laughter that most fully employ the motifs of liminality. From romance to satire to the grotesque, these genres are built on transgression and inversion, disguise and masquerade, sexual reversals, the deflation of ideals, and the leveling of hierarchies. It is to these motifs, which are also the motifs of the carnivalesque, that B. Ruby Rich refers when she advocates the feminist potential of the "Medusan film," a type of film about sexuality and humor.[12] She argues that comedy should not be overlooked as a weapon of great political power, which women should cultivate for "its revolutionary potential as a deflator of the patriarchal order and an extraordinary leveler and reinventor of dramatic structure" (353).[13]

The name "Medusan" is borrowed from Hélène Cixous's "The Laugh of the Medusa," an essay that might well have inspired *A Question of Silence*. Medusa, of course, is a mythological woman whose story bears important implications for theories of sexuality, spectacle, and cinema. When Medusa boasted of her beauty to Athena, Athena became jealous and changed Medusa and her sisters into monsters with fangs for teeth, snakes for hair, and staring eyes that could transform people into stone. Perseus killed her by looking at her reflection in his mirrorlike shield and then beheading her. The blood from her left side was fatally poisonous, and that from her right could restore life to the dead. Medusa remains an evocative symbol in contemporary culture, appearing, for instance, as an evil woman who threatens an androgynous male hero and the furry creatures who follow him in *Captain E-O*, a Michael Jackson video shown in the early 1990s in Disneyland.[14] One could say that among the many things Medusa embodies is extreme ambivalence toward women—toward their bodies, their beauty, their celebration of self, and their blood.

Whereas for Freud, Medusa incarnates male fears of castration, Cixous uses her to mock those theories built on such notions of female lack. In the most widely quoted passage from the essay, she writes that what Perseus averted his eyes from was not a deadly monster but a woman without the deformities "male" theories attempt to inflict on her: "You have only to look at the Medusa straight on to see her. And she is not deadly. She's beautiful and she's laughing" (255). While underscoring yet another failure, like that of Bakhtin, to "hear" women's laughter, this rewriting of Medusa's story exemplifies the kind of creative destruction Bakhtin associates with the grotesque. Cixous describes her own work as seeking "to break up, to destroy; and to foresee the unforeseeable, to project" (245). Given only an "arid millennial ground to break," an apocalyptic annihilation of the Law—of all that classifies, divides, names—must occur to clear the space for female writing, female bodies, and female desire, and that destruction is released, as in *A Question of Silence*, through a violent but productive laughter: "Now, I-woman am going to blow up the Law . . . to break up the 'truth' with laughter" (257, 258). Cixous has been criticized, and rightly, for her essentialism. However, her essay, like *A Question of Silence*, can still be appreciated for its rhetorical and poetic power.

Feminist film theory has yet to pursue fully the implications of Medusa's power both to draw Perseus's gaze as spectacle and to fix her own gaze, her "staring eyes," on him.[15] By using her power to draw his gaze, she can halt his quest for his Oedipal patrimony, robbing him, in fact, of his own eyes. From Cixous's perspective, that power becomes deadly only because of Perseus's refusal to meet her gaze. A more courageous meeting of her gaze would allow Perseus to apprehend not petrifying monstrosity but beauty: "You have only to look at the Medusa straight on . . ." As long as men avert their eyes from her, fearing the sight of her *and* her gaze, "woman" can be only a phantasm of castration for them, deadly and grotesque. And more important, as long as women do not look at *each other* straight on, they can see only distorted reflections of themselves.

Medusa creates a spectacle of herself with unruly laughter when she turns her gaze from her image reflected in Perseus's shield to Perseus himself, the Other, with his averted eyes. She laughs like the women in *A Question of Silence* and like another dead woman, Rebecca in Alfred Hitchcock's 1940 film *Rebecca,* who, as Mrs. Danvers reports, "used to rock with laughter at the lot of them"—at men. I am not arguing that the sight which inspires Medusa's laughter, or Rebecca's, somehow escapes determination by the material conditions of their gaze, or that any unmediated vision is possible. What I am suggesting is that for now we might turn from the images of dead women that indeed dominate cinema and listen to this laughter for what it tells us about women's power to look and to know.

Medusa, like Bakhtin's grinning pregnant hags, contains some of the earliest outlines of the unruly woman, an ambivalent figure of female outrageousness and transgression with roots in the narrative forms of comedy and the social practices of carnival. The unruly woman represents a special kind of excess differing from that of the femme fatale (the daughters of Eve and Helen) or the madonna (the daughters of Mary), whose laughter, if it ever occurred, no longer rings in the myths still circulating around them. Like Medusa, the unruly woman laughs. Like Roseanne Arnold, she is not a "nice girl." She *is* willing to offend and be offensive. As with the heroines of the romantic film comedy, from Ellie in *It Happened One Night* (1934) to Loretta in *Moonstruck* (1987), her sexuality is neither evil and uncontrollable like that of the femme fatale, nor sanctified and denied like that of the virgin/madonna. Associated with both beauty and monstrosity, the unruly woman dwells close to the grotesque. But while mythology taints and dooms Medusa, the unruly woman often enjoys a reprieve from those fates that so often seem inevitable to women under patriarchy, because her home is comedy and the carnivalesque, the realm of inversion and fantasy where, for a time at least, the ordinary world can be stood on its head.

As I will argue in this book, the figure of the unruly woman contains much potential for feminist appropriation, for rethinking how women are constructed as gendered subjects in the language of spectacle and the visual. The parodic excesses of the unruly woman and the comedic conventions surrounding her provide a space to "act out" the "dilemmas of femininity," in Mary Russo's words (225), to make not only "fantastic" and "incredible" but also laughable those tropes of femininity valorized by melodrama. Russo asks in what sense women can produce and make spectacles of themselves *for* themselves. The unruly woman points to new ways of thinking about visibility as power. Masquerade concerns itself not only with a woman's ability to look, after all, but also with her ability to affect the terms on which she is seen.

Such a sense of spectacle differs from the one that shaped early feminist film theory. Granting that visual pleasure and power are inextricably bound, this position would see that relation as more historically determined, its terms as more mutable. It would argue that visual power flows in multiple directions and that the position of spectacle isn't necessarily one of weakness. Because public power is predicated largely on visibility, men have long understood the need to secure their power not only by looking but by being seen, or rather, by fashioning—as subject, as author, as artist—a spectacle of themselves. How might women use spectacle to disrupt that power and lay claim to their own?

The connection between spectacle making and power was clear in Hellenic Greece, where men played out their existence in a public sphere sharply demarcated from the invisible private sphere, in which women and slaves tended to the body. It was understood in early Christian culture which worshipped God through "graven images" and spectacular cathedrals. In Renaissance England, Elizabeth I consciously manipulated her image to consolidate her power; and throughout the courts of Europe, the upper-class body was celebrated by adorning it with sumptuous clothing. Yet as capitalism tightened the structure of the patriarchal family, Protestantism and the Enlightenment fostered a turn from the pleasure of the image toward visual austerity and utilitarianism. The sartorial flamboyance men shared with women through the eighteenth century became increasingly restricted to women. Women retained their attachment to spectacle, but a spectacle exiled to the private sphere and severed from the exercise of official power. One could argue, following Michel Foucault, that as power has become more dispersed, the need to display it has diminished; however, in a postmodern culture of the image and the simulacra, power also lies in possession and control *of* the visible.

I want to suggest that women might begin to reweave the web of visual power that already binds them by taking the unruly woman as a model— woman as rule-breaker, joke-maker, and public, bodily spectacle. Such a move would be similar to what de Lauretis advocates when she calls for the strategic use of narrative to "construct other forms of coherence, to shift the terms of representation, to produce the conditions of representability of another—and gendered—social subject" (*Technologies of Gender* 109). Mary Russo notes that the category of the grotesque is often projected on the female body when it makes a spectacle of itself through pregnancy, age, or other violations of proper feminine bodily containment. She asks how this category might be used "affirmatively to destabilize the idealizations of female beauty or to realign the mechanisms of desire" (221). In acts of spectatorial unruliness, I believe, we might examine models of *returning* the male gaze, exposing and making a spectacle of the gazer, claiming the pleasure and power of making spectacles of ourselves, and beginning to negate our own invisibility in the public sphere.

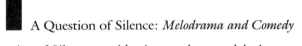 A Question of Silence: *Melodrama and Comedy*

In many ways, *A Question of Silence* provides just such a model. An example of the twofold project Cixous describes as her own ("to break up, to destroy; and to foresee the unforeseeable, to project"), the film sets out both to demolish the logical underpinnings of an "arid millennial ground" and to outline, however tentatively, the possibility for a new and more fertile one. In doing so, it depicts the conflict between the law—the monumentally repressive force at the heart of narrative conflict—and the women's desire that opposes it. The only outcomes of that desire the film allows are a life-draining repression of feelings or a violent release of them, and the women move from silent suffering to violence and finally to a laughter that momentarily transcends both.

Partly because the representation of women's anger is so rare, the film resists easy categorization by genre. Within the film itself, the therapist Janine wrestles with a similar puzzle: In what "genre" can she place the story of the three women? What traditional narrative makes sense of their behavior? Although the film can be read as a mystery, a courtroom drama, a thriller, or a reverse slasher movie, no conventional interpretive strategy quite works. The film's formal elements, including its absence of point-of-view shots, heighten this ambiguity by preventing the kind of spectator engagement classical Hollywood cinema fosters. Melodrama is the most familiar of genres for many women, and the first drafts of advertising posters presented to a women's group distributing the film in Britain emphasized the themes of victimization, imprisonment, and violence. The group—appropriately, I believe—rejected these drafts in favor of an image based on the women's laughter at the film's end.[16]

A *Question of Silence* clearly operates in the realm of fantasy Doane calls for, yet unlike works based on similar transgressive material, such as Cecelia Condit's *Possibly in Michigan* (an experimental video made in 1983 about female revenge, murder, and cannibalism), it avoids the appearance of fantasy or surrealism.[17] This strategy forces its viewers into the more difficult position of dealing with the pivotal event of the film, the murder of the shopkeeper, in the context of realism, as the representation of an actual event. Rather than seeing that event as the mystery it initially poses for Janine, however, the murder is better understood as a narrative device to divide the audience along gender lines, much as Brecht wished to do in terms of class. By doing so, the film raises crucial issues about the differing epistemologies of subcultural groups and dominant cultures.

From a perspective uninformed by or hostile to feminism, *A Question of Silence* might well appear a ludicrous and poorly done fable, a melodramatic depiction of the villainies of patriarchy. This perspective is represented in the film by the relatives, friends, and disciplinary institutions that surround its central female characters—above all by the discourses of the law and medicine that interrogate and process their lives. Confronted with the women's violence, the court first attempts to find an explanation within its own logic, but as the film unfolds, the women's epistemology—their own logic—proves beyond the court's grasp. Both law and medicine conspire here to explain away their behavior as pathological and outside reason. The label of "insanity" denies the women even a criminal's capacity for agency, guilt, and moral responsibility and attempts to reduce the dimension of their story from tragedy to melodrama, a typical strategy for narrating the events of women's lives and one to which I will return in Chapter 3. In the eyes of the court, the women are deranged fools, not heroic transgressors against an incomprehensible moral order like the various romantic male criminals of literature and film, from Raskolnikov in Dostoevski's *Crime and Punishment* to Meursault in Camus's *The Stranger* to the heroes of any number of gangster and outlaw films.[18]

A Question of Silence has also been interpreted as a feminist counter to the slasher movies and porn flicks that play on male fantasies of brutalizing and mutilating women's bodies. But here Medusa seizes Perseus's shield and sword, carves him up, and throws her image of him back at him in the form of the film itself. No wonder many men don't like it. Documented in vignettes from the women's lives, the women's anger encompasses lifetimes of repressed and generalized frustration and rage. Andrea's denial that she felt angry when she killed the shopkeeper does not negate her long-simmering rage. Instead it removes the possibility of dismissing her violence as an act of passion rather than a coolly committed execution of feminist justice. Some critics have argued that the film's depiction of revenge does not offer "sadistic pleasure" to female viewers (for instance, Murphy 105), but I am not so sure. It is important to remember that expressions of women's anger are disturbing to women and men alike because they challenge an ideology of heterosexuality that identifies sadism with men and masochism with women. Films such as *A Question of Silence* are powerful precisely because they address female spectators in ways that disrupt those norms and offer pleasures normally denied to women. Indeed, much of the controversy about *Thelma and Louise* arose from the film's juxtaposition of femininity and violence and from the apparent incongruity of seeing women "acting like men."

For my purposes, *A Question of Silence* is most interesting in its transformation of the raw material of melodrama into a feminist comedy of sorts, and in its use of female unruliness and the grotesque in a narrative about "very ordinary, very normal" women. As this book will eventually argue, melodrama and comedy—in particular, romantic comedy—are linked by common ideologies that limit the plots available for narrative representations of female desire, and the proximity of these forms offers much fruitful ground for feminist cultural production. In *A Question of Silence*, the comedy that emerges is certainly not a traditional one. It neither produces laughter through conventional sight gags and verbal jokes nor replicates the "boy meets girl" structure of romantic comedy. However, it does follow the movement "from law to liberty" that Northrop Frye identifies as fundamental to the genre. What distinguishes *A Question of Silence* from traditional comedy is that its critique of law and definition of liberty are made from the perspective of an uncompromising—and, in fact, radical—feminism, and that its passage from law to liberty turns on the recognition of a single, unspoken joke.[19]

Eventually the film's absence of pathos, starkness of moral polarities, and flatness of style move it from melodrama to the didacticism of allegory, but melodrama is where it begins, with its ominous opening chords, its setting in intimate domestic space, and its overriding concern with women's suffering and desire. In its opening scene, the film establishes the conflict between that desire and an oppressive order built around masculine power when Janine's husband is too immersed in his books to respond to his wife's sexual advances. She playfully wields her pen—an instrument of language and law—as a play-knife or weapon against their most visible representative, her lawyer husband. The scene shows how close the gestures of violence and heterosexual love are when later the women slash the shopkeeper in a similar neck-to-groin movement and when Janine eventually withdraws from sexual intimacy with her husband as she discovers the psychic violence he inflicts on her.

The first part of the film is an exploration of silence, a strategy of purity. Initially—when Christine sinks into catatonia because of her isolation in the home, and when Andrea's words in the business meeting are, in effect, stolen from her—silence does not represent a choice for the women in the film. After the murder of the shopkeeper, however, they take up silence on their own terms as a brilliant gesture of revolt, a refusal of patriarchal language and the silence it imposes on them. Christine's refusal to speak galvanizes the women's anger and is repeated by the silence of the women who witness the murder but don't report it. Yet even such radical silence is ultimately a negation, and so the second half of the film belongs to "danger" and to sound—the sound not of spoken language but of laughter, which Janine elicits repeatedly with her questions and which she replays again and again on her tape recorder.[20] From the beginning, the film explores various ways men and women use laughter. When Ann's male customers insult her with crude jokes and she refuses to laugh, they ask her, not unexpectedly, if she's lost her sense of humor. For these men, laughter is a means of asserting what they consider their rightful dominance. Conspicuously absent from this scene, women's laughter is heard throughout the rest of the film—Andrea's laughter of disdain at the man she picks up and has sex with; giggles when the women are introduced to each other; ironic laughter when Andrea tells her own story; and Ann's manic laughter throughout.

Janine cannot join in that laughter, however, because she simply does not see the incongruities, or understand the frustrations, that provoke it. As a professional woman, she has a different, and more privileged, relation to patriarchal power than do the working-class women on trial.[21] Class compounds the indignities they suffer and so they understand their oppression intuitively and can communicate it, as they did in the boutique, instantly and wordlessly. Janine, on the other hand, has gained the most and suffered the least under patriarchy. The men in her social and professional circles have literally too much "class" to heckle her as Ann's customers do, or to patronize her with the blind arrogance of Andrea's boss. Bourgeois men have the luxury of concealing their sexism until their privilege really *is* threatened—as, for example, when Janine's refusal to play by the rules threatens to draw unfavorable attention to her and cost her husband clients. Again and again, the film contrasts her appearance of sophistication with her naiveté about women's oppression. Her frustration that she cannot understand the women shows itself in her increased tension as the film progresses. As she begins to understand what is so obvious to the other women, she moves toward a feminist consciousness, but one that is initially liberal—accommodating, adapting to, and working within the system.[22] To protect her own investment in that system, she hangs on to her faith that her position and credentials will enable her to make a difference in the outcome of the trial.

While Christine touches Janine's heart, it is Andrea, the secretary, who is most like her in social class and intellectual skills and who guides her through her re-education. A first turning point in that process occurs in a sexually charged scene between the two women toward the end of the film. The scene ties the massive shift about to take place in Janine's consciousness with a potential realignment of her sexual desire around women, suggesting lesbianism as an alternative to heterosexuality. Their encounter is interrupted and its potential unexplored, however, and finally it isn't erotic love among women that topples the conceptual edifices of patriarchy but something more abstract—the women's recognition of the hopeless clash between two epistemologies, their awareness that while they understand men's thinking, men cannot begin to understand theirs.

They express that recognition in the film's second major turning point, the explosion of laughter that carries them out of the courthouse and into an implicit politics of a radical, separatist feminism. This laughter not only comments on the depth and absurdity of the women's oppression, but it binds them together. Once Janine recognizes that no compromise is possible, the tension on her face gives way to a smile and at last she joins in their laughter. The film finally suggests that understanding patriarchy means understanding a monumental joke. Janine's education is complete when she finally "gets" it. This joke has perplexed Janine throughout the film and caused her to listen repeatedly to the sounds of Ann's raucous laughter on the tape. For while Andrea laughs often and cynically, it is Ann whose laughter most insistently troubles her. Three times she replays

Ann's hysterical response to the question of whether she misses a man or wants to remarry. "You gotta be kidding!" Ann shrieks.

Of all the women in the film, Ann is the one most strongly coded with unruliness. Her excessive body, speech, and behavior are signs of danger rather than purity. Unlike Janine's body, which is static, slender, and self-contained, Ann's body calls to mind Bakhtin's senile pregnant hags and the disruptive potential of the grotesque. Coarse in appearance and manner, her body bears the signs of change, age, fluid boundaries. She makes a spectacle of herself because she is loud and "talks too much," as Janine says. She's fat and celebrates the murder with the festive activities of drinking and feasting. When we see a memory of her surrounded by her family, her own grotesqueness becomes heightened by theirs. She is the oldest of the three women on trial, unable to leave her job because, as she says, no one wants to hire an old woman. Her age gives her not only the perspective to laugh but also the freedom to do so. Ann is the first to laugh at the end of the film, and she is followed by an even older woman, then by a black woman. Farthest from the center of patriarchal power, and most vulnerable in their marginality to its punitive powers, these women are also closest to the license of the unruly. They drop without hesitation the "divine composure" of femininity which our culture expects of "well-adjusted, normal women" (Cixous 246) like Janine. In their laughter, they reveal that composure to be a mask.

A Question of Silence challenges Doane's analysis of the joke, for here, while the structure of the joke remains the same, the positions occupied by the men and women within it shift. Women both initiate the joke and complete it with their laughter. At first, it is clear that the trial is set up to maintain the court's power by presenting the women as passive spectacles, specimens, deviations from the norm. Men call the women a "battalion of high-heeled boots"; women "like them," they insist, can be recognized "a mile away." But the women turn the tables on the men. The men, squirming and outraged, become the objects of a gaze that reduces them to fools, victims of a laughter they cannot comprehend. First, the women redefine the terms of the spectacle they represent in the courtroom; rather than remaining passive objects of male scrutiny, they actively redefine themselves through their laughter as spectacle-for-themselves, invading the space of the courtroom and overturning its decorum. Moreover, they aggressively use the power of their own gaze not only to reverse the performer/audience relations in the courtroom but to put the dynamics of a feminist joke into motion. By turning their gaze onto the men, they make them, the law, and patriarchy itself the objects of their derisive laughter, the butts of a joke that exposes the fact that the emperor has no clothes. Norman Holland describes laughter as a disguise—or a masquerade, if you will—that makes those who share it aware of mutual, and often forbidden, identifications (84). When the women in *A Question of Silence* laugh, they confirm their common epistemology, a shared understanding of the rage that led to murder and silence. By turning their gaze on each other, the women continue the wordless communication that occurred most notably in the earlier scene in the boutique. Through a relay of glances, they establish the essential connection between joke-maker and laugher that completes the circuit of the joke.

The real test of this feminist joke, and of the film itself, comes with the attempts to extend that circuit from screen to spectator, to draw us into its dynamics, to maneuver us into a position where, like Janine, we must respond. If we laugh, the joke, and the film, have succeeded. For many, of course, they have not, and I don't wish to argue that the line distinguishing those who laugh from those who don't is entirely determined by gender. While the film gives no examples of laughing men, Janine stands out as an example of the woman for whom such laughter is hard-won. Critics have noted the heated discussions that often follow screenings of the film and the hostility male reviewers have almost universally expressed toward it. In part, their anger may be the result of the film's lack of compromise, its denial of the possibility of change within existing social systems.

Like radical feminism itself, *A Question of Silence* is limited by its inability to imagine how differences—not only between men and women, but among women—can be negotiated apart from language or the symbolic. The film indeed sketches out a range of differences among women, differences of age, class, race, and sexual orientation. Yet ultimately these differences *are* only sketched out, not fully articulated. For example, the black woman's story, unlike those of the three white defendants and Janine, remains untold. By addressing itself primarily to the professional white woman like Janine, *A Question of Silence* illustrates some of the limitations of radical feminism, which likewise has been charged with a failure to move beyond its rhetorically powerful analyses of "woman" toward more nuanced accounts of the circumstances and desires of "women," to borrow de Lauretis's suggestive distinction. Are silence and laughter, the only alternatives the film really explores, adequate to the task it sets for them?

I believe that the anger that some men feel at the film, whatever its cause, shares something with the anger that women feel at certain jokes directed at them. It is another example of the kind of reaction that Modleski, in *The Women Who Knew Too Much*, attributes to female victims of sexist jokes: they get the joke to the extent that they know it's on them, and at the same time they get angry. In both cases the object of the joke finds laughter difficult or impossible. The important difference is the shock that may occur when women assume the position of joke-maker. When men make jokes about women, they assert their already-existing social power over them. When women make jokes about men, they invert—momentarily—the social hierarchy.

In the chapters that follow, I consider how the figure of the unruly woman—too fat, too funny, too noisy, too old, too rebellious—unsettles social hierarchies. As I will show, the unruly woman crosses the boundaries of a variety of social practices and aesthetic forms, appearing most vividly in the genres of laughter, or those that share common structures of liminality and inversion. Rather than attempting to redefine these genres, so often neglected and discounted in our culture, I will consider what we might learn from them about female resistance—and pleasure—and about how they might help lay the groundwork for the production of more emancipatory feminist theories.

While I use examples from other historical periods and areas of popular culture, my emphasis is on contemporary U.S. media, primarily Hollywood film and television. This emphasis has imposed certain limitations on my study. The prejudices that have made Roseanne Arnold such a deviation from the norm on prime-time TV have even more forcefully excluded other, potentially more disruptive, women's voices from mainstream media—those of the lesbian, the mestiza, and other "border people" who test not only the boundaries of gender and class, like Arnold, but those of race, sexual orientation, and other forms of difference as well. For example, romantic comedy—as this book will show—has provided one of the few outlets for representations of female unruliness in Hollywood film. But while the genre has used its focus on the heterosexual couple to explore differences of gender and class, it has avoided those of race almost altogether, because of deep-rooted taboos on miscegenation. Similarly, while lesbians working in independent film and video are making inspired and often hilarious use of comedy to critique the institution of heterosexuality, these critiques have rarely found their way, as yet, into mainstream channels of distribution.

This book has two sections, "Part One: The Unruly Woman" and "Part Two: Female Unruliness in Narrative Cinema." Narrative necessarily and notoriously constrains representations of female desire, and its effect on the image of the unruly woman is no exception, so I begin this book by taking a semiotic approach to female unruliness. By identifying signifiers of unruliness from the social and literary traditions of the carnivalesque, I create a sharper picture of the unruly woman than that which might emerge from a narrower focus on narrative form. More important, this section grounds the second part of the book in a theoretical framework that emphasizes the social meanings of comedic practices and forms.

Part One, then, identifies certain characteristics—among them, fatness, rebelliousness, a sharp tongue, and an association with pigs—that have come to be associated with comedic forms of female transgression. I make no claim for exhaustiveness in the examples I use throughout this book, but instead have chosen those that strike me as most provocative. While I draw several of these from early modern Europe, a historical period that bears considerable relevance to studies of the carnivalesque, I reserve my most extended analysis for two examples from contemporary U.S. culture: Miss Piggy and Roseanne Arnold. In doing so, I make no claims that these recent examples are tied by historical causality to the earlier ones but instead suggest a more subtle relation of intertextuality.[23] This claim is particularly appropriate to the genres of laughter, which have long been recognized as highly conventionalized, built out of enduring character types, gags, and plot devices. By applying the insights of feminism to these traditions, I hope to carve out of them a convention, or set of conventions, that has previously been overlooked.

Part Two moves from carnival to comedy, and from television and the tabloids to film, for while both Miss Piggy and Arnold appear in narrative films, their impact arises primarily from the circulation of their images in a range of other media, from trademarked Muppet toys in Miss Piggy's case to TV talk show appearances in Arnold's. Thus, Part Two begins with a discussion of narrative and the options it provides for representing female unruliness. Narrative film, I argue, confines the unruly woman primarily to the genres of melodrama and romantic comedy, which are closely related but which take the "problem" of female desire to significantly different ends. The remainder of the book tracks the interplay in Hollywood cinema between the figure of the unruly woman and the genre of romantic comedy, from the screwball comedy of the 1930s to the postclassical comedy of the present. I conclude by returning briefly to Arnold's career in an afterword that considers the implications of recent changes in her image, following her identification of herself as an incest survivor and her efforts to reshape her body through diet and cosmetic surgery.

Throughout, I attempt to keep in mind the contradictions and ambivalences of these comedic forms—how they play on our desire to laugh when we shouldn't and to keep faith when we have little reason to. To see these forms only in terms of the ideological work they do, however, is to overlook the more utopian and transformative impulses also within them and the opportunities they provide for imagining a social world in which laughter occurs less often to "break apart," as Cixous describes, than to bring together.

Part The Unruly Woman

Pig Ladies, Big Ladies, and Ladies with Big Mouths
Feminism and the Carnivalesque

Perhaps the image of carnival can be used to move out of the immediate issues at stake here, the problem of the politics of the Oedipus complex, its relation to women, language and the symbolic order, to extend the argument to the problem of the politics of myth, its relation to change, language and historical experience.

—LAURA MULVEY ("CHANGES" 168)

And if an ill-informed bookseller attempted to convince me to substitute for it [Miss Piggy's Guide to Life] *some flossy novel about sad people in big houses by a woman with three names, I would reject it politely but without hesitation. "Take back your flossy novel about sad people in big houses by a woman with three names," I would insist, indicating with a quick movement of my hand in what contempt I held such trash. And then, helping him from the floor, I would ask him in the nicest pos-*

In a 1,000-piece jigsaw puzzle of Jim Henson's Muppets, Miss Piggy's face, coquettishly tilted to one side, beams out from a group of close to twenty of the puppets. She stands behind her beloved frog Kermit who, as hero of the Muppets, occupies front row center and whose sympathetic presence sets the tone of their adventures. Yet Miss Piggy rises a full head above him to the visual center of the puzzle. This dominance over the apparent leader of the Muppets is central to Miss Piggy's persona. It is also central to a larger tradition of female unruliness—that of the woman on top—which resonates in her image.

As a group, Henson's puppets encompass a range of human and animal characteristics.[1] Some, such as the old men Statler and Waldorf, are clearly human. Others, such as Kermit the Frog, Miss Piggy, and, of course, Animal, are clearly animal. However, the distinction between animal and human blurs in a sea of fuzzy textures, bright fabrics, and similar voices (spoken primarily by a handful of men). In fact, it seems irrelevant in the whimsical vision of their creator, who endowed his creatures with qualities that are meant to be seen as, above all, human. While Kermit may muse on the difficulties of being a frog ("It's not easy being green," he sings, in one of the most lyrical ballads in the classic Muppet repertoire), the source of that pain is really not his frogginess but his humanness, his awareness of how a certain alienation is the price of being human. (If it's possible to miss this point when Kermit sings the song, it certainly isn't when Frank Sinatra does.) And while such sensitivity and pain might seem reminiscent of the romantic male hero, Kermit's masculinity—even in his courtship of Miss Piggy—is never the focus of our attention. His gender is as unobtrusive as his attire, which, except on rare occasions, consists only of a subdued green, jester-like collar.

Indeed, at first glance, the distinction between female and male appears to be as irrelevant among Henson's puppets as the one between animal and human. Except for the humanoids, who are marked as humans by their unambiguous gendering as male or female, the rest of the puppets, the animals, are "generic" humans—that is, male. There is one important exception, however: Miss Piggy. As her name indicates, two aspects are basic to her identity: she is a "Miss," both the most strongly gendered of the main Muppet characters and the only female among them; she is also "Piggy." It is no accident that the most obviously gendered Muppet is a female, that the female is an animal, and that the animal is a pig. Gender is Miss Piggy's raison d'etre, and the issues of sexuality in the Muppet world condense most extravagantly around her porcine body (cf. Kinder 65).

Like her name, Miss Piggy's persona and her humor arise from the tension between two precariously combined qualities: an outrageously excessive, simpering, preening femininity and a wicked right hook. Miss Piggy's femininity is evident in her awareness of her "to-be-looked-at-ness." With cleavage-baring costumes, wigs, jewelry, coy and flirtatious body language (leg-crossing, hair-flouncing), she cultivates an appearance designed to appeal to males. She also uses her voice to enhance her femininity by adopting a mannered, whispered French. She calls herself "moi."

The essence of conventional femininity is the pursuit of heterosexual love, and wherever Miss Piggy is, the story of her love affair with Kermit is not far behind. A sequence in *The Muppet Movie* (1979) depicting the origin of their romance parodies the conventions of romantic love, from love at first sight to storybook weddings. Love is one of the few areas where Hollywood allows women to take charge, and the Muppets are no exception: Miss Piggy initiates her affair with Kermit. On stage, after establishing herself as female spectacle par excellence by winning a home-town beauty contest, she deploys her gaze like one of her famed karate chops when she first lays eyes on Kermit. The camera zooms in on his face in a point-of-view shot, as romantic music swells. A reverse shot shows a bright flash issuing from her eye, emphasizing not only the "sparkle" of love but the fact that she is the one who first looked. What follows is a montage of clichéd courting scenes, from slow-motion romps in flowery meadows, to rowing by waterfalls, to a rendezvous on a foggy London street, to a wedding. The sequence closes with the couple framed in a heart-shaped iris like the one made famous by *I Love Lucy*, while Miss Piggy screeches the finale of the love song, "Never Before and Never Again." In *The Kermit and Piggy Story* (1985), mostly songs and production numbers from *The Muppet Show* compiled for home video release, she and Kermit continue to spoof romantic love. As in the screwball comedy film, their declarations of love take the form of verbal sparring and actual screaming.[2] Even the film's B-movie title is mock-heroic, casting their story in the context of the great love affairs of history, and the myths and movies they have generated.

At the same time, however, Miss Piggy's apparent femininity is constantly undermined aurally and visually. Her voice, a tremulous falsetto, is provided by a man, Frank Oz. Even more strikingly, Miss Piggy physically dwarfs Kermit. She is enormous beside him, and her body is voluptuously physical. In the courting sequence of *The Muppet Movie*, for example, the

Miss Piggy shows the cultural ideals of femininity to be both artificial and comical through her exaggerated performances of them. She also undermines her poses of coyness and passivity by frequent outbursts of vigorous physical aggression. From The Muppet Movie, © *1979 Associated Film Distribution (AFD).*

two lovers run to each other across a meadow. Instead of meeting in an embrace, Miss Piggy plows into Kermit and continues to bulldoze him across the field. When they finally fall to the ground and disappear beneath the eye of the camera, she is on top. Fat jokes are sprinkled through *The Kermit and Piggy Story*, and while Miss Piggy isn't exactly fat she is undeniably large, and she loves to eat. One scene in the film shows the two characters seated at a cozy, romantic dinner. On the table in front of Kermit is a modest salad. Miss Piggy has a huge platter of spaghetti and meatballs. The film repeatedly detours from the dinner to their memories then returns to the dinner. With each return, the mountain of spaghetti gets smaller and smaller until it disappears. The movie ends with Miss Piggy bolting from the table to get pizza and assigning the dish-washing to Kermit.

As Judith Williamson has argued, Miss Piggy's unabashed hedonism subverts the ideologies of both capitalism and patriarchy. In *Miss Piggy's Guide to Life*, a mock self-help and etiquette book, Miss Piggy borrows *Cosmopolitan* magazine's style of using imperatives and checklists ("do this, check that") to tell women how to improve themselves. On the surface, she seems to accept the norms of femininity. But when she tells women how they can "snack" their way to "slimness," she abandons *Cosmo*'s line on deferred gratification in favor of the pleasure principle, mocking the bourgeois Protestant ethic of work and investment that pervades women's magazines and that helps support the identity of self-sacrifice and masochism with femininity (Williamson 55–61).

Miss Piggy only barely conceals the power, coarseness, and aggressiveness of her physicality beneath a simpering and submissive mask of femininity, which she drops the moment her own interests are threatened. These interests are defined largely but not exclusively in terms of her love object, Kermit. When such threats occur, she responds verbally with one-line insults delivered in a clearly masculine voice. (She calls a chicken "Buzzard Beak" and a rival pig "Bacon Brain.") She also displays her well-known skills in the martial arts. In one episode in *The Kermit and Piggy Story*, she wears a black belt and violently demonstrates her skills on a hapless Kermit. More typically, it is his enemies or hers that she tosses around. In *The Muppet Movie* she bursts her own chains to rescue a bound Kermit and demolishes a crew of bad guys with a series of violent lunges, punches, leaps, and karate kicks. In *Miss Piggy's Guide to Life*, she uses a "quick movement" of her hand to knock to the floor a bookseller who tries to sell her a romance novel instead of her own book (xii). Miss Piggy will have nothing to do with melodrama. Yet, despite her disdain for such a feminine genre, she also appears generally content to operate within the confines of conventional heterosexuality. That is because for her, femininity is a masquerade, a costume like any other, which she can relish—or wallow in, if you will—but discard in an instant. Feminine passivity and weakness are artificial ploys, tools to utilize toward her own ends.

More an image than a character fleshed out in narrative, Miss Piggy exists in a hazy realm, triggering multiple and contradictory responses. No one could deny that on one level she provides the occasion for laughter at women. Yet at the same time, she mobilizes laughter against the posturing and illusoriness of a femininity that encourages such silliness as diminutive names ("Piggy") and girlish ways for full-sized, fully grown women. It is this masquerade more than the feisty and funny "woman" who plays it that she renders ridiculous. In one study of children and television, girls said they liked Miss Piggy the best of the Muppets. It was her aggressiveness, not her femininity ("She crashes Kermit the Frog to pieces," one girl said), that seemed to appeal to them (Hodge and Tripp 150–157).

The Muppets have had enormous popularity in our culture, their images widely circulated through television shows, movies, books, records, toys, games, clothing, and other products. Yet consider how Peter Jennings described three of the most popular of them when he eulogized Henson on the ABC Evening News after his death in 1990: Cookie Monster taught us that "monsters can be lovable"; Big Bird showed us "grace in awkwardness"; and Miss Piggy was "a study in self-centeredness." Miss Piggy is admittedly self-centered, but she is other things as well. Moreover, her self-love draws attention to the self-*denial* we expect to accompany all the other signs of femininity Miss Piggy exhibits so abundantly. Jennings's reading—misreading, really—overlooks the exuberance and humor in the Miss Piggy character, which was modeled on Mae West, another female female impersonator. It also shows how easily the feminine—even among puppets—is held to a different, and harsher, standard than is the masculine.

Historian Natalie Zemon Davis might explain this phenomenon by identifying Miss Piggy as an unruly woman, a topos (a "place" or stock rhetorical theme) of female outrageousness and transgression which often evokes such ambivalence—on the one hand, delight; on the other, unease, derision, or fear. Davis first identified this figure in "Women on Top," an essay in her book *Society and Culture in Early Modern France*. The topos of the unruly woman isn't limited to the historical period Davis examines, however, but reverberates whenever women disrupt the norms of femininity and the social hierarchy of male over female through excess and outrageousness. Davis does not provide an inventory of qualities associated with female unruliness but instead a wide-ranging collection of examples of "women on top" and a powerful theoretical framework for understanding them.[3] Still, from her examples and others, such as Miss Piggy, a cluster of qualities tends to emerge:

1. The unruly woman creates disorder by dominating, or trying to dominate, men. She is unable or unwilling to confine herself to her proper place.

2. Her body is excessive or fat, suggesting her unwillingness or inability to control her physical appetites.

3. Her speech is excessive, in quantity, content, or tone.

4. She makes jokes, or laughs herself.

5. She may be androgynous or hermaphroditic, drawing attention to the social construction of gender.

6. She may be old or a masculinized crone, for old women who refuse to become invisible in our culture are often considered grotesque.

7. Her behavior is associated with looseness and occasionally whorishness, but her sexuality is less narrowly and negatively defined than is that of the femme fatale. She may be pregnant.

8. She is associated with dirt, liminality (thresholds, borders, or margins), and taboo, rendering her above all a figure of ambivalence.

These are some of the tropes or signifiers of female unruliness. Ideology holds that the "well-adjusted" woman has what Hélène Cixous has described as "divine composure" (246). She is silent, static, invisible—"composed" and "divinely" apart from the hurly-burly of life, process, and social power. Such is not the case with the unruly woman. Through her body, her speech, and her laughter, especially in the public sphere, she creates a disruptive spectacle of herself. The tropes of unruliness are often coded with misogyny. However, they are also a source of potential power, especially when they are recoded or reframed to expose what that composure conceals. Ultimately, the unruly woman can be seen as prototype of woman as subject—transgressive above all when she lays claim to her own desire.

 The Carnivalesque

The unruly woman has cackled at the margins of Western history for centuries, but perhaps never more insistently than in medieval and early modern Europe. Examples of unruly women from that time are unrivaled in their clarity and outrageousness and have helped produce a semiotics of unruliness that persists into contemporary U.S. culture. For that reason, I will make what may appear to be a somewhat lengthy detour into that period to investigate some of the theoretical perspectives its study has produced. The first of these comes from the work of Russian linguist and semiotician Mikhail Bakhtin, especially his analysis of the social meanings of comedy and the carnivalesque in *Rabelais and His World*.[4] Later, I will return to some of the most pressing questions that have been raised by Bakhtin's study.

According to Bakhtin, the carnivalesque is the social and literary tradition which, more than any other, expresses the dynamic nature of language and the relativity of power in all aspects of social life. As the purest expression of popular culture, it contests the institutions and structures of authority through inversion, mockery, and other forms of travesty. Carnivalesque practices retain the critical and cultural tools of the dominant classes but in order to degrade and mock the forms of high culture. For Bakhtin, these practices contain a blueprint for a future socialist state, conceived not in any teleological or totalizing sense but in terms of the utopian dimensions of everyday life.

The carnivalesque can refer to actual performances and events or to texts which sublimate its festive and oppositional impulses. Both are licensed by authorities to mark important events in communal life and to allow competing discourses to meet, contradict, and relativize each other. In Rabelais's time, carnivalesque events included such rites and festivals as the Feast of Fools and the Feast of the Ass. In contemporary culture, they might include parades, Superbowl parties, festive celebrations for rites of passage such as weddings, and political rallies and conventions. Roseanne Arnold carnivalized the discourses of patriotism and sports with her "scandalous" performance of the national anthem in 1990 at a San Diego Padres baseball game, subverting the dominant culture with its own tools. The carnivalesque is thus not a form of "mere" play but involves matters of philosophical and social import—struggles over social and political power, the triumph of the material over the abstract and the communal over the individual. It rejects abstraction and "eternal spirit" as defenses against life's terrors in favor of laughter and an immersion in what Bakhtin calls "the material principle of life."

This material principle of life and the values of becoming and relativity, which Bakhtin sees in the dialogic play of language, are epitomized in an aesthetics of the *grotesque*. The grotesque exaggerates incompleteness, process, and change, maintaining a kind of moral neutrality or *ambivalence* toward time and death. When life is understood from a collective rather than individual perspective, time becomes the necessary link in the process of communal growth and renewal, and death the "other side" of birth rather than a source of terror which irrevocably separates the individual from all others. For that reason, dismemberment, horror, death, and taboo are essential elements of the grotesque. They are reminders of the totality of life, possessing a demonic power to unsettle all that would conceal the democratic materiality of the body. Fear exists only when the part is separated from the whole, the individual cut off from history and community. Today, the Fox TV sitcom *Married With Children* draws on the aesthetics of the grotesque in the implied blood that drips down its titles and the exaggerated grossness of its characters. The two recent Batman films make similar use of the grotesque with the Joker, the deformed and demonic villain of *Batman* (1989), and the menacing circus freaks of *Batman Returns* (1992). Whenever a film breaks taboo by making comic use of corpses, it ventures into the grotesque.

Because human bodies bear the traces of social structures, they can be read in terms of this aesthetic. The "grotesque body" exaggerates its processes, bulges, and orifices, whereas the static, monumental "classical (or bourgeois) body" conceals them. The grotesque body breaks down the boundaries between itself and the world outside it, while the classical body, consistent with the ideology of the bourgeois individual, shores them up. The classical body is the body of Janine in *A Question of Silence*. The grotesque body is that of Ann—or Arnold Schwarzenegger, Sylvester Stallone, and Jackie Gleason; or Tammy Faye Bakker, Bette Midler, Dolly Parton, Miss Piggy, and Roseanne Arnold. Where the classical body privileges its "upper stratum" (the head, the eyes, the faculties of reason), the grotesque body is the body in its "lower stratum" (the eating, drinking, defecating, copulating body). Whenever the body is engaged in the functions that bring it closest to the thresholds of life and death—being born, having intercourse, giving birth, and dying—it is grotesque. An aesthetics of the grotesque helps explain the angry and moving work of performance artist Karen Finley, who uses simulated excrement and semen for political commentary. It also explains why comedy makes such abundant use of scatological jokes and sexual humor.

It is this notion of the grotesque body which bears most relevance to the unruly woman, who so often makes a spectacle of herself with her fatness, pregnancy, age, or loose behavior. The grotesque body is above all the female body, the *maternal* body, which, through menstruation, pregnancy, childbirth, and lactation, participates uniquely in the carnivalesque drama of "becoming," of inside-out and outside-in, death-in-life and life-in-death. Bakhtin acknowledges as much when he writes about the pregnant senile hags on the terra-cotta vases or about the popular comic tradition in general:

> *In this tradition, woman is essentially related to the material bodily lower stratum; she is the incarnation of this stratum that degrades and regenerates simultaneously. She is ambivalent. She debases . . . and lends a bodily substance to things, and destroys; but first of all, she is the principle that gives birth. She is the womb.* (Rabelais and His World 240)

However, this passage also points to an important limitation regarding gender in Bakhtin's work. Although Bakhtin has much to offer feminist scholarship, his interest lies in class, not gender, and he does not depart significantly from traditional representations of the feminine.[5] His idealization of the women as the "incarnation" of the "lower bodily stratum" falls into one of the most enduring and misogynist of philosophical traditions, that of relegating the feminine to matter and the masculine to spirit, and then privileging the latter. Bakhtin fails to take into account the social relations of gender, where the identification of women with reproduction has rarely worked to their advantage. Like so many theorists of transgression, he once again finds his models in the masculine—the author Rabelais, and his creatures Gargantua and Pantagruel. Men transgress in their actions; women transgress in their being, through the very nature of their bodies, not as subjects.[6] He never asks, as Mary Russo notes, why the old hags are laughing. It remained for Natalie Zemon Davis to incorporate gender into the carnivalesque and take a closer look at Gargamelle, the mother of Gargantua.

 The Woman-on-Top: Female Unruliness

Whereas Bakhtin's study of carnivalesque inversions emphasizes social class, Davis extends Bakhtin's principles to gender. Because the subservience of female to male was a critical element in the rigidly hierarchical thinking of medieval and early modern times in Europe, its inverted, carnivalized form was powerfully disruptive, and during this period the figure of the woman on top flourished.[7]

Davis tracks the woman on top across a range of social and symbolic fields, finding examples in paintings and theatrical productions as well as in books, proverbs, poems, and broadsheets which were often read aloud to the poor. The woman on top could appear in several variations, all of them violations of the "natural order": women who allow their "lower" unruly impulses to control their "higher" ones; women, such as Joan of Arc, who assume male positions of authority (and masculine clothing); and men who masquerade as women for various reasons. Cross-dressing by both men and women was a common means of effecting gender inversion, despite Church sanctions against it. Yet gender inversion had somewhat different implications for men than it did for women. By disguising himself as a woman, a man could appropriate the inherent unruliness and dangerous disorderliness of women but in the safety of his own disguise, thus becoming twice as transgressive as he would be disguised as a male official. For a woman, gender inversion meant not so much disguising herself as a man but, more radically, giving rein to the "wild" lower part of herself and seeking power over others.

In social practice, gender inversion occurred at fairs and other festive occasions licensed by civil and religious authorities. It also occurred in actual riots and protests against those very authorities, such as the Wiltshire riots of 1641, which were led by "Lady Skimmington," a man dressed as a woman carrying a ladle. (A "skimmington" was a public mockery of henpecked husbands, whom wives beat with "skimming" ladles.) Women had fewer opportunities than men for their own festivals of inversion, but they did participate in riots despite prohibitions against public action by women, and, as Davis notes, the authority of husbands wasn't entirely rigid. Some women accepted their husbands' authority, others got around it by deceit, still others openly rebelled by cursing, badgering, and thrashing their husbands (Davis 145; see also Underdown). These rebellious women were ambiguous figures. They could be seen simultaneously as "shameful and outrageous" and "vigorous and in command" (140). In practice, an unruly woman who thrashed and henpecked her husband could be both the leader of festivity and its butt. Sometimes she might be ducked in ponds and paraded with a muzzle to curtail her presumably excessive or sharp speech, and at other times urged to continue her fight.

Davis identifies several categories of unruly women, drawing examples from folklore and literature. One group permanently dominated men, and included such characters as Chaucer's Wife of Bath in *The Canterbury Tales*, Rabelais's Gargamelle in *Gargantua and Pantagruel*, and various other husband-thrashers. Davis describes Gargamelle as "a giant of a woman, joyously and frequently coupling, eating bushels of tripe, quaffing wine, joking obscenely, giving birth in a grotesque fecal explosion from which her son Gargantua somersaults shouting 'Drink, drink'" (134). Gargamelle embodies the material principle of life. She is huge. She eats, drinks, and has sex voraciously. She is a maker of jokes, and obscene ones at that. She represents the maternal body, the body ever in process, on the threshold of life and death. In contemporary culture, Roseanne Arnold has cultivated a similar Rabelaisian image with her accounts of wild sex, food orgies, and jokes based on public displays of her body.

Other women on top, such as the heroines of Shakespeare's romantic comedies, dominated men by denouncing their abuses of power but only until those abuses were corrected. The witty Rosalind in *As You Like It* educates Orlando and so limits his power over her. In the 1949 film *Adam's Rib*, Katharine Hepburn beats Spencer Tracy in court. Both women on top then retreat to their proper places as wives. Still other unruly women were directly licensed social critics, such as the folk figure *Mère Folle* (Mother Folly or the Mother of Fools), prominent in late medieval and early Renaissance traditions of carnival and in *The Praise of Folly*, an immensely popular satiric tract written by the Dutch humanist Erasmus in 1511. Mother Folly mocked masculine secular and religious authority. She also followed the path of danger rather than that of purity, allowing the representation of certain unruly feminine traits—anger, whorishness, and talkativeness—which the Church repressed in favor of chastity, silence, and meekness, virtues fostered by the Cult of the Virgin.[8] But whatever form the woman on top took, her presence created strong intertextual links across a range of social and symbolic discourses. Every time a "great pregnant woman" at the front of a crowd cursed grain-hoarders or cheating authorities, Davis writes, the "irreverent" Gargamelle was part of her tradition (147).

 *Mrs. Noah: Stubbornness and Speech*

Abundant examples of other unruly women can be found in Western cultural history—Socrates's shrewish wife Xantippe; Kate, the "shrew" in Shakespeare's *The Taming of the Shrew*, who remains unrivaled as a rebellious romantic heroine; and Sarah of the Old Testament, in effect a senile pregnant hag, whose laughter at her discovery that she is pregnant by her 100-year-old husband stands out in a book noted more for its mirthlessness and sobriety of tone.[9] However, two unruly women from the period I have been discussing bear particular relevance to Miss Piggy and exaggerate qualities that recur more mutedly in contemporary culture. In the enormous, greasy Ursula the Pig Woman of Ben Jonson's play *Bartholomew Fair* (1614), the grotesque body of the unruly woman takes on an especially carnivalesque cast that is replayed not only in Miss Piggy but in

Roseanne Arnold's star persona. Likewise, the various Mrs. Noahs of the medieval mystery plays, who torment Noah with their tongues, their disdain for his authority, and even their fists, anticipate not only Miss Piggy in her violence against Kermit but also the heroines of the romantic film comedy and the television sitcom, who more gently disrupt the orderly lives of their husbands and lovers. Lucille Ball probably knew nothing about Mrs. Noah; the connections I'm suggesting aren't ones of direct influence and causality. Yet Lucy Ricardo did not take shape in a cultural vacuum, but was fashioned out of the storehouse of types and conventions that comprise the topos of the unruly woman.

As many of the preceding examples suggest, the woman on top is often characterized by excessive size, excessive garrulousness, or both—from Miss Piggy, to the joking "great giant" Gargamelle, to the "great pregnant woman" cursing the authorities, to the women paraded through the streets wearing muzzles.[10] That the unruly woman eats too much and speaks too much is no coincidence; both involve failure to control the mouth. Nor are such connotations of excess innocent when they are attached to the *female* mouth. They suggest that the voracious and shrewish female mouth, the mouth that both consumes (food) and produces (speech) to excess, is a more generalized version of that other, more ambivalently conceived female orifice, the vagina. Together they imply an intrinsic relation among female fatness, female garrulousness, and female sexuality.

The reason for this connection, according to Patricia Parker in her study of "literary fat ladies," is the desire in patriarchal culture to control both women's bodies and the production of cultural texts or ideologies. Fatness and excessive speech represent productiveness in terms of expansion. Just as the expansive vagina is associated with (re)production, so the eating mouth produces a bodily expansion in space and the speaking mouth produces a linguistic or textual expansion in time. By tying the notion of fatness to excessive speech and projecting these qualities on the female body, patriarchal ideology exerts control over both women's bodies and the production of texts. Not surprisingly, this fatness or expansiveness is ambivalent, carrying positive associations of abundance on the one hand and negative ones of loss of control on the other. The "fat lady" thus can represent both fertility and the *vagina dentata*.[11] Similarly, the "fat text"— the dangerously seductive, invariably feminized, "talky" text that resists or delays closure—is both pleasurable and dangerously resistant to proper restraint. In the romantic comedy of the classical Hollywood period, playful and out-of-bounds speech becomes one means by which the female hero takes control of the narrative. Ellie in *It Happened One Night* prolongs the liminal period of her freedom and defers the film's resolution through talk. In *Bringing Up Baby*, Susan sets the course of the plot through her anarchic use of language.

Mrs. Noah of the mystery-play cycles serves as a particularly vivid example of gender inversion brought about largely through female speech.[12] Mrs. Noah doesn't speak in the Bible, but in these plays she acquires a sharp tongue for the sheer pleasure of tormenting her husband. In her character, female speech is inseparable from female rebelliousness, anger, and obstinacy. And while fatness is not part of the Mrs. Noah tradition, physical strength—by implication, size—is. Like Miss Piggy walloping her opponents and disdaining notions of femininity not to her liking, Mrs. Noah exchanges blow for blow with her husband. And like Miss Piggy, she doesn't laugh herself, but becomes the occasion for ambivalent laughter.

In the Noah plays, Noah has been warned to build an ark and get his sons and wife on board. Mrs. Noah refuses to obey him for various reasons—she's too busy weaving and she resents men telling their wives what to do; she wants to stay and drink with her friends, the "gossips" or sinners about to die; or she insists that her relatives be allowed to come. Mostly, she is portrayed as cantankerous, rowdy, stubborn, and irrational, indifferent to the impending doom of the flood and willing to do anything rather than obey her husband.

Mrs. Noah's refusal to budge provokes a riotous battle which often encompasses everyone else on stage. She and Noah hit and scream at each other. In the Wakefield play, where she is called Uxor, Noah addresses the men in the audience, and Uxor addresses the women. Each heaps abuse on the other, Noah calling her names like "ram's shit" and Uxor scorning him for his fearfulness and gullibility. Uxor strikes the first blow, and their brawl ends in a draw, with Noah calling for a truce. He says, "My back is near in two," and she replies, "And I am beat so blue" (Bevington, lines 12–13). Perhaps the most shocking lines occur when Mrs. Noah wishes her husband dead and appeals to the women in the audience for understanding:

> *Lord, I'd be at ease, and cheerful in my heart, if I might for once enjoy a widow's lot [have a helping of widow's pottage]. To benefit your soul, [Noah,] truly, I'd gladly distribute mass-pennies [pay for masses in honor of your departed soul]. So would others, doubtless, whom I see in this place [that is, among the audience]. (lines 388–394)*

Uxor eventually agrees to get on the ark, and her submission marks the turning point in the story of the Flood. God doesn't cease his destruction of the sinful world until she ends her rebellion.

Traditional accounts of these plays insist that Mrs. Noah's behavior is not meant to be taken sympathetically, even though it is comical, nor is her loyalty to her friends meant to be seen as a virtue. By framing the story of Mrs. Noah's rebellion in a story of apocalypse, female unruliness takes on a cosmic and frightening significance. Mrs. Noah bears the representational burden of a humanity so willfully blind to salvation, so stubborn, angry, and disorderly that it can be purged only through apocalyptic destruction. And by reducing the story of the Flood to a wild domestic battle between Noah and his wife, the plays suggest that more than just a religious message about the need to repent is at stake. The chastening of an unruly wife by her henpecked husband also teaches a social message about the submission of wife to husband.

At the same time, these plays provided both men and women with a comical look at marital discord. By transforming the silent wife of the Bible into a woman on top created out of stock comic traditions, folk tales, and misogynistic literary sources, the playwrights and members of each community who performed in these plays took part in a carnivalesque poaching of official culture.[13] Mrs. Noah offered women in particular a brief but utopian glimpse of the "unruly option," in Davis's words. This option suggested what it might be like to escape the authority of husbands, priests, and a destructive patriarchal God. It offered female autonomy in place of submission; festivity in place of punishment and mortification; and the claims of a woman's blood relatives and female friends over those of a husband. It also emphasized productive work—weaving—over reproduction, or breeding like the other beasts paired on the ark.

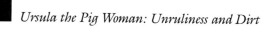

Ursula the Pig Woman: Unruliness and Dirt

Of those beasts, one has a special position in traditions surrounding the unruly woman. It is no accident, I suggested earlier, that the most prominent female Muppet is Miss Piggy and not Miss Horsie or Miss Doggy. Western literature and folklore contain numerous examples of what Parker calls the "sisterhood of swine," women whose association with the pig revives an ancient Greek and Latin slang term, often used degradingly, for the female genitals (24).[14] Much of the ambivalence surrounding the unruly woman derives from her relation to margins and boundaries and from the power inherent in them. That relation is exemplified in the pig, an animal considered in folklore to be a "creature of the threshold"—above all, the threshold between animal and human. While today the term pig is used to express anger (and applied to police, fascists, and male chauvinists), the pig has also been a traditional symbol of festivity, as in Jonson's *Bartholomew Fair*. The play depicts the experiences of a cross-section of London society that leaves the orderly world of the city to enter a chaotic gathering of hucksters, prostitutes, puppeteers, and other lowlifes at the Bartholomew Fair. At its center is the booth of one of the most colorful members of the sisterhood of swine, Ursula the Pig Woman, who presides as the fair's reigning "enormity."

Ursula is a fat, greasy, sweaty woman who breeds and roasts pigs at the fair and around whose booth much of the action of the play revolves—eating, drinking, stealing, brawling, urinating. She beats her pimp and leaves a trail of grease behind her. Standing for the abundance of the fair, and the world itself, Ursula embodies the energy and vitality that can be attached to the "gross" unruly woman. A "sow of enormity" (Jonson, V.vi.51) whose booth is "the very womb and bed of enormity," she is, in Stallybrass and White's words, a "celebrant of the open orifice . . . belly, womb, gaping mouth, udder, the source and object of praise and abuse . . . Above all, like the giant hog displayed at the fair, she is excessive" (64). Her description of herself recalls Eve: "I am all fire and fat. I shall e'en melt away to the first woman, a rib again" (II.ii.46−48). As Parker notes, she is not only fat but perpetually "in heat" (24), a sign of greedy incontinence and sexual desire. Ultimately, she represents a world that is "all vanity" (III.vi.30), and, like that world, she is a fearsome "bog" where a man "might sink . . . and be drowned a week, ere any friend he had could find where he were" (II.v.83−85).

Ursula derives her cheerful grotesquerie through her association with the pig, an animal widely both praised and reviled.[15] On one hand, as Jonson's play suggests, Western traditions of festivity honor the pig. "Carne-val" is at root an honoring or valorization of "carne"—meat, flesh, food, the life of the body—and in medieval times it was presided over by a fool carrying a scepter made of a pig's bladder. As feudalism declined, the pig came to be valued for virtues esteemed in early capitalism: industriousness and utility ("the Husbandmans best scavenger, and the Huswifes most wholesome sink" [quoted in Stallybrass and White 45]). At the same time, the pig is also considered a filthy abomination. It eats and digests garbage and excrement, both human and its own, and it wallows in mud which it often makes with its own urine to protect its skin from the sun. Judaism codified the pig's "uncleanness" in its dietary law. Christianity saw the pig in moral terms and associated it with sin, especially drunkenness, lechery, and greed. In bourgeois culture, the pig came to represent boorishness, bad manners, and other violations of taste, as in Lewis Carroll's *Alice's Adventures in Wonderland*, where Alice scolds the Duchess's grunting "baby" for improper manners.

While for Bakhtin such ambivalence is a mark of the grotesque and affirms the inescapable, creative/destructive powers of time, others take a less idealized view. Anthropologist Marvin Harris explains the taboo on pigs in cultures throughout the world—pig love and pig abomination—as a means of regulating complex ecological systems governing the production and allocation of limited material resources. Others, such as Mary Douglas, complicate Bakhtin's notion of ambivalence by locating it in social tendencies to order the world conceptually and control deviance. From such a perspective, the pig's semiotic status, especially its proverbial dirtiness, arises less from its actual habits than from its symbolic location in a place of ambiguity, its association with a *liminality* close to the symbolic boundaries that order social experience and mark the frontiers between nature and culture.[16] The pig mixes feces and food, animal and human, the household and the barnyard, inside and out. More than most domestic animals, it blurs the line between animal and human because it lives in such close proximity to human households and because its habits—eating human garbage and excrement, for example—involve it so intimately in human life. This ambiguity is heightened in European culture, where the hairless pink skin of the pig bears an unsettling resemblance to the flesh of children.[17]

Miss Piggy's uncanny effect occurs, then, because more than any of the other Muppets she destabilizes the line between animal and human. With Miss Piggy, the animal is already almost human, and the human—especially the female—is already close to animal ("the lower stratum, the material principle incarnate"). Miss Piggy's body is both animal and human: the snout in close proximity to the ultra-feminine lashes, the little pig ears in the mane of hair, and the hoof-feet in dainty high heels. Her personality also mixes the animal and human. Her masculinized aggressiveness undermines a femininity that would render her more "human," and instead she becomes a hybrid which in another context might be deemed monstrous. In contrast, Kermit's mixture of animal and human is reassuring rather than disturbing because he so clearly preserves the demarcation between the animal and human. In his case, the animal remains connected exclusively to his body—but discreetly and unobtrusively; and the human, in his sensitive spirit, is untainted by any hint of the bestial.

The liminality that accounts for the pig's status is also the source of the demonic power the unruly woman taps into—the power to destabilize old frameworks and create new ones. "To have been in the margins is to have been in contact with danger," Douglas writes, "to have been at a source of power" (*Purity and Danger* 97). That power, attributed to the socially marginal, is ambivalent, however, and is often turned against those presumed to have it. Annie, the female lead in the recent horror film *Misery* (1990), for example, is a fat "pig woman" quite different from Ursula and Miss Piggy; the film invests her with sadistic power to justify the brutal death it inflicts on her. As Douglas explains, societies identify whatever resists their conceptual categories as "dirt," or "matter out of place." Like water, dirt often stands for creative formlessness. Societies enforce adherence to their belief systems and control deviance by placing pollution taboos on whatever lies closest to their margins.[18]

All marginalized groups are vulnerable to pollution taboos that stigmatize them as less than human and their bodies as "dirty," "foul," "greasy." In a society that sees itself as predominantly white, heterosexual, Gentile, and middle class, those groups include lesbians and gay men, Jews, people of color, immigrants, the working class. Because social structures intensify their pollution taboos when they are under the greatest stress, the volatility surrounding two "body" issues of the 1980s and 1990s—abortion and AIDS—suggests the perceived threats feminism and the gay rights movement pose to the body politic. In the case of abortion, conservative political and religious groups zero in on the ambiguity of the fetus and the pregnant woman. Both woman and fetus confound the distinction between inside and outside, human and not human. Both are in liminal, transitional states—the fetus less, the pregnant woman more, than a fully-formed human individual. Both are therefore taboo—dangerous and set apart from normal rights and regulations. Perhaps even more clearly, the discourse around AIDS exploits the fears about the taboo-laden bodily fluids—matter that issues from orifices—to demonize and control homosexuals and drug-users.

The unruly woman is especially vulnerable to pollution taboos because by definition she transgresses boundaries and steps out of her proper place.[19] Women who do so, intentionally or not, have always risked punishment, from accusations of witchcraft, hysteria, and madness to the more subtle forms of social ostracism and job discrimination. Angry women, Douglas suggests, are dangerous and vulnerable not because of their intentions but because their anger unsettles ideologies about gender. When pollution taboos attach to the unruly woman, these taboos are likely to take on a sexual cast. It seems, as Parker suggests, that the orifices of women's bodies cannot be conceptually disentangled from each other. Ursula's sweat and grease are one step removed from the more sexual, swamplike connotations also associated with her. Or consider the following passage from Georges Bataille's account of eroticism: "The low prostitute, because she has become a stranger to the taboo without which we should not be human beings, falls to the level of the beasts; she generally excites a disgust like the one most civilizations claim to feel for sows" (*Death and Sensuality* 134). The sexually available woman, in other words, blurs the line between human and animal, evoking a particular animal associated with gluttony and filth.

The unruly woman's rebellion against her proper place not only inverts the hierarchical relation between the sexes but unsettles one of the most fundamental of social distinctions—that between male and female. The woman on top is neither where she belongs nor in any other legitimate position. When she rises above the male, she neither takes his place and becomes a "man" nor quite remains a "woman." The taboos placed on her suggest that her power arises less from male fears about castration and female sexuality than from the need to enforce conformity to a particular set of beliefs in which gender is a critical linchpin. What most threatens that set of beliefs is not (or is not *only*) the vagina, but the female mouth and its dangerous emanations—laughter and speech.

 The Decline of Carnivalesque Ambivalence

One of the most intriguing implications of studies of the carnivalesque such as Bakhtin's and Davis's concerns the practice of theory itself. Much contemporary cultural criticism, especially on the left, conveys a sense that cultural critique must be somber and ascetic—or at best scathingly and condescendingly ironic—to have political import. The same could also be said of some feminist criticism strongly shaped by deterministic readings of Freud and Lacan. In contrast, the laughter produced by the examples Bakhtin and Davis draw on undermines the notion that oppositional intellectual work must be, by necessity, a gloomy enterprise. However, the application of the theoretical insights of Bakhtin and Davis to contemporary U.S. culture is not without problems and is vulnerable to at least two major objections, which I would like to consider in some detail in the rest of this chapter. The first concerns the assessment of the oppositional potential of carnivalesque practices in the past, and the second, the historical gap between those cultures and our own.

One of the most common charges against Bakhtin and critics influenced by him concerns a tendency to romanticize "the people" and to overestimate both their power and their good will.[20] If in one sense *Rabelais and*

His World looks ahead to a realization of ideals out of reach in Bakhtin's own life, in another sense it looks backward with nostalgia toward a folk culture that no longer exists. Many historians and anthropologists have been largely skeptical about the value of carnival as a transformative model because its inversions are invariably righted and its temporary suspensions of boundaries appear only to reinforce existing social frames. For example, Peter Stallybrass and Allon White caution against an uncritical appraisal of the liberating potential of any transgressive social practices, rightly warning against the dangers of "displaced abjection" during the suspension of normal social restraints—the turning of one oppressed group on another that is even weaker (19, 53–54). As Emmanuel Le Roy Ladurie notes, "The feast and social change do not always go in one direction" (350), and in Europe, women and Jews have been pilloried, raped, stoned, and even killed during anarchic festivals. In the Los Angeles riots of 1992, more Korean-Americans than wealthy Caucasians suffered as the targets of black outrage. This warning is crucial. Transgressive women never escape their vulnerability, either in times of general license or in those of restraint. Nor did women enjoy greater freedom during the times Bakhtin and Davis describe than they do today. Carnival and the unruly woman are not essentially radical but are ambivalent, open to conflicting appropriations.

Yet it is also important not to discount the impact of the symbolic, the lingering and empowering effect of the *sign* of the woman on top outside and beyond privileged moments of social play. As I have tried to show, images of female unruliness were widely circulated in earlier historical periods and carried charges that were ambivalent, strongly positive as well as negative. As Davis writes: "Rather than expending itself primarily during the privileged duration of the joke, the story, the comedy, or the carnival, topsy-turvy play had much spillover into everyday 'serious' life" (143). There it could "widen behavioral options for women within and even outside marriage" and "sanction riot and political disobedience" for both men and women (131). The image of the woman on top in the world of play made the "unruly option" a "more conceivable" one, especially in the family (145). It could even "facilitate innovation in historical theory and political behavior" (131).

As for the historical gaps that separate those cultures in which the sign of the woman on top flourished from our own, Davis carefully defines the limits of her own particular study, and Bakhtin himself would probably argue that the evolution of capitalism has severely diminished whatever power the unruly woman once possessed. Indeed, along with a veiled attack on Stalinism, *Rabelais and His World* also contains a powerful critique of modernity and capitalism. According to Bakhtin, the ambivalent unity of the carnivalesque—the ability not only to tolerate contradiction but to revel in it—has become increasingly elusive under late capitalism, which has separated parts from wholes and replaced the organic "material principle of life" with "thingness." Without such ambivalence, dualities become oppositions and laughter alienated, ironic, and detached. Popular culture no longer stands for vulgarity and vitality but only for vulgarity. From this perspective, then, the degradation *and* regeneration once associated with "woman" can now mean only degradation *or* regeneration; Miss Piggy can be eulogized *only* as a "study in self-centeredness." Women's privileged relation to the grotesque body—already fraught with misogyny—becomes even more disturbing when that ambivalence disappears, leaving only dread or idealization.

Such a loss of ambivalence helps explain the conjuncture in this century of the discourses of both fascism and popular culture with a notion of femininity as "loose" and "dirty." In Weimar Germany, as Klaus Thewelheit has explained, the ambivalence or undecidability of blood as a carrier of life and death produced a phobic effort to separate it into two categories: one signifying racial purity, the other dissolution and loss of identity, a filth projected on all groups—women, Jews, Communists, and homosexuals—perceived as threats to the dominant Aryan masculine culture. The Frankfurt School expressed its fears about mass culture in language that cast on it a dangerous femininity whose disruptive powers threatened the boundaries between an oppositional high culture and the uncontrolled and dirty masses (Kintz, "Gendering the Critique of Representation"). In much cultural criticism on the left, popular pleasures, from the romances of the nineteenth century to game shows on television, only "debase" and "destroy," they no longer "revitalize" and "re-create" as well. This tainting of popular culture with such a negatively conceived femininity continues to surface in the debates about postmodernism (Armstrong; Rowe, "Class and Allegory").

The twentieth century has likewise witnessed ever more audacious attempts to separate the "regenerative" and the "degenerative" powers of women, to transfer the power to create life from women's bodies to men's technologies. The 1980s cartoon show *The Smurfs* appropriates the name of Gargamelle, Gargantua's unruly mother, for its villain, a wicked *male* sorcerer; all that remains of her regenerative/destructive power is the destructiveness, and even that is severed from her femininity.[21] The show reduces the feminine to a single girl, Smurfette, who depends entirely on the protection of the legion of little blue male Smurfs. A similar (and ancient) fantasy about men giving birth is at work in the development of reproductive technologies. The controversial case of Mary Beth White-head and Baby M, which spawned several made-for-TV movies, recalls primitive and even classical concepts of reproduction and genealogy, in which the mother provides only the blood that nourishes the child and the womb that incubates her. Baby M's "real life"—her social legitimacy—was provided by her father, who enforced his claim to her with a legal contract.

Modern efforts to theorize the utopian aspects of laughter and trans-gression similarly suffer from a loss of the ambivalence central to the cul-tures Bakhtin studied. Instead, many tend to collapse into attempts to valorize destruction apart from its opposite term. This tendency can be found in a strain of theory that finds a redeeming nihilism in postmodern culture (e.g., Lyotard; Baudrillard), and even more so in the earlier ex-ample of Georges Bataille, whose interests overlap those of Bakhtin in many ways. Both Bataille and Bakhtin seek to escape the oppressive total-izing of dialectical reasoning and to explore the relation between sex and death. Both valorize laughter as a weapon of transgression and liberation, and the lower body over the upper. (Bataille belonged to a secret society called the "Acephales," or the Headless.) Bataille's analysis of the destruc-tive power of laughter is similar to director Marleen Gorris's in *A Question of Silence* and to Hélène Cixous's in "The Laugh of the Medusa." Instead of negating official culture, Bataille seeks an "explosion" of all categories of reason and meaning. For him, laughter leads to "sovereignty"—a re-fusal to submit to reason, much like that of the women in *A Question of Silence*. Like ecstasy and poetry, laughter collapses all meaning. We truly "break up" with laughter, he writes, exceeding and destroying the confines of the self. To "laugh at dying" is to "die of laughter."

However, Bataille also provides a reminder of the costs of romanticiz-ing transgression and bears out Le Roy Ladurie's warning about the vul-nerability of the weak when anarchic impulses are set loose. Whereas Bakhtin's vision is comedic and social, Bataille's is tragic and asocial, in the tradition of Nietzsche, for whom the excesses of carnival enable a euphoric surrender of self into a larger philosophic whole rather than into a social community. If *A Question of Silence* falls short of envisioning a language or symbolic means by which women can express their differences, such a lapse looms even larger in Bataille's thinking. He advocates discarding the critical tools of the dominant culture—the legacy of the Enlighten-ment, for example—without fully considering the dangers of doing so. His assertion that the "explosion of repressed violence transforms it into something with religious significance" (*Literature and Evil* 26) may be true. However, it is also ominous for groups that have more often been victims than perpetrators of such explosions. Bataille could return safely from his Acephales rites in the woods without the fear of being hunted down for witchcraft.[22]

It would appear, then, that Bakhtin is right and that the oppositional power of the carnivalesque has been a victim of late capitalism. But how would he account for Miss Piggy? Or a film like *A Question of Silence*? Both seem to indicate that the tropes of female unruliness are alive and still triggering intense and widely varied responses.

I believe it is a mistake to look only to philosophic discourse for clues to the vitality of the carnivalesque as a cultural tradition. Instead, we should continue to examine the kinds of popular sources that inspired Rabelais and Bakhtin. Of course, the texts Bakhtin examines as carnivalized and dialogic (*Gargantua and Pantagruel*, *The Praise of Folly*, *Don Quixote*, Dostoevski's novels) were addressed to a literate, and therefore restricted, audience when they were written. Yet while Erasmus was writing *The Praise of Folly* and Rabelais *Gargantua and Pantagruel*, on the popular stage Mrs. Noah was savaging Noah and Ursula the Pig Woman was reveling in the grotesque body; while erudite male authors were already absorbing carnivalesque motifs into literary works available to the few, more egalitarian rites and festivities were keeping them alive and generating new ones for the many (see Weimann). These festivities were participatory, the hallmark, according to Pierre Bourdieu, of all popular culture. They were also performative, allowing an outlet for female unruliness in disruptive spectacle.

It is also a mistake not to pursue the threads of intertextuality when they lead into earlier historical periods. Recent cultural criticism has stressed the need for historical specificity as opposed to an idealism that obscures difference under the guise of a universal subject, and indeed the nostalgia of *Rabelais and His World* can be explained by the historical conditions of *its* production. Postmodernism rightly seeks the fissures and discontinuities of culture, and enormous ones separate the times I have discussed in this chapter from our own. Yet there is another danger in hesitating to examine as well the continuities and the lessons that history teaches. The detailed and stable hierarchy of the Great Chain of Being no longer exists, leaving behind it something more fluid and less visible. But hierarchy has hardly disappeared from contemporary culture. And if the rigid gender division and social symbolism Davis describes can no longer be found in industrialized Western countries, the oppression of women and the projection of the feminine as a symbolic category on vast areas of culture do, however, persist. Popular culture is deeply conventionalized, and comedy even more so, many of its most familiar elements having endured for centuries. For that reason, Mrs. Noah's violence and Ursula's hedonism help explain the standing of Miss Piggy and Roseanne Arnold as contemporary figures of ambivalence and taboo.

One helpful way of extending the insights of Bakhtin and Davis into contemporary culture is by placing the carnivalesque under the larger umbrella of liminality, the concept Victor Turner uses to describe social moments of transformation and play, when a culture explores the "subjunctive" rather than the "indicative" mode of its being, the "what might be" rather than the "what is." In such moments, a culture reflects on its codes, often through performative or dramatic forms such as gesture, music, and dance. In earlier historical periods, festivals and rituals served this function. Today, cinema studies, cultural studies, mass communication, and philosophy have all found evidence of carnivalesque tendencies in modern culture from their various vantage points (see, for instance, Stam; Newcomb; Fiske; Baudrillard; and Lyotard).[23]

For some, this tendency exists on the fringes of dominant Western culture—in Third World cinema, which is closer to its own folk traditions, or in pornography and the avant-garde, which are freer than the mass media to venture into the oppositional, the transgressive, and the grotesque. Others find it in performance forms such as clowning or the circus, when they take on the task of political satire.[24] Others find it in postmodern philosophy, which often describes its oppositional potential in language that recalls the carnivalesque. Still others seek the carnivalesque closer to home, in popular film and television, our modern equivalent of Bakhtin's streets and marketplaces. Thus, John Fiske describes contemporary popular culture—excessive, "broad, bright"—as a "deep modeling of a pleasurable ideal of the people that is at once both utopian and counter-hegemonic" (101). It is this thread of performance and liminality that I will follow to the popular culture of today and the stage it provides for the spectacle of the unruly woman.[25]

Rather than arguing for or against the survival of the carnivalesque and its subversive potential, I want to suggest instead that contemporary popular culture has sustained at least one site of insurgency in the unruly woman. It is not surprising that she appears in her most extreme forms on the margins of popular culture, in underground and avant-garde film, video, theater, and performance art; *A Question of Silence*, after all, circulates as an art film among limited audiences. At the same time, the popular media have provided Miss Piggy to an enormous number of viewers across a broad spectrum of ages and classes. While Miss Piggy may not possess the vitality and outrageousness of an Ursula or a Mrs. Noah, she also escapes the nastiness of Bataille's monstrous prostitute. The feminist potential of her image lies in its copiousness, or fatness, if you will—the chain of associations that link it to Mae West, and West to other vamps and female impersonators. For the culture at large, the unruly woman continues to signify the "ultraliminal," the danger that "anything *may* go" (Turner 41). For women in particular, she continues to offer herself as a sign available for recoding and reauthoring the notion of "Woman."

Roseanne
The Unruly Woman
as Domestic Goddess

Sometime after I was born in Salt Lake City, Utah, all the little babies were sleeping soundly in the nursery except for me, who would scream at the top of my lungs, trying to shove my whole fist into my mouth, wearing all the skin off on the end of my nose. I was put in a tiny restraining jacket. . . . My mother is fond of this story because to her it illustrates what she regards as my gargantuan appetites and excess anger. I think I was probably just bored.

—ROSEANNE BARR (ARNOLD) (*ROSEANNE* 3)

Last week, America's patience snapped. With a single voice the nation thundered, "Intolerable!" We are a people slow to anger but fierce when galvanized, as by Pearl Harbor or, as last week, by Roseanne Barr's rendition of "The Star Spangled Banner." Barr is a star and a slob. She is a star because the country has a robust appetite for slob television, the theme of which is: Crude is cute. Up to a point. There are limits.

—GEORGE WILL
("CITIES GLEAM WITH GUNFIRE")

In July 1990, Roseanne Barr Arnold, star of the top-rated ABC sitcom *Roseanne*, was invited to sing the national anthem at a double-header between the Cincinnati Reds and the San Diego Padres. Tom Werner, co-producer of the TV show and owner of the Padres, thought that the fat and noisy comedian would give a boost to his losing team. It was Working Women's Night at the San Diego stadium, and Arnold was nationally known for her depiction of working-class family life in *Roseanne*. With thirty-thousand fans in the stands, Arnold screeched out the song, grabbed her crotch, spit on the ground, and made an obscene gesture to the booing crowd. Werner had been right; the team won its next two games. But the performance, intended as a parody of baseball rituals, unleashed a firestorm in the press. CNN broadcast the story with interviews of outraged "people on the street." In one segment, baseball fans drove a steamroller over a boom box containing a tape of her voice. Angry calls flooded the switchboards at ABC. On national television, President George Bush called her performance "disgraceful." Arnold received threats on her life.

The incident boosted media coverage of the already controversial Arnold from the tabloids to the establishment press and from the gossip columns to Page One. Headlines joked about "the fat lady singing" or the "Barr-mangled banner," while the tabloid *Star* more graphically exclaimed "Barrf!" and then listed "Her 10 most gross moments." From sports writers to political commentators, all felt compelled to say something about the incident. William C. Rhoden wrote in the *New York Times*: "Barr is merely the symptom of the excesses of greed in American sports. . . . One gets what one pays for" (B9). Opera singer Robert Merrill, who had sung the anthem at Yankee Stadium for eighteen years, spoke of "this woman, who obviously has no taste at all. . . . It was like, 'Here I am, and to hell with you.' . . . I almost upchucked my dinner. . . . I don't know if I've ever felt so angry" (quoted in Georgatos A4). Perhaps the most virulent reaction was that of conservative columnist George Will. Leading his column with quotations from five news stories about children killed or critically injured that summer by gunfire in New York City, he linked Arnold's performance not only to the horrors of American cities in decay but to the sneak attack on the nation by the Japanese at Pearl Harbor. What seemed to distress him most was that, in his view, she was feeding the nation's fatal appetite for "slob television." First paraphrasing the American epic poet Walt Whitman ("I hear American bullets singing"), he then lamented the "alabaster cities" of "America the Beautiful" which no longer "gleam, undimmed by human tears!" (A15).

Obviously Arnold had struck a nerve. Other singers have been criticized for their highly stylized renditions of "The Star Spangled Banner"— among them Jose Feliciano, Bobby McFerrin, Marvin Gaye, and Willie Nelson. And one could argue that Arnold, as a comedian, was doing nothing more than they had, shaping the performance according to her own comedic artistry. But none provoked a reaction comparable to this one. Arnold jested about it—"I must be the greatest singer. My voice can stop a fucking nation." But a year later she said more reflectively:

> *It's because I'm a woman. And I was making fun of men and, you know, we have to remember, that's really dangerous. It still is. I really thought I was to that point in my career where I had broken all those barriers down, and it served to remind me that it's still dangerous to be a woman who makes fun of men, or a woman who is funny, or a woman who does any social criticism, or a woman who has a brain, or a woman who has anything to say, or, you know, a woman, period. . . . It's dangerous and frightening. (Arnold, Interview)* [1]

In other words, as Will insists, there are indeed limits or barriers, especially for women who behave as Arnold does. His description of her as a "star and a slob" only dimly suggests the powerful and contradictory status she has achieved by whining, wisecracking, munching, mooning, screeching, and spitting her way into the national consciousness. If it is dangerous "to be a woman, period," it is especially so to be an *unruly* woman, and Arnold's performance in San Diego that summer confirmed her status as such.

Women rarely have the opportunity to claim the kind of public space that Arnold did that day, and her experience offers abundant lessons about the relation between social power and public visibility. Invisibility helps constrain women's social power; as long as women are not seen in the public sphere, they do not exist. Arnold heightened her visibility by forcing herself from one—less visible—category of popular discourse into another usually unavailable to women—from "soft news" to "hard news." Soft news includes gossip, the tabloids, *People* magazine, lifestyle and entertainment sections of the newspaper; hard news covers events clearly in the public sphere and appears on the front pages and op-ed pages of newspapers and at the beginning of newscasts. If sports is not exactly hard news, it's not soft either, because of its particular status in masculine culture. When Arnold walked into that stadium, she made herself the subject of hard news, subject to those voices that had never touched her when she was safely contained in a place marked "sitcom" or "HBO Comedy Special," or in the feminized discourse of gossip columns and tabloids.

Implicit in the unruly woman's heightened visibility is her potential to bring about a process Erving Goffman describes as "breaking frame." Goffman suggests that social life is an "endless negotiation" about which cultural frame should surround, and thereby give meaning to, various events and bits of behavior. He argues that the meaning of a social situation can be radically altered by changing the frame in which it is perceived and that frames are most vulnerable at their margins. Because she is dangerously situated in the margins of social life, the unruly woman enjoys heightened "frame-busting" power.

Arnold entered a space that day already defined as liminal or sacred in patriarchal culture. Baseball is not merely a game, something that is played, but a collective, public, and masculine ritual, a quasi-religious re-affirmation of patriarchy, patriotism, and the myth of our nation's Edenic history. Unlike football, its rival in the national mythology of sports (at least until the rise of basketball in the past twenty years), baseball, with its grace and decorum, is the game of choice for intellectuals and the upwardly mobile. It is George Will's favorite sport. Free of the narrative constraints of her television series, Arnold staged a joke that reframed that ritual event and turned it into something else—a carnivalized moment of leveling, mockery, and inversion. By exceeding the limits of play tolerated on that diamond, parodying the gestures of the Boys of Summer, and singing the national anthem less than reverentially—in effect, by being who she was, a comedian, joke-maker, and unruly woman—she violated the space of that ritual and, indeed, the national airwaves that had been given over to its celebration. What might have been a harmless spoof of the tropes of masculinity and patriotism became a threat to the sanctity of all American institutions, invoking that "perilous realm of possibility," in Victor Turner's words, where "'anything *may* go'" (41).

According to Turner, at times of dramatic social change, sacred symbols—such as baseball, the national anthem, and the flag—burst into the public arena to mobilize people to defend their cultures. In the summer of 1990, the U.S. government was laying the groundwork for its showdown with Saddam Hussein and preparing to deploy sixty thousand troops in Kuwait. Flag-burning had become a controversial issue, with proposals in

Congress for a constitutional ban against it. Arnold's performance made her vulnerable to the official voices of masculine authority, the voices of news and government from George Will to George Bush, which projected onto her all perceived threats to the dominant culture. Indeed, Will's near loss of control over his own rhetoric exposed his column's subtext—the range of repressed fears this disorderly fat woman released about racial threats to the nation's "alabaster" cities, about mass culture with its "slob" values encroaching on the tidy domain of those who know Walt Whitman's poetry well enough to paraphrase it.[2]

Not only in this incident but throughout her career Arnold has used the semiotics of unruliness to break frame, to disrupt, to expose the gap between, on the one hand, the New Left and the women's movement of the late 1960s and early 1970s, and on the other, the realities of working-class family life two decades later. On one level, of course, Arnold's joke backfired. On another and more important one, however, it succeeded as a powerful demonstration of the disruptive power of the unruly woman. Even as fans were booing her in the stadium, others were cheering.[3] As Arnold's career has unfolded, her fat, unruly body—and her noisy, angry, funny persona—have shape-shifted into forms that might appear less transgressive than the ones that first defined her. A new history shaped by her disclosures of incest, a new body shaped by dieting and cosmetic surgery, and even a new name when she dropped Barr for Arnold have created what might be considered a new Roseanne, whose power to continually re-create herself as a boundary breaker remains to be seen. I will return to these changes at the conclusion of this book, where I discuss them in terms of genre and the pressure to rewrite unruly women's stories as melodrama rather than comedy. But for now I wish to emphasize how she created her definitive persona (re-created nightly on syndicated reruns of *Roseanne*) through an inspired use of the semiotics of unruliness. Throughout this discussion, I use "Arnold" to refer to Roseanne Barr Arnold not as a "real" person but in Richard Dyer's sense, as a sign created by her various public roles, performances, and interviews and by the commentaries about them. I reserve "Roseanne" to refer more narrowly to the character she plays by that name. Together, these elements evoke an ambivalence that has both produced and threatened her popularity.

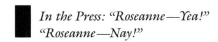 *In the Press: "Roseanne—Yea!"*
"Roseanne—Nay!"

The cover of the December 1990 issue of *Vanity Fair*—headlined "Roseanne on Top"—shows Arnold holding the wrists of her husband Tom

Arnold to pin him beneath her. Her mouth is open in what appears to be a laugh. She is wearing a low-cut red dress, a strawberry-blonde wig, diamonds, and a white fox fur, a look that parodically recalls the blonde bombshells and gold diggers of early classical Hollywood film. The photograph, a medium shot, centers on Arnold's massive cleavage. Tom Arnold's face, looking at the camera and registering little emotion, is upside down.

The words and images of the cover suggest that Arnold wields power in multiple dimensions—power over men, financial power, celebrity power, sexual power. These words and images also acknowledge that she has achieved that power by cultivating a particular persona defined by gender inversion. Inside, more photographs give Arnold's outrageousness, vulgarity, and excesses the validation of high style. Shots of her mud wrestling with Tom Arnold in playful, sexually suggestive poses literalize her "earthiness." One photograph, captioned "filthy rich," shows the couple covered with mud and bathed in golden light. It brilliantly displays the ambivalence and danger—the "dirt"—represented by the convergence of money and sexuality in the person of the unruly woman. Beneath the "Roseanne on Top" cover headline, however, is a smaller subhead asking, "But Who's the Boss?" While recognizing, and even celebrating, Arnold's status as one of television's highest-paid performers, the magazine still has trouble fully granting that this monumental figure is indeed the boss.

Arnold's rise to such success began in Denver in the early 1980s, when she worked first as a wisecracking cocktail waitress and then as a performer in local comedy clubs. After auditioning for the Comedy Store in Los Angeles, she was invited to perform on *The Tonight Show*. A concert tour followed, and her national career took off. Here, briefly, are some of her personal and professional milestones of the next few years.

Arnold produced her first HBO special, "The Roseanne Barr Show," in 1987, and in January 1988 signed on with producers Marcy Carsey and Tom Werner. Carsey/Werner, who had developed the top-rated sitcom *The Cosby Show* (1984–1992) out of Bill Cosby's standup comedy act, hired Matt Williams as executive producer, but almost immediately Williams and Arnold started battling over artistic control of the show. According to Arnold, he wanted to name it *Life and Stuff* so that it would not become a star vehicle for her. The show made its debut in October of that year as *Roseanne* and became one of the top three television series of the year. In January 1989, Williams was forced off the show and two weeks later it hit number one. That spring, the tabloid press pried open confidential records and identified a daughter Arnold had given up for adoption eighteen years earlier. In July she filed to divorce her first husband, Bill Pentland. In

September, she published her autobiography, *Roseanne: My Life as a Woman*, which became a best-seller. In December, she made her film debut in Susan Seidelman's *She-Devil*, also starring Meryl Streep. The film was a critical and box-office failure.

In January 1990 Arnold married her longtime friend, standup comedian Tom Arnold. (The *New York Times* noted that he was six years younger than she.) Meanwhile, the turmoil on the *Roseanne* set continued. In March Jeff Harris, the executive producer who had replaced Williams, resigned, taking out an ad in *Variety* about leaving for a vacation "in the relative peace and quiet of Beirut." On July 25, Arnold touched off a national scandal by her rendition of "The Star Spangled Banner." In September, *Little Rosey*, an animated Saturday-morning children's show, made its debut, with Arnold providing the voice for the show's main character. She described the cartoon show as the only one on television with a girl hero, no violence, and no sexism. The show lasted only one season because she refused to comply with the network's insistence that more boy characters be added.[4] In December, Amy Heckerling's film *Look Who's Talking Too* was released, with Arnold providing the voice of the wise-cracking girl.

Arnold's second HBO special, "Roseanne Barr: Live from Trump Castle," was aired in January 1991. In June, she and Tom Arnold settled a $35-million lawsuit against the *National Enquirer* and the *Star*, the terms of which were not disclosed. Tom Arnold converted to Judaism, the couple renewed their vows in a religious ceremony, and Roseanne Barr changed her name to Roseanne Arnold. In September, she announced that she was an incest survivor at a conference in Denver attended by 1,100 people. *Backfield in Motion*, a made-for-TV movie starring Roseanne and Tom Arnold, was broadcast in November of that year, and her third HBO comedy special, "Roseanne Arnold," in June 1992. By 1992, *Roseanne* had reached number one in the United Kingdom, a sign of the international success Arnold had achieved, and she was now one of the highest-paid performers on television, earning about $100,000 per episode. In 1992 she and Tom Arnold completed a deal with ABC, which included the series *The Jackie Thomas Show* for him. When *Roseanne* finished its fourth season in 1992, it went into syndication, reportedly earning Arnold at least $30 million (Hirschberg 186), while continuing to run at or near the top of the ratings in prime time.

Despite this record, Arnold's success has not generated universal enthusiasm, as the national-anthem incident made clear. Nor was that incident an isolated event, but merely the most provocative in a series of episodes that included dropping her pants at other public events, cracking jokes about menstruation on national television, and generally "making a spectacle of herself." Many people find Arnold's persona deeply offensive, and controversy has followed her up almost every rung of the ladder to success. She and her series have been trashed by the tabloids, snubbed by the Emmies, and condescended to by media critics.[5] At the same time, her fans have been loyal and numerous enough to propel her to, and sustain, her success. In a *People* magazine poll, readers voted her their favorite female television star and the one most likely to have a flourishing career in the year 2000. The August 1989 issue of *Esquire*, on its favorite (and least favorite) women, concisely displayed this ambivalence, or difficulty in placing her, by running two stories by two men, side by side—one called "Roseanne—Yea," and the other, "Roseanne—Nay."

While this ambivalence cuts across media and class lines, the supermarket tabloids have perhaps played the largest role in creating and popularizing Arnold's unruly persona. The tabloids are the carnivalesque of the popular print media, giving heightened representations of the kinds of "weirdness or disjunction" their readers experience in everyday life (Fiske 114). They are popular with the same demographic group targeted by Arnold's show, women aged 18–34, or, as comedian Alan King more colorfully describes them, "the hopeless underclass of the female sex. The polyester-clad, overweight occupants of the slow track. Fast-food waitresses, factory workers, housewives—members of the invisible pink-collar army. The despised, the jilted, the underpaid." "In other words," as Arnold replies, "the coolest people" (both quoted in O'Connor B27). Arnold shares with the tabloids a taste for the self-consciously excessive, vulgar, and sensational. Both Arnold and the tabloids carnivalize, invert, and mock the norms of bourgeois taste.

Consider this description of Arnold's wedding to Tom Arnold:

> *Hilarious five-page photo album*—ROSEANNE'S SHOTGUN "WEDDING FROM HELL"—*Dad refuses to give pregnant bride away*—*"Don't wed that druggie bum!" Maids of honor are lesbians—best man is groom's detox pal. Ex-hubby makes last-ditch bid to block ceremony. Rosie and Tom wolf 2 out of 3 tiers of wedding cake.* ("Roseanne's Shotgun 'Wedding from Hell'")

The headlines cover a simulated photo of her tossing her bridal bouquet. With her tongue protruding, she is grotesquely shot from below to exaggerate her size. Other tabloid headlines proclaim additional atrocities: "ROSEANNE TELLS KIDS 'DROP OUT OF SCHOOL.'" "ROSEANNE BEAT UP

HER HUSBAND—AND HAD AFFAIRS WITH SIX MEN (She often ignored her children, leaving it up to Bill to fix the youngsters' meals and wash their clothes)." "ROSEANNE INVESTIGATED FOR CHILD ABUSE." "STAR-SPANGLED SICKO ROSEANNE: 'DON'T SEND ME BACK TO THE PSYCHO WARD'." "ROSEANNE'S DISGRACE! THE *REAL* REASON TV'S STAR IS MAK-ING AMERICA HATE HER." "ONE OF THE MOST HATED WOMEN IN AMER-ICA." "BEFORE, HER ADVISERS WOULDN'T LET HER GO OVER THE BOR-DER OF DECENCY, BUT WITH TOM THERE ARE NO BORDERS!"

It is hard not to see much of Arnold's treatment by the tabloids as tongue-in-cheek, as in the remarkable list of taboos called up by the de-scription of her "wedding from hell," or the inversion of the classical wife-beating story that elicits sympathy for her husband as victim (for having to "fix the youngsters' meals and wash their clothes"). However, that tone often conveys a scarcely concealed condescension. Granted that the tab-loids are *about* excess and about showing celebrities in revealing or com-promising poses, there is an edge of cruelty to their treatment of Arnold, especially in photographs that exaggerate her fatness and her willingness to show her anger or to ignore the conventional standards of female beauty. The media have betrayed the same mixed bag of emotions toward a group of wealthy, aging women (among them, Imelda Marcos, Leona Helmsley, Tammy Faye Bakker, Elizabeth Taylor, and Zsa Zsa Gabor) who have shared the tabloid covers and gossip columns with Arnold.

The tabloids can be cruel to everyone, but when that cruelty is directed against the transgressive older woman it often takes the form of comedy, turning her into a grotesque clown. For example, Zsa Zsa Gabor's advanc-ing age has increased her unruly standing. Her circus-like trial (at the age of seventy-two) for slapping a Beverly Hills police officer coincided with Arnold's anthem episode and made her a rival for coverage in the gossip columns. After her trial, she was booed and called a floozy when she rode her horse in a parade. The case of Leona Helmsley is even more suggestive since, unlike Gabor, she does not work in show business and so would seem protected from the excesses of publicity associated with stardom. *Newsweek* brought considerable criticism on itself for the tone of its cover story about the 69-year-old billionaire when she was charged with tax eva-sion. The story used her age and sex to ridicule her. Headlined on the magazine's cover with "Rhymes with Rich" and written as a take-off on *Alice's Adventures in Wonderland*, the article described "Leona-bashing" as "summer's most fashionable sport" (Waters et al. 46). The story elicited angry letters from women complaining that powerful male figures charged and convicted of much more serious crimes are never trivialized in such a manner. As sociologist Jack Leven said in the article, "Here's this abrasive, aggressive, stubborn, wealthy person who happens to be a woman. If Donald Trump behaved in the same way, people would overlook it or might even admire it" (51).

In Arnold's case, especially in the early years of her career, the tabloids displayed an effort to wrest her definition of herself from comedy—where she asserts her power to be the subject of laughter—and transfer it to melodrama, where she becomes an object, a victim. When Tom Arnold gets the "credit" for Roseanne's transgressions, she becomes a victim of her own powerlessness, simply a woman out of control. Melodrama, unlike much comedy, punishes the unruly woman for asserting her desire. Such parodies of melodrama make the unruly woman the target of *our* laughter, while denying her the power and pleasure of her own.

Arnold hardly fared better among more sophisticated commentators. In an early review of *Roseanne*, Elvis Mitchell noted in the *Village Voice* how "startled" he was to see "this kind of arrogance so early in the run of a TV series" (47). He criticized the general lack of "class" or "taste" in television viewers and reviewers, describing her show as the "1040 EZ, low-income, no deductions" version of *The Cosby Show*. And according to Joyce Maynard, Exeter- and Yale-educated author of the syndicated column "Domestic Affairs," Arnold was "obnoxious and insulting to the average American wife/mother and homemaker" (C1). Both commentators displayed certain recurring problems in contemporary cultural criticism—the left's difficulties with gender, and middle-class feminism's with class. While Mitchell appreciated the "tastelessness" of *Married With Children*, finding the show a hip send-up of working-class family life, *Roseanne*, with its strong female character and feminist content, was "arrogant." Maynard's difficulty in understanding Arnold's appeal began with her unthinking assurance that she could speak for the "average American wife/mother and homemaker," despite the class privileges that she enjoys.[6]

One explanation for the contradictions that have characterized Arnold's reception in U.S. culture lies in the phenomenon of stardom itself. As Dyer has explained (*Stars*), people become stars because their images play on—and magically resolve—ideological contradictions of their times. In Arnold's case, her copious body could be seen as a site which makes visible, and reconciles, the conflicts women experience in a culture that says consume (food) but look as if you don't. Or it makes visible the conflict any member of the working class might experience in a culture that says consume (goods—conspicuously and lavishly) but don't expect a job that provides you with the means to do so. This explanation is apt, but it doesn't fully explain the extreme ambivalence that has marked Arnold's career from its outset.

Such an explanation, I believe, would locate Arnold in the historical and theoretical context of female unruliness. In an article on the op-ed page of the *New York Times* ("What Am I, a Zoo?"), Arnold describes her own awareness of the carnivalesque heterogeneity of her image by enumerating the groups she has been associated with—the regular housewife, the mother, the postfeminist, the "Little Guy," fat people, the "Queen of Tabloid America," the "body politic," sex, "angry womankind herself," "the notorious and sensationalistic La Luna madness of an ovulating Abzugian woman run wild"—and so on. All are valid, she believes, although many people insist on reducing this multivalence to a single truth:

> *Some people, they look at me, and they'll see a real person that's "down," you know, earthy or (what are some of the nasty things they say about me?) "crude." They'll say that. And it is there. And then other people will see that there's some spiritual or deeper meaning, and they'll see that. Some people will just see one and then other people will see both of them, because I think that what I'm really trying to do is project both of them at the same time, because I think they are equally here and equally valid and equally human. (Arnold, Interview)*

She projects both that "crudeness" and that "deeper meaning" most exuberantly and defiantly by inscribing across her body the signifiers of female unruliness.

 Arnold's Carnivalesque Body

Arnold's unruliness is more clearly paradigmatic than syntagmatic, less visible in the stories her series dramatizes than in the image cultivated around her body: Roseanne Arnold-the-person who tattooed her buttocks and mooned her fans, Roseanne Conner-the-character for whom farting and nose-picking are as much a reality as dirty dishes and obnoxious boy bosses. It is Arnold's *fatness*, however, and the *looseness* or lack of personal restraint her fatness implies, that most powerfully define her and convey her opposition to middle-class and feminine standards of decorum and beauty. Indeed, the very appearance of a 200-plus-pound woman on a weekly prime-time sitcom is significant. More than anything, I believe, her fatness is the source of the hostility directed against her. Even if a fat

The tabloid press did much to construct Arnold as a figure of carnivalesque excess. Here, the National Enquirer
portrays her as a physically aggressive and sexually voracious woman on top whose behavior is "shocking" because it inverts conventional patterns of domestic violence
and marital infidelity.

woman says or does nothing, her very appearance, especially in public
space, can give offense. Fatness has carried more positive implications for
women in other historical periods and among other ethnic and racial
groups, but in white, late-twentieth-century America, it signifies a disturbing unresponsiveness to social control.

As Michel Foucault has shown, social groups exercise control over their members by inscribing standards of beauty and perfection, of social and sexual "normalcy," on their bodies. At the same time, the body serves as a vehicle for communication from subject to social world—a nonverbal communication that is often hidden by the social privileging of speech (Douglas, *Implicit Meanings* 87). Body language conveys the individual's relation to the social group along a continuum of control, from strong to weak, from total relaxation to total self-control. Among the socially powerful, relaxation signifies "ease." Among those deemed in need of social control, it signifies "looseness" or "sloppiness." The body that "refuses to be aestheticized," that does not control its "grotesque, offensive, dirty aspects," can thus communicate resistance to social discipline (Fiske 97). George Will could find no better way to express his reaction to Arnold's rebelliousness than by describing her as a "slob."

Arnold's body epitomizes the grotesque body Bakhtin described, an affinity that is clear from the first paragraph of *Roseanne: My Life as a Woman* (Barr), where her description of her "gargantuan appetites" even as a newborn baby brings to mind Bakhtin's study of Rabelais. Arnold compounds her fatness with a looseness of body language and speech. She sprawls, slouches, and flops on furniture; her speech—even apart from its content—is loose, its enunciation and grammar "sloppy," and its tone and volume "excessive."

In twentieth-century U.S. culture, these qualities have long lost the positive charges they might have carried in the cultures Bakhtin described. Our culture stigmatizes all fat people by psychologizing or moralizing their obesity.[7] For *women*, body size and bearing are governed by especially far-reaching standards of normalization and aestheticization, which forbid both looseness and fatness. Women of ill-repute, whether fat or thin, are described as "loose," their bodies, especially their sexuality, seen as out of control. Similarly, fat women are seen as having "let themselves go." To protect themselves against the threat of rape, violence, come-ons, and offensive male vulgarity, poor women, especially women of color, may assume a bearing that is "stiff" and "ladylike." Anita Hill displayed extreme dignity and reserve during the 1991 Senate hearings on the appointment of Supreme Court Justice Clarence Thomas, although that bearing did not protect her from sexual innuendoes by men or charges of "aloofness" by women.

The cult of thinness is among the most insidious means of disciplining the female body in contemporary U.S. culture. Because a woman's social well-being is largely dependent on her appearance, heavy women suffer more than heavy men from the culture's tendency to stigmatize fat people.

Comedians make fat jokes about Arnold but they usually spare John Goodman, the equally fat actor who plays her husband on her sitcom. While other cultures have considered round and fleshy women as sensuous and feminine, our culture considers them unfeminine, rebellious, and sexually deviant, either undersexed or oversexed. In her studies of women's relation to food (*Fat is a Feminist Issue* and *Hunger Strike*), Susie Orbach has described anorexia as the "metaphor of our times," an expression of the extreme contradictions women experience when they are socialized to tend to the needs of others but deny their own. Femininity is gauged by how little space women take up; women who are too fat or move too loosely appropriate too much space, obtruding upon proper boundaries (Henley 38). It is no coincidence, Orbach writes, that since the 1960s, when women accelerated their demands for more space in the public world, the female body ideal has become smaller and ever more unattainable. At the same time, the incidence of anorexia has sharply increased. The anorectic takes the imperative to deny her desire and "aestheticize" her body beyond healthful limits, her emaciated form becoming a grotesque exposure of the norms that seek to control women's appetites in all areas of their lives.

The transgressive, round female body is also the maternal body, and maternity ties women to the process of generation and aging. As a result, the figure of the grotesque old woman often bears a masculinist culture's projected fears of aging and death. While Arnold is hardly an old woman and the media do not attempt to portray her as such, fatness and age are closely related because both foreground the materiality of the body. Warning against a misogyny she finds in camp aesthetics and certain postmodern tendencies in general, Tania Modleski argues that the "disembodiment" or "body without organs" celebrated by some theorists of postmodernism (such as Gilles Deleuze and Felix Guattari) remains a uniquely *male* body. The "essentially 80s figure of masculinity," she writes, is Pee Wee Herman, who remains pre-adult and pre-sexual while the "fat lady" and "aging actress," stock figures in the camp aesthetics Pee Wee draws on, must get old, get fat, and die (*Feminism Without Women* 99–103).

Women are expected to keep not only their bodies but their utterances unobtrusive. As Henley notes, voices in any culture that are not meant to be heard are perceived as loud when they do speak, regardless of their decibel level. The description of feminists as "shrill"—with voices that are too loud and too high-pitched—quickly became a cliché in accounts of the women's movement. Dominant cultures characterize minorities among them as loud—Americans in Europe, Japanese in the United States. In white U.S. culture, the voices of blacks are characterized as not only "loud" but "unclear," "slurred," and "lazy"—in other words, loose. Farting, belching, and nose-picking convey a similar failure—or refusal—to restrain the body. While boys and men can make controlled use of such "uncontrollable" bodily functions to rebel against authority, such an avenue of revolt is generally not available to women. But, as Henley suggests, "if it should ever come into women's repertoire, it will carry great power, since it directly undermines the sacredness of women's bodies" (91).

Expanding that repertoire of revolt is entirely consistent with Arnold's professed mission. She writes of wanting "to break every social norm . . . and see that it is laughed at. I chuckle with glee if I know I have offended someone, because the people I intend to insult offend me horribly" (Barr, *Roseanne* 50). Arnold describes how Matt Williams, the producer she eventually fired from her show, tried to get *her* fired: "He compiled a list of every offensive thing I did. And I do offensive things. . . . That's who I am. That's my act. So Matt was in his office making a list of how gross I was, how many times I farted and belched—taking it to the network to show I was out of control" (quoted in Jerome 85–86). Of course she was out of control—*his* control.

By being fat, loud, and ever willing to "do offensive things," the star persona "Roseanne Arnold" displays, above all, a supreme ease with her body—an ease which triggers much of the unease surrounding her because it diminishes the power of others to control her. Pierre Bourdieu describes such a manner as an "indifference to the objectifying gaze of others which neutralizes its powers . . . [and] appropriates its appropriation" (208). It marks her rebellion against not only the codes of gender but those of class, for a culture's norms of beauty or the "legitimate" body—fit and trim—are accepted across class boundaries while the ability to achieve them is not. Ease with one's body is the prerogative of the upper classes. For the working classes, the body is more likely to be a source of embarrassment, timidity, and alienation.

While her body bears the coding of the working-class woman's "alienated" body, Arnold rejects what that coding signifies. Her indifference to conventional readings of her body exposes the ideology underlying them. Concerning her fatness, she resists any efforts to define and judge her by her weight. Publicly celebrating the pleasures of eating, she argues that women need to take up more space in the world, not less. She similarly attacks the "legitimate" female body, which conceals any traces of its reproductive processes. On national television she announced that she had "cramps that could kill a horse" and described the special pleasure she took from the fact that she and her sister were "on their period"—unclean, according to Orthodox Jewish law—when they carried their grandmother's coffin. And in her autobiography she writes about putting a woman, a mother—her—in the White House: "My campaign motto will be 'Let's vote for Rosie and put some new blood in the White House—every twenty-eight days'" (Barr, *Roseanne* 117).

A woman's relation to cultural standards of female beauty, Arnold suggests, is complex, created from an interplay between her internalized body image and her external resources. Arnold often appears in public and on her series fashionably dressed and immaculately groomed, and in her second HBO special, "Roseanne Barr: Live from Trump Castle," she parodies glamorous stars by appearing convincingly glamorous herself. Yet in the more typical style of the Domestic Goddess, her basic character, she also shows why the overworked housewife may not have the time or money to spend on the regime of personal beauty required by a patriarchal consumer culture. She rejects the barrage of ads that tell women they can never be young, thin, or beautiful enough and that their houses—an extension of their bodies—can never be immaculate enough. She denies the pollution taboos that foster silence and self-hatred in women by urging them to keep their bodies, like their bathroom fixtures and kitchen appliances, deodorized, anticepticized, and "April fresh." Instead, she reveals the social causes of female fatness, irritability, and messiness in the strains on working-class family life. For "Roseanne Conner," junk food late at night may be a sensible choice for comfort after a day punching out plastic forks on an assembly line.

 Authorship and Standup Comedy

Out of Arnold's ease with her body comes her power not only to resist objectification but also to name her own experience, to create herself. Perhaps her greatest unruliness lies in the presentation of herself as *author* rather than actor or comedian, and indeed as author of a self over which she claims control. "Roseanne" is a persona she has created *for* and *by* herself. Her insistence on her authority to create Roseanne is a claim to subjectivity, an unruly act par excellence, which has provoked derision or dismissal much like Jane Fonda's earlier attempts to "write" her self did, albeit in the genre of melodrama. Building on the transgressiveness already inherent in her body, Arnold defines her self in the genre of comedy, taking advantage of its capacity to express anger by disguising it.

Arnold has created Roseanne in part by effacing the lines that separate her various roles. Her show, and the character she plays on it, bear her name, and in interviews she describes her act as who she is. She sees Roseanne as a work of comedic artistry fashioned out of her interviews, performances, public appearances, and television series, which together give expression to her consciously developed perspectives on ethnicity, gender, and social class.[8] Nowhere has Arnold asserted her power to create her self less ambiguously than in her 1989 autobiography, *Roseanne: My Life as a Woman* (Barr). The book fits comfortably into the genre of star biography, describing her triumph over adversity and key turning points of her life. But by its very existence, it also grants a historicity to Roseanne and helps legitimize her claims for authorship. Like any autobiography, it is valuable less for its factual authenticity and completeness than for the portrait it creates of the author as she wishes to present herself. (Indeed, the memories she later uncovered about her childhood abuse darken much of the book's account of her early family life and explain its occasionally elliptical references to violence [for instance, 163].) The book contains an eclectic array of poems, jokes, and meditations sprinkled throughout a loosely organized account of her life up to her move to Hollywood. It reveals a side of Arnold not immediately evident in her performances—a side as comfortable with the language of the poetic as with that of the comedic, and as ready to discuss her views on spirituality as to explain the reasons why "fuck" is her favorite word.

In *Roseanne: My Life as a Woman*, Arnold identifies the significant events in her life before her move to Hollywood. She learned about female strength when for the first time in her life she saw a woman, her grandmother, stand up to a man, her father, after he struck one of his children. Growing up as a Jew in Utah among relatives who remained haunted by memories of the Holocaust taught her about marginality and fear. She learned about madness and institutionalization at the age of sixteen when she spent eight months in a mental hospital because of nightmares and other symptoms of psychological trauma she experienced after being hit by a car. Like other labels of deviancy, madness is often attached to the unruly woman, and it is a leitmotif in Arnold's autobiography and the tabloid talk about her. As she points out, madness is uniquely uncooptable by the "normal" world, especially when it can be concealed behind the guise of "writer, comedian, storyteller, artist or whatever."[9] Later, she became disillusioned with feminism and counterculture politics when the women's movement was taken over by women unlike herself, "hand picked," she writes, to be acceptable to the establishment.

Co-existing with the pain of her childhood and early adulthood was a love of laughter, the bizarre, a good joke. While she always had a strong desire to write, it was only in performance that she felt safe. And because, since her childhood, she could always say what she wanted to as long as it was funny, *comic* performance allowed her to be a writer, in effect to "write" herself. She has often described comedy, as practiced by Lenny Bruce, Dick Gregory, and other rule-breaking, limits-testing comedians, as the "last free speech form," "mightier than the pen AND sword," a "street-fighting art form" that is not supported by grants. Comedy opens up space for the expression of anger. It can both wound and heal. At first she was afraid of comedy, feeling "unworthy," she writes, perhaps put off by the masculine aura about the aggressive comedy she admired. So she aspired instead to create herself in the familiar, feminine genre of melodrama, as "some poetess tragically and forlornly trying to scrape some piece of misery off the sole of my soul and write some touching little fat girl shit about it." What finally convinced her to cast her lot with comedy was "the thought of a woman, any woman, standing up and saying NO . . . a huge, cosmic NO." She explains, "The first time I went on stage, I felt *myself* say it, and I felt chilled and free and redeemed" (Barr, *Roseanne* 152). This "no" draws on laughter's power to negate. It refuses the affirmation men often like to attribute to women, as in Molly Bloom's famous, unconditional, rhapsodic "yes" at the end of James Joyce's *Ulysses*.

In her book's acknowledgments, Arnold thanks twenty-eight women who have inspired her, from Mae West, Moms Mabley, Marilyn Monroe, and Judy Holliday to Gilda Radner and Elaine May. They helped her discover what she calls "funny womanness"—"a brand new theory that we women have our own way of thinking, really different from the way men think, and really different from the way they think we think" (Barr, *Roseanne* 175). In other words, as in *A Question of Silence*, the different experiences of men and women produce different epistemologies. Yet finding a female tradition in which to locate her own voice was not easy. Early in her career, she rejected academic feminism because it seemed "dead" and so she declined to speak from a middle-class position, choosing instead the voice of a "working-class woman who is a mother" (Barr, *Roseanne* 161). At the same time, she chose to work in the popular media rather than the avant-garde. These choices explain the difference in tone between the Domestic Goddess, the character she would ultimately create, and the housewife "Judith Beasley," a similar character created by Lily Tomlin. Where Tomlin's humor is campy and appeals to the taste for irony of her more upscale audience, Arnold's humor is more direct.

Arnold discovered her stance (or attitude, if you will) when she realized that she could take up the issue of female oppression by adopting its very language. Helen Andelin's *Fascinating Womanhood* (1965) was one of the most popular femininity manuals for the women of her mother's generation. Part of a movement that exalted homemaking as a form of self-expression, the book taught women to manipulate men by becoming "domestic goddesses." Yet, Arnold discovered, such terms might also be used for "self-definition, rebellion, truth-telling," for telling a truth that in her case is both angry and affirmative (Barr, *Roseanne* 172). So she built her act and her success by exposing those "tropes of femininity" stylized and valorized, as Mary Ann Doane explains in *The Desire to Desire*, in the women's melodrama. Arnold attacked the ideology of "true womanhood"—how to be the perfect wife and mother—by cultivating the opposite, an image of the unruly woman. Appropriating Andelin's words but to very different ends, she called this figure the "Domestic Goddess."

It is no accident that a tradition of funny, angry women is hard to find, for the closeness between laughter and anger produces deep constraints on how women may express or participate in both. These constraints are illuminated by Freud's theory of wit (*Jokes and Their Relation to the Unconscious*), which points to the importance of gender in much comedy and laughter. For Freud, joke work arises from the unconscious much as dream work does. It has three related forms—the joke itself, the comic, and the humorous—which all release energy otherwise spent in repression. In brief, the joke produces pleasure by releasing inhibitions, and, unlike the comic, it is "made," not "found." The comic arises from the recognition of human dependence on external factors, often social in nature. Humor gives pleasure by substituting itself for more distressing emotions, such as anger. The most tendentious of the three is the joke, which is also the only one structurally dependent on gender.

In Freud's account, the joke in its basic form requires three parties—two men and a woman. The first man initiates the joke to release an aggressive impulse, originally sexual, toward the woman. He forces her to participate in the joke through her embarrassment, her acknowledgment that she understands its content. (Such was the case when Anita Hill was made to repeat Clarence Thomas's remarks to her about pubic hair on a Coke bottle.) Through its cleverness, the joke veils and makes socially acceptable its underlying aggression. The joke does not exist until the laughter of the second man confirms it; the woman, as the joke's passive butt, thus enables the formation of a bond between the two men. According to Freud, the replacement of an actual woman by a symbolic substitute marks the advance of civilization, as does the joke's evolution from smut to content that is less overtly sexual.[10]

Freud's account of the joke suggests why so much laughter is directed *at* women and why so much comedy is misogynistic. It also explains why women so often feel alienated from many traditions of comedy, whether the slapstick of early silent film or the routines of standup comedians from Andrew Dice Clay to Eddie Murphy. For this reason, standup comedy—highly dependent on the dynamics of joke making—has, until the 1960s, been an unfriendly place for female performers. Until then, women rarely appeared in a comic act without a male partner. Even after the sixties, women who succeeded as standup comedians tended, in a sense, to occupy the "male" position by directing their jokes at themselves in self-deprecating barbs, or at other women. Much of the humor of Phyllis Diller and Joan Rivers falls into this category.

Freud's analysis explains how precariously the unruly woman is poised between serving as a target of hostile laughter herself and hurling that laughter back at its sources. It also gives yet another explanation for the furor Arnold provoked in San Diego. Not only did she violate the space of baseball, but she encroached on another sacred masculine territory—that of the joke-maker. Arnold "made" a joke, and a tendentious one, containing a thinly veiled message of aggression. Refusing to play the passive victim herself, she forced men into that role. As in her standup routine, she used the social pressure mobilized by the joke to force men to assume a perspective, even if only briefly, they ordinarily would not—to laugh at their symbols of masculine pride. In order to laugh, men had to adopt the double perspective that characterizes women's lives, experiencing the joke as both subject and object, as butt and complicitous second party. For many, obviously, that was impossible.

Women's comedic traditions, whether in print or performance, have tended toward the less aggressive form of what Freud calls humor, which preserves the ego by denying or transforming threatening or painful emotions. Because anger is one of the most socially unacceptable emotions for women, it provides fertile ground for being reworked into humor (see Mellencamp, "Situation Comedy"). The tradition of woman's comedy, then, is aptly described as "domestic humor." Mostly written, this tradition is typified by the columns of Erma Bombeck, which chronicle a woman's life as wife and mother, after the rosy illusions promised by the narratives of romantic comedy have been replaced by a very different reality. Domestic humor or "matriarchal laughter" expresses accommodation and resignation, according to Judith Wilt, by piling "sandbags of wit against the flood of anger and pain" (192). Freud believed humor to represent the highest and most mature form of human development. But, as Arnold's joke making suggests, the accommodation of humor may not always be the ideal response to the pain produced by situations that can be changed. Through the persona of the Domestic Goddess or unruly matriarch, Arnold takes up the traditional issues of the domestic humorist—housework, children, men, husbands, aging—but with the harder, sharper, tougher voice of the feminist joke-maker.

Success in comic performance has often required the creation of a persona strong enough to endure from performance to performance. Jackie "Moms" Mabley and Sophie (first "Red Hot Mama" then "Big Fat Mama") Tucker both established well-known personae in their vaudeville routines—in both cases, those of bawdy older women.[11] With the exception of Mae West and the salty, warm-hearted prostitute she played throughout her career, however, female comedians have rarely been able to use their personae to anchor a series of films, as male comedians from Charlie Chaplin to Woody Allen have done (Fischer, "Sometimes I Feel Like a Motherless Child").[12] Arnold's success with the Domestic Goddess is perhaps most significant in that it gave her a critical entry not into film but into prime-time network television. Arnold introduced the Domestic Goddess to a national audience in 1987 with "The Roseanne Barr Show," her first HBO special, and within a year Marcy Carsey and Tom Werner, producers of *The Cosby Show*, signed her on.

"The Roseanne Barr Show":
The Domestic Goddess

Arnold's move to network TV can be attributed in part to the symbiotic relationship between standup comedy and cable television. Because standup comedy is cheap to produce, it helps feed cable's enormous appetite for programming, and an explosion of standup comedy accompanied cable's expansion during the 1980s. Indeed, standup comedy has become a staple on cable television, giving exposure to aspiring performers from comedy clubs throughout the country. Cable has also helped open the door for women in comedy, familiarizing U.S. audiences with such performers as Elayne Boosler, Rita Rudner, Carol Leifer, Louise Duart, and Stephanie Hodge. As a privately owned medium, cable is not subject to the same content regulation as the broadcast networks, and so it allows standup comedians the freedom to test limits essential to the form. Pay cable also does not need to keep sponsors happy by avoiding controversy. On HBO, Arnold's act retained its edge of vulgarity and anger. Its success paved the way for her network series, where she softened the edges of the crude, outspoken Domestic Goddess in exchange for massive exposure.

"The Roseanne Barr Show" is not a conventional standup act merely performed before television cameras. Instead, it is designed as a television show that both parodies the medium and takes advantage of its inherent intertextuality. The show shifts from domestic drama or soap opera to horror film to TV advertisement to live standup comedy. It respects then disregards an invisible proscenium between the audience and the performer. In its generic structure, the show parallels the tensions that comprise its thematic content: between the levels of Arnold's persona, between a woman's experience of the private and the public, between narrative and performance, and between melodrama and comedy.

The show opens outside a suburban stucco house at night with its windows invitingly lit up, and then it cuts to a woman's hands in a sink washing dishes. The woman is "Roseanne," wearing a frown on her face and rollers in her hair. She calls to her family seated at a nearby table. "Hey, you guys, I got this joke," she yells. She tells it to them, but they are distracted and don't pay much attention. Aunt Grace, a large, outspoken, and sour old woman with bright red hair, warns her that she shouldn't swear so much when she performs. "And don't do any of those uterus jokes," she says. Roseanne protests, "But what I do is more like an *act*— it isn't really about jokes." When Roseanne mutters a complaint to her husband about his aunt, he protests that Grace is *her* aunt. A TV newscast interrupts the conversation by announcing that Grace "The Aunt" Klotsky has just escaped from a mental institution. Aunt Grace vanishes, and the husband locks the door. The camera moves outside the house again, the wind picks up, and Freddy Krugar from the *A Nightmare on Elm Street* horror films appears by the window, holding an ax. He runs past a trailer to the stately house next door. A woman's voice calls, "Is that you, Richie?" and then screams.

This sequence establishes the essential themes of the show, from its setting in domestic space to its self-reflexivity. It begins by locating its own origins, which are the origins of Arnold's career, somewhere between the hands in the sink and the furrowed brow, between the drudgery of housework and the frustrated ambition of the housewife. When Arnold says, "It's more like an *act*," she sets herself apart from those comedians who mainly tell jokes, cuing the viewer not only about what to expect in the next hour but about how all of her work should be understood. Beginning with her opening appearance, when she seems to be playing herself, she interweaves elements of historical truth about her own life and career with a fictional narrative, playing with the boundaries between Roseanne Barr Arnold, Roseanne the character, and the Domestic Goddess. This ambiguity is complicated by the presence of actors, relatives, and friends in the show.[13]

The sequence's use of genre, especially horror and melodrama, both deepens this ambiguity and dramatizes the view of domestic life that lies at the heart of Roseanne's act. When within moments the cozy world of the domestic drama becomes *A Nightmare on Elm Street*, we see how horror haunts the family, which can be infiltrated by insane strangers who pass themselves off as long-lost relatives or stalked by monsters that terrorize those unwary enough to keep their doors unlocked. Like Arnold, Aunt Grace draws on the iconography of the unruly woman, but by emphasizing its grotesqueness she creates a peculiarly threatening image. Yet the horror film remains within the framework of comedy, suggesting that if domestic life can be a nightmare, it can also have its share of laughs and happy endings. The show changes tone with a fast-motion drive down the freeways of Los Angeles accompanied by the theme song "I Am Woman." This drive alludes to Arnold's own trip to success, which she identifies with her move to Los Angeles. The trailer that had been parked in the driveway of the stucco house pulls up by a Santa Monica theater with Arnold's name on the marquee. A male voice-over makes a pitch for "FemRage—for the one time in a month you're allowed to be yourself," and Arnold makes her appearance on a stage as the Domestic Goddess.

At this point, Arnold shifts into the mode of standup comedy, and while her act may not be "about jokes," she now makes heavy use of them. This shift in emphasis from narrative to standup comedy allows her to sharpen her critique of the family, showing that it is threatened less by external monsters than by those from within. In the mode of standup comedy, Arnold continues to invite identification with her character, but through moments of *recognition* delivered by each punch line rather than through the emotional engagement and resolution of narrative. Using the direct address of standup comedy aimed at a visible studio audience, she delivers a monologue about men, fatness, children, yuppies, male impotence. She establishes a perspective and style that are resolutely working class and uses sarcasm to puncture sentimental illusions about domestic life. She is aggressive and vulgar. Here, as in the national-anthem episode, she uses the joke to express the socially unacceptable emotion of anger toward men. She does not mediate her position by simulating feminine coyness, flakiness, or deference, as more feminine comedians such as Elayne Boosler and Rita Rudner often do. She recounts how when someone criticized her for not being more feminine, she answered, "Well, suck my dick."

Moments into her routine, Roseanne is interrupted by two of her children who walk on stage to complain to her about how their father is neglecting them. She talks with them and sends them back to what we learn later is the trailer, parked behind the stage. Throughout the act, the children interrupt Roseanne, never understanding that she is working. At one point, she excuses herself from the studio audience to tend to them, apparently abandoning the onstage Domestic Goddess persona for the Roseanne of the opening melodrama. The camera follows her offstage to the trailer. She mutters, "Jeez, I have to do everything myself. I have to do everything around here. Some big star I am." While her husband snores in an easy chair before the TV, she begins to clean up the kitchen. The two settings—trailer and stage—literalize the deep and familiar conflict many women experience between the private and the public, between home and work. Throughout the show, Roseanne moves between the two. She is never able to escape the demands of her family. They follow her everywhere, remaining always only a few steps away.

The show concludes by returning to the stucco house. This return to the private also shifts the generic emphasis back to narrative. Roseanne's performance is over, but nothing has changed. Aunt Grace is back. She gives Roseanne a prescient warning—"I warned you about your language, young lady. They may go for that sort of thing on cable, but you'll never get your own show." The daughter answers, "Yes, she will." Again, the wind picks up, and this time it is Jason from *Friday the Thirteenth* who skulks outside. A different female voice calls out from the house next door then screams. The scenario is the same but different. The return to narrative is also a return to a particular kind of narrative—that of the soap opera, laced with tropes of horror which themselves become domesticated within the context of family life. The soap opera is defined neither by recognition, like the joke, nor by resolution, like the conventional narrative, but instead by repetition and familiarity, like domestic life itself.

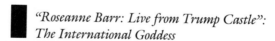

"Roseanne Barr: Live from Trump Castle": The International Goddess

In "Roseanne Barr: Live from Trump Castle" (1991), her second HBO special, Arnold again both comments on her career and presents herself in at least two voices or personae. Yet the changes that have occurred in her career allow her to intensify her anger significantly. With her sitcom *Roseanne* a smash hit and into its third season, she is now not only "one happy fat" woman, but "one happy, smart, fat, rich" woman, or, as Tom Arnold said, "America's worst nightmare—white trash with money" (both quoted in O'Connor). Out of that money and success she creates a new persona, the International Goddess or Diva, who plays one performance mode—the sadism of many male comedians toward their audiences—against another, the highly emotional relationship of many female stars with theirs.

The Diva dominates the first half of the show, allowing Arnold to examine the new status she now enjoys. In the second half, Arnold draws on her success—and the power it has brought her—to abandon *both* personae, the Domestic Goddess and the Diva, and to speak as "herself," Roseanne (Barr) Arnold, Standup Comedian and Joke-Maker. Of course, this Roseanne is a persona too, with the backdrop of the Diva ever present, but one that engages more directly with its audience, fully utilizing the direct address of standup comedy to heighten the impact of her voice. Speaking with the authority of an international star who knows her audience has paid forty dollars per ticket to see her, this Roseanne makes visible the power that allows her to speak as she does—more clearly than ever in the mode of standup comedy and the tendentious joke.

Opening with aerial shots of Atlantic City and the glitzy Trump Castle ablaze with light and filmed as a cabaret act before a live audience, this show appears strikingly different from the first. Arnold makes her entrance in the role of the Diva, driven on stage by Donald Trump in a classic Deusendorfer car and opulently dressed in a sequined gown, with a white fur draped over her shoulders. "Oh, you're *all* my friends," she says in a husky, dramatic voice. Then she dramatically poses and displays her body to be adored in an act of mock generosity with undertones of aggression that persist throughout the show. For the rest of the first half, she moves through the clichés of a celebrity making a comeback, blowing kisses, and telling her audience how *they* are what "happened" to her in the four years that have passed since her last special. Several times, she refers to her "awakening political consciousness." The Diva appears to be a composite of such stars as Elizabeth Taylor and Judy Garland, whose tempestuous private lives contributed to their highly emotional relationships with their audiences. A recurring theme in Arnold's work concerns the effects of sudden wealth on ordinary people. The Diva persona enables her to criticize the feigned sincerity of many celebrities who forget who they are once they become famous, who adopt political causes because they are fashionable, who even become Republicans.[14]

As the Diva, Arnold doesn't abandon the issues the Domestic Goddess addressed but presents them in a setting appropriate for the new character. For example, she uses a series of popular ballads that sentimentalize traditional notions of gender to point out its social construction. First she addresses the women: "Sometimes it's hard to be a woman . . . Oh Mandy, you came and you gave without taking, and I sent you away . . . Whether I'm right or whether I'm wrong." Then she sings to the men: "How do you thank someone who has taken you from crayons to perfume? . . . Davy, Davy Crockett, king of the wild frontier . . . To Sir, With Love."

She sings each medley to a prop of life-size photographs—a group of men, dressed in bikinis, striking beefcake poses, and another of women wearing the clichés of men's working uniforms, such as hard hats and briefcases. The juxtaposition of images and words dramatizes the arbitrariness, and the foolishness, of our culture's notions of gender.

Early in the show the Diva fires off a series of "classic jokes, the jokes that made me the *huge* star that I am today," while Tom Arnold stands on the side of the stage by a drum set, giving a snare roll and cymbal crash for each punch line ("The other day on *Donahue* I saw these men who dress up like women, and when they do, they can no longer parallel park" [CRASH!]). In this segment Arnold makes a joke *of* these jokes, but she doesn't dismiss the Domestic Goddess so much as add another layer to her. The movement from Domestic Goddess to Diva expands the scope of the character's influence and concern from the private to the public, just as Arnold's life has brought her into the public world in increasingly wider circles, from trailer-bound housewife to international star, and, indeed, as the U.S. women's movement has expanded its concerns from its early emphasis on the home and the workplace to such global issues as international peace and the environmental well-being of the planet.[15]

In the earlier HBO special, Arnold deflects much of the anxiety that men in her audience might feel by directing many of her jokes at "generic" men or a fictional husband. In this show, however, she tests the tolerance of her audience by eliminating much of that distance and repeatedly setting up her audience, both male and female, as butt. This sharper tone asserts itself even less ambiguously in the second half when we discover that Arnold's new voice is not tied to the persona of the Diva. A persona forms a buffer that protects the audience from the direct force of her jokes.[16] Moreover, the strong working-class coding of the Domestic Goddess further distances middle-class audiences from her critique. In the second part of the show, Arnold sheds most of the signs of the Domestic Goddess that she usually displays in other public appearances. Her voice becomes less tentative and her diction more articulate. Now she is dressed in an understated "power outfit" of black silk and high heels. By assuming the transparent style of the middle class, she furthers the impression that, unlike the earlier Roseannes, this fearless woman on stage is unconstructed, her message unmediated, and her anger real.

No longer having to filter her anger through the Domestic Goddess or any other persona, she lists the groups who annoy her, and there are few exceptions. "Women are jerks, too," she says. She describes the "relationship experts" who judge other women who don't meet their standards for liberated behavior, or "women who are mean to other women," like Wellesley students who protested Barbara Bush's visit to campus, or lesbians who disapprove of women who are with men. Most of these complaints are directed at women who use their "awakened political consciousness" or social privilege self-righteously to judge other women.

Arnold's anger, along with the show itself, reaches its climax in its last moments, when she delivers a long and furious challenge to comedian Arsenio Hall for his repeated use of "Roseanne fat jokes" on his Fox TV talk show. She grounds this display of her own strength in yet another version of her autobiography, one which stands as the basis for her broader critique of women's oppression. In doing so, she recasts the events of her life into a nightmarish monument to her own survival:

> *Excuse me, Arse. I'm thirty-seven years old. I got four kids. I'm Jewish and I was raised in Salt Lake City, Utah. My Dad sold crucifixes door-to-door to Mexicans. When I was seven I fell down, tore off my whole lip, had to have it sewed back on. When I was sixteen, I was hit by a car and my head was impaled on the hood ornament . . . I got pregnant the first time I had sex. My parents made me give her up for adoption. I found her eighteen years later when her face was splashed across the cover of the* National Enquirer. *I spent eight months in a state institution, a mental institution. I hitchhiked three times across the country by myself, with hepatitis. I lived in a car, a cabin, a cave. I married a guy just because he had a fucking bathtub. I had three more kids. He treated me like shit every day for sixteen years, and when I finally got the guts to dump that sonofabitch, I have to pay him half the money I make for the rest of my goddamn life, Arsenio.* FUCK *WITH ME!*

Such a narrative of her life casts a compelling light on the success that is so much a subject of the show. It also transforms a potential narrative of *victimization* into one of power. While it is important to note that Hall's race makes him an easier target than, for example, Johnny Carson might have been, Arnold in effect shows women, and all who experience social injustice, that they need not contain their pain and internalize their anger but instead can direct them outward toward their sources. Her eyes flash when she flings her final challenge at Hall and walks off stage. The audience roars its approval, many in it rising to their feet.

▮ Roseanne: *The Domestic Goddess and the Sitcom*

One year later, in January 1992, Arnold's face appeared on the cover of *TV Guide* wearing a red Lucille Ball wig. The headline asks, "Is Roseanne the New Lucy? Not since the '50s has one woman so dominated television" (see Murphy and Swertlow). Like Ball, Arnold has achieved her success through comedy and wields considerable power behind the scenes. The most important connection between the two, however, arises from Ball's influence (with her husband Desi Arnez) in determining the shape of the sitcom and in carving out a place in it for the unruly, funny housewife. It is on this tradition that Arnold builds in her ABC series *Roseanne* (1988–).

Like television itself, the rise of the sitcom is tied to the development of highways and flight to the suburbs during the 1950s, but its origins lie in popular forms from earlier in the century, such as the repeatable narratives of newspaper sketches, comic strips, vaudeville, and radio shows. By offering regular characters and settings, these forms were readily adaptable for TV, with its institutional need to attract and maintain a regular audience which it could sell to advertisers. The comedy film short of the 1920s and 1930s, which increasingly emphasized domestic situations, marital conflicts, and the everyday realities of its targeted middle-class audiences, was also a forerunner of the TV sitcom (Neale and Krutnik 226–227). The sitcom eventually evolved into two general categories—the domestic sitcom, such as *I Love Lucy* (1951–1961) and *Roseanne*, and the workplace sitcom, such as *The Mary Tyler Moore Show* (1970–1977), *M*A*S*H* (1972–1983), and *Cheers* (1982–1993), in which the workplace and coworkers serve, in effect, as surrogates for home and family. In the context of American comedy since the 1940s, the sitcom has come to occupy what David Marc describes as the "oceanic middle" between the two extremes of standup comedy—one based on social consciousness, such as Lenny Bruce's work, and the other on social consensus, such as Bob Hope's. A "something for everyone" form of television drama, the sitcom often teaches a kind of cheerful resignation to one's lot in life (*Laverne and Shirley* 1976–1983) or adjustment to prevailing institutions (the Norman Lear sitcoms). But it can also subvert or discredit those institutions, and such is the case with *Roseanne*.

One of the most suggestive thematic sources for the domestic sitcom, I

In her sitcom Roseanne, *Roseanne Arnold plays a working-class wife and mother who doesn't hesitate to express her feelings for her husband, Dan (played by John Goodman). Much of the sitcom's activity takes place in the cluttered kitchen of the family's bungalow.*

believe, is the romantic comedy of classical Hollywood cinema. The remaining chapters of this book will track the unruly woman's position in this classical and postclassical film genre, but for now I wish mainly to point out that both romantic comedy and the sitcom center on the relation between the sexes and provide a clearly delineated space for female disruptiveness.

In classical romantic comedy (e.g., *It Happened One Night* [1934], *Bringing Up Baby* [1938], and *The Lady Eve* [1941]), narrative pleasure arises from conflict between the sexes generated in large part by the female character's rebelliousness, unconventionality, and sense of play. These qualities are also the essence of her appeal, which was enhanced by the conventions of classical Hollywood cinema, including the star system. If such a romantic heroine seemed unsettlingly out of bounds, audiences knew from their experience with the genre that she would be eventually brought to the altar and domesticated there. By the 1940s, female unruliness took on a more troublesome cast, however. The romantic heroine's desire for a career became a frequent source of friction between the couple, along with the couple's familiarity with each other, as films turned from

Roseanne often asserts her authority in the household by teasing Dan, but the show does not compromise his essential dignity.

the tensions of courtship to the battles of married life (although without the trappings of domesticity, such as children). This pattern, which can be seen as early as *The Philadelphia Story* (1937) and *His Girl Friday* (1940), characterizes many of the Hepburn-Tracy films (*Woman of the Year* [1942] and *Adam's Rib* [1949]).

It also characterizes the situation of Lucy and Ricky Ricardo in television's *I Love Lucy* (1951–1961). For, as the drive toward domestication and containment associated with the 1950s was closing down familiar options for representing female unruliness on the big screen, others were opening up in TV, modified to suit the needs of the new medium. The married couples of the late screwball comedy provided an important model for the squabbling couples of the domestic sitcom (cf. Schatz, *Hollywood Genres*). But TV's intimate scale, its mode of consumption in the home, and its need to attract and maintain regular viewers required the development of narrative forms different from those of film—forms, such as the series and serial, that were ideally suited to explorations of domestic life.[17]

While film placed the unruly woman in plots about romantic love that made use of the medium's capacity to tap the Imaginary, TV placed her in situations that reflected its own consumption in the home and the issues of family life that presumably concerned its largely female audience. In her new incarnation on television, the unruly woman became anchored in the family like television itself, no longer a bride but a wife, a mother, a *matriarch*; no longer in the realm of fantasy and the erotic, but part of the everyday. Taking up the woman's story *after* the high drama of courtship and the wedding that resolves romantic comedy, the domestic sitcom explores what follows: children, the routine of family life, and marital discord with no promise of a magic, total reconciliation of difference.

Early TV attracted viewers not only by introducing new stars such as Sid Caesar and Imogene Coca, but by recycling and adapting radio and film stars, many of them middle-aged. One of these was Lucille Ball, whose career provides an instructive example of the consequences of channeling female unruliness from film into TV. As Alex Doty has argued, TV domesticated and infantilized her screen image, but it also never fully eradicated the "glamour, high style, wealth, wit and independence" she brought from her earlier career on film, and she eventually became one of the few female stars to combine sexuality, slapstick comedy, and domesticity.

Television, of course, is an overwhelmingly conservative institution, rigorously containing the excesses of its Lucys and Gracies. However, television also possesses other attributes that have made it in many ways more open than film to representations of female unruliness. For one, television might well be considered the quintessential postmodern medium, emerging in a time of crisis about male authority and the erosion of models of narrative, spectatorship, and subjectivity associated with classical Hollywood cinema. Television's "flow," in contrast to the tight causal logic and textual "integrity" of narrative film, releases women from the confines of the Oedipal plot and her positioning within a heterosexual couple into the more loosely constructed image of the sitcom family. This image, while appearing to uphold the authority of patriarchy, might in fact be seen as masking the crumbling of its power.[18]

Moreover, TV's lack of visual intensity frees female performers from the cinematic drive to position them as passive, eroticized spectacles and opens up opportunities for more active modes of performance such as joke making and even slapstick (as, for instance, in Lucy's mugging at the camera). In its early years, as Denise Mann has argued, TV undermined the stability of the woman's image through programs such as *The Martha Raye Show*, which challenged dominant values of femininity and domesticity by parodying Hollywood scenarios of romance and melodrama: television thus induced "an arena of liminality between the old and the new sets of values, between the gendered power relations typically associated with the classical Hollywood film . . . and the as yet unformulated power relations being set forth in television's address to women" (61).

Above all, TV has historically taken its female audience seriously, addressing women as active (if only as active *consumers*), rather than as passive objects of spectacle. In such figures as Lucy, Gracie (*The George Burns and Gracie Allen Show* 1950–1958), Samantha and Endora of *Bewitched* (1964–1972), and above all Roseanne, it has taken advantage of the culture's willingness to grant women a certain degree of autonomy in the private sphere in exchange for what it denies them in the public.

The pleasure of situation comedy does not arise primarily from narrative suspense about the actions of its characters or from its one-liners, but from the economy or wit with which it brings together two opposing discourses (Woollacott). With both its story lines and its jokes, *Roseanne* juxtaposes two discourses on family life—one based on the liberalism that underlies most popular culture, and the other on the hard-hitting, joke-making "proletarian feminism" of the Domestic Goddess.[19] In effect, Arnold tests the schema proposed by Marc by simultaneously speaking to the "oceanic middle" and expressing the kind of "social consciousness" more often found in standup comedy. The clash between these two discourses was dramatically played out during Arnold's much publicized battles for artistic control of *Roseanne* in its first season. In her account, Matt Williams, the show's first producer, wanted what she had always seen on television—"a male point of view coming out of women's mouths . . . particularly around families" (quoted in Jerome 85–86).[20]

Despite television's interest in a female audience, that male point of view informs most classics of the domestic sitcom genre, from *I Love Lucy* and *Leave It to Beaver* (1957–1963) to *All in the Family* (1971–1979). And while the domestic sitcom is founded on male/female conflict, the degree of female unruliness each series allows is tempered by the ethnic, class, and racial differences it attempts to negotiate. Sitcoms set in middle-class WASP families (*Leave It to Beaver, The Donna Reed Show* [1958–1966], *My Three Sons* [1960–1972], *The Brady Bunch* [1969–1974], and *Father Knows Best* [1954–1960]) tend to leave the authority of the husband/father largely unchallenged. The same is true of *The Cosby Show*, which replicates many of the values of the WASP upper-middle-class family. Tolerance for a wife/mother's disruptiveness tends to increase when a sitcom plays across ethnic or class difference. A husband's authority can be tested more boldly when he is non-WASP, like the Cuban Desi Arnez or the Jewish George Burns, or if, like Darren in *Bewitched*, his wife makes use of extrahuman sources of power. The working-class sitcom also opens up more room to demystify the idealized WASP family and to mock the male, but in its best-known examples, *The Honeymooners* (1955–1956) and *All in the Family*, it has still supported masculine authority in the home and conveyed that "male point of view coming out of women's mouths." Edith may be the moral center of *All in the Family* and she gains stature and respect in later seasons—but we remember her as the "dingbat."[21]

Arnold wanted something different. In expressing a *woman's* point of view on the family, *Roseanne* acknowledges the frustrations of the wife and mother but also affirms her strength and commitment to her husband and children: "I'm not Lucy trying to hide 20 bucks from Ricky, or June Cleaver gliding around in a dust proof house in pearls and heels. I'm a woman who works hard and loves her family, but they can drive her *nuts*" (quoted in Hicks 4). One episode explicitly alludes to *Leave It to Beaver* by playing its theme music and switching to black and white when Aunt Jackie, who has been a substitute wife and mother to the Conner family during Roseanne's absence, hands the children their lunches and books with a beatific smile as they skip out the door on their way to school. While *Roseanne* is often praised for seeming more "real" than most other television sitcoms, the world of the Conners, like that of the Ricardos and Cleavers, is, of course, a fiction as well—but one based on an explicitly feminist and working-class point of view. In Arnold's vision of family life, the children talk back, the house is a mess, money is always in short supply. The Conners, a blue-collar family, live in a tract of bungalows in the mill town of Lanford, Illinois. Dan works in construction and eventually starts up a small cycle business. Roseanne moves from one pink-collar job to another and is often out of work. The series has followed goody-goody Becky and tomboy Darlene through their rebellious adolescence, with DJ, the little brother, mostly staying out of the way. Deviating from the television norm (evident in such recent examples as *Wonder Years* [1988–1993], *Doogie Howser, M.D.* [1989–1993], and *Brooklyn Bridge* [1991–1993]), *Roseanne* gives greater attention to the stories of the daughters than to those of the son.

In its first season, the show presented its dramatic conflicts starkly, relying primarily on one-liners and blunt confrontations between its characters ("That's why some animals eat their young") for its humor and its bite. By the fourth season (1991–1992), the Conners had acquired a lengthy history, and the show approached the emotional range of the domestic drama or soap opera. For example, in an early episode, fifteen-year-old Darlene appears in a funk, and she remains that way for most of the season, dressed in black, lying on the couch, radiating gloom. The series did not attempt quickly to explain or remedy her depression.

Roseanne has followed the two Conner daughters through adolescence and into adulthood, giving unusual attention to female rites of passage. Darlene (Sara Gilbert) spent much of the 1991–1992 season dressed in black and sprawled on the living-room couch, suffering from a generalized depression that the series did not attempt to explain or quickly resolve.

As in the soap opera, the wife/mother in *Roseanne* is ultimately responsible for the emotional well-being of the family, and in the title sequence (which changes only slightly in the series' fifth and sixth seasons), family life is shown to be a circle which literally begins and ends on her. Roseanne sits at a cluttered kitchen table with her husband, children, and sister Jackie. The group is playing cards. The camera begins on Roseanne, then moves around the table, until it finally returns to Roseanne and stops. Meanwhile, the show's folksy theme song plays. Roseanne wins the hand, appears to burst out laughing, and sweeps up her earnings, clearly delighted to be the "woman on top." As the music fades into silence, its sound is replaced by her exuberant laughter, which continues a few moments longer. The sequence provides a backdrop of resilient, uncomplicated laughter for the more sardonic laughter that usually follows in each episode.

Jackie, played by Laurie Metcalf, holds a special place in that family circle. Husbands and wives typically discuss family issues together in a sitcom, and *Roseanne* is no exception. But Jackie provides Roseanne with a *female* confidante and ongoing opportunities for "girl talk." The series motivates Jackie's casual, regular presence in the household with the simple fact of dirty laundry; she drops in to use the Conners' washer and dryer. As a character in her own right—the thirty-something single woman who can't find any track, never mind a fast track—she provides interest and comedy through her efforts to find "meaningful" relationships with men and "rewarding" jobs primarily in male-dominated fields, first as a cop, then as a truck driver. Through her presence, the series examines the ambivalences of sisters' relationships with each other in adult life. Most important, Roseanne's regular conversations with Jackie allow her to address her audience as women, and to continually provide female-to-female commentaries on the events that unfold in the series.

While the Conners' social circle is casually integrated, *Roseanne* leaves the issues of race, ethnicity, and its own whiteness unexamined. Instead, it mines the terrain of class and gender, showing how the Conners' class position affects their lives at home and in the workplace. Home life deteriorates when Roseanne is out of work; the family suffers financially and emotionally from her anxiety and loss of self-esteem. Home life also suffers when she *does* have a job, since most of the ones available to her make no allowances for her needs to tend to her family. Every visit to school when a child is in trouble means time off without pay and an angry boss. In one of the strongest episodes about the oppression of working-class women, Roseanne confronts her threatening and patronizing new boss at Wellman Plastics, where she has worked on an assembly line for eleven years. He has increased the quota of piecework beyond what the workers can do. He resents Roseanne's refusal to be intimidated by him and when she asks him privately to lower the quota, he agrees, as long as she displays a new, subservient attitude toward him. For a while, she goes along with his public humiliations but then he raises the quota anyway, teaching her that it was not productivity he wanted but power. She saves her self-respect by quitting the job.

That episode ends with a triumphant celebration at the Lobo Bar. But subsequent episodes trace the trials of Roseanne's unemployment and her demoralizing search for a new job, continually interweaving the politics of gender and class. Roseanne enters the pink-collar ghetto of phone sales and fast food. She is disqualified from one appealing job because she hasn't learned to use a computer. Her boss at a fast-food restaurant is a spoiled and arrogant teenage boy. Her search ends for a while when she takes a

Halloween provides a chance for Roseanne *to indulge its taste for the carnivalesque. Gender stereotyping is the theme of this episode, in which Dan tries to stop son DJ from dressing up as a witch and Roseanne appears in drag at the neighborhood bar, where she joins a group of men playing pool and boasting about their sexual conquests.*

job at a beauty shop sweeping the floor, answering the phone and making coffee. The job is not ideal; she must walk Mrs. Wellman's dog and pick up her dry cleaning—even though after eleven years Mrs. Wellman still calls her "Roxanne Conway." "The work is degrading," she tells Dan after he makes an insensitive joke about the triviality of being a "shampoo girl," "but nobody there makes me feel like it is. That is *your* job." Her female boss, on the other hand, treats her with respect and appreciation. "I like the people, they like me, and that makes sweepin' hair not so bad." By the fourth season, the series has muted its treatment of worker/management conflict by creating her new boss, a gay man, as a sympathetic character.[22] Whether at Chicken Divine or Rodbell's Coffee Shop, however, these are Roseanne's "jobs," which she distinguishes from her career—the work she does at home raising her family. One episode focuses on exposing the hidden work of that career. When Dan is invited to discuss his work on Career Day at Darlene's school, Roseanne protests that she wasn't also invited to discuss hers. She then takes Darlene's home economics class on a field trip to the grocery store, showing them how to juggle limited money and time to produce a meal for five between errands and loads of laundry.

Roseanne treats gender and issues related to the female body with particular candor, wit, and poignancy. In one Halloween episode (and Halloween seems to hold a special place in the series), the holiday's invitation to masquerade and transgression becomes the means for commentary on the social construction of gender. The episode combines one story line about DJ's insistence on dressing as a witch with another based on Roseanne's disguise as a man. DJ's costume distresses the normally easygoing Dan, who urges him to be a warlock or wizard—a "guy witch"—instead, and to carry a fire poker instead of a broom. Roseanne reminds Dan that he thought Darlene was cute when she dressed up as a pirate for three years. Later, when Roseanne's car breaks down, she stops at the Lobo Bar in costume. In her beard, scruffy hat, overalls, and bulky jacket, she infiltrates the male culture of the bar, exposing the tropes of masculinity by exaggeration and direct challenge. She swaggers, struts, grunts, and mocks the sexual tall tales men tell each other.

In the course of its first four seasons (1988–1992), the series followed the Conner girls from late childhood to the brink of adulthood, and it gave a degree of attention unusual in American popular culture to female rites of passage. An episode about Darlene's first period acknowledges her fears about growing up and losing the easy equality she has had with boys before either have moved into their adult heterosexual roles. Her first pe-

Roseanne often exposes the hardships of working-class family life and gives dignity to women's domestic labor. When Dan is invited to Darlene's school to give a talk about his work in construction for career day, Roseanne protests that taking care of a family is a career, too. Here, she takes Darlene's female classmates on a field trip to the grocery store and teaches them how to stretch a housewife's limited money and time.

riod makes her angry, sad, and afraid that she will take up the detested feminine traits of her older sister. Dan doesn't help when he congratulates her with an awkward "Good job." "My life is over and he congratulated me," Darlene tells Roseanne, when the two talk together in Darlene's room. Yet the episode uses this occasion to make a powerfully positive statement about femininity. Roseanne, conscious of the negative feelings her own mother conveyed to her about her body, tells her, "It's not a disease. It's something to celebrate. You've become a full-fledged member of the Woman Race." Darlene is not convinced. "I'm probably going to start throwing like a girl, anyway." Roseanne answers: "Definitely. And since you got your period, you're going to be throwing a lot *farther.* . . . Now you get to be part of the whole cycle of things."

The Conners rarely convey their love for each other directly, but here

Roseanne comes close when she ties her own participation in "the cycle of things" with having Darlene as a daughter. The episode is a favorite of Arnold's, and she has been thanked for it by mothers who have used it in conversations with their own daughters. In another episode, Becky asks her mother for birth-control pills. Roseanne agrees, but with extreme reluctance. By the end of the episode, Roseanne learns that Becky has already had sex with her boyfriend. She gives her a long hug, Becky says, "Mom, let go," and Roseanne answers, "In a couple of years." The moment captures the complexity of a mother's feelings about the eventual, inevitable separation between parent and grown child.

In other episodes the series looks at PMS and false-pregnancy alarms. In one, PMS motivates Roseanne's transformation into a demonic, husband-terrorizing woman on top. The episode, which recycles material from her standup routine, is told from Dan's point of view in a takeoff on the film *Apocalypse Now* (1979). Its opening allusion to the film also calls up film noir, with its evocations of macho toughness and angst. In a point-of-view shot from Dan on the bed, we see a ceiling fan and its shadows (which in the film become the blades of a helicopter). In a voice-over, Dan describes the house in terms of a combat or war zone. "Today's the day. Twenty-four hours of hell. I must get out of the house. Far from ground zero." He then looks into the camera: "The horror! The horror!" In another episode, Roseanne fears that she is pregnant. The family reacts selfishly. The girls complain about the extra work they'll have to do and the money they won't be able to spend on themselves. Dan blames her for getting pregnant. At the end, the test results are negative. The children are delighted. Roseanne, however, is not so sure. While relieved, she also feels a sense of loss, which she conveys when she flatly tells Dan the names she had picked out for the baby.

One unusually stylized episode ("Sweet Dreams") warrants a more detailed look because it so effectively defines Roseanne's unruliness against its opposite, the ideology of the self-sacrificing wife and mother. It depicts this clashing of discourses by playing three styles against each other: a realist sitcom style for working-class family life; a surreal dream sequence for female unruliness; and a musical sequence within the dream to reconcile the "real" with the unruly. Dream sequences invariably signal the eruption of unconscious desire, and in this episode, the dream is linked with the eruption of female desire, the defining mark of the unruly woman.

The episode begins as the show does every week, in the normal Conner world of broken plumbing, incessant demands, job troubles. Roseanne wants ten minutes alone in a hot bath after what she describes as "the worst week in her life" (she just quit her job at the Wellman factory). But between Dan and her kids, she can't get into the bathroom, and she falls asleep waiting. At this point, all the marks of the sitcom disappear. The music and lighting tell us we are in a dream. Roseanne walks into her bathroom, but it's been transformed into an opulent, Romanesque pleasure spa where she is pampered by two bare-chested male attendants ("the pec twins," Dan later calls them). She's become a redhead. Even within this dream, however, she's haunted by her family and the law that stands behind it.[23] One by one, the members of her family appear and continue to nag her for attention and interfere with her bath. And one by one, without hesitation, she kills them off with tidy and appropriate means. (In one instance, she twitches her nose before working her magic, alluding to the 1960s sitcom *Bewitched*). As *A Question of Silence* suggests, revenge and revenge fantasies are a staple of the feminist imagination. In this case, Roseanne murders not for revenge but for a bath.

Roseanne's unruliness is further challenged, ideology reasserts itself, and the dream threatens to become a nightmare when she is arrested for murder and brought to court. We learn that her family really *isn't* dead, and, along with her friends, they testify against her, implying that because of her shortcomings as a wife and mother she's been murdering them all along. Crystal says: "She's loud, she's bossy, she talks with her mouth full. She feeds her kids frozen fish sticks and high-calorie sodas. She doesn't have proper grooming habits." And she doesn't treat her husband right, even though, as Roseanne explains, "The only way to keep a man happy is to treat him like dirt once in a while." The trial, like the dream itself, dramatizes a struggle over interpretation of the frame story that preceded it: The court judges her desire for the bath as narcissistic and hedonistic and her barely suppressed frustration as murderous. Such desires are taboo for good self-sacrificing mothers. For Roseanne, the bath (and the "murders" it *requires*) are quite pleasurable, for reasons both sensuous and righteous: Everyone gets what they deserve.[24] (Coincidentally, during this episode ABC was running ads for the docudrama *Small Sacrifices*, aired November 12–14, 1989, about a real mother, Diane Downs, who murdered one of her children and tried to kill the other two.)

Barely into the trial, it becomes apparent that Roseanne severely strains the court's power to impose its order on her. The rigid oppositions it tries to enforce begin to blur and alliances shift. Roseanne defends her children when the judge—Judge Wapner from *People's Court*—yells at them. Roseanne, defended by her sister, turns the tables on the children and they repent for the pain they've caused her. With Dan's abrupt change from prosecutor to crooner and character witness, the courtroom becomes the stage for a musical. Dan breaks into song, and soon the judge, jury, and entire cast are dancing and singing Roseanne's praises in a bizarre production number. Female desire *isn't* monstrous; acting on it "ain't misbehavin'," her friend Vanda sings. Even though this celebration of Roseanne in effect vindicates her, the judge remains unconvinced, finding her not only guilty but in contempt of court. Dream work done, she awakens, the sound of the judge's gavel becoming Dan's hammer on the plumbing. Dan's job is over too, but the kids still want her attention. Dan jokes that there's no place like home, but Roseanne answers "Bull." On her way, at last, to her bath, she closes the door to the bathroom to the echoes of the chorus singing "We Love Roseanne."

The requirements for bringing this fantasy to an end are important. First, what ultimately satisfies Roseanne isn't an escape from her family but an acknowledgment from them of *her* needs and an expression of their feeling for her—"We love you, Roseanne." I'm not suggesting that *Roseanne* represents a miraculous transcendence of the limitations of primetime television. To a certain degree this ending does represent a sentimental co-opting of her power, a shift from the potentially radical (what if Roseanne woke up and walked out?) to the liberal. But it also indicates a willingness to engage with the contradictions of women's lives. Much of Roseanne's appeal lies in the delicate balance she maintains between individual and institution and in the impersonal nature of her anger and humor, which are targeted not so much at the people she lives with as at what makes them the way they are. What Roseanne *really* murders here is the ideology of "perfect wife and mother," which she reveals to be murderous itself.

The structuring—and limits—of Roseanne's vindication are equally significant. Although the law is made ludicrous, it retains its power and remains ultimately indifferent and immovable. As usual (whether at Wellman Plastics or even at the Padres game), Roseanne's "contempt" seems ultimately her greatest crime. More important, whatever vindication she does enjoy can happen only within a dream. It cannot be sustained in real life. The realism of the frame story inevitably reasserts itself. And even within the dream, the reconciliation between unruly fantasy and ideology can be brought about only by deploying the heavy artillery of the musical. Few forms embody the utopian impulse of popular culture more insistently than the musical, and within musicals, contradictions difficult to resolve otherwise are acted out in production numbers (see Altman; Feuer).

That is what happens here. The production number gives a fleeting

resolution to the problem Arnold has typically played with in her tumul-
tuous career, the problem of representing what in our culture still remains
largely unrepresentable: a fat woman who is sexually "normal"; a sloppy
housewife who is also a good mother; a loose woman who is tidy, who
hates matrimony but loves her husband, and who can mock the ideology
of true womanhood yet consider herself a Domestic Goddess.

Part **2**

Female Unruliness in Narrative Cinema

Narrative, Comedy, and Melodrama

Poetics must begin with genre.
—MEDVEDEV/BAKHTIN (*THE FORMAL METHOD IN LITERARY SCHOLARSHIP* 175)

If on the high dramatic plane it is the son who kills and robs, it is the wife who plays this role on the plane of comic Gallic tradition. She will cuckold the husband, beat him, and chase him away.
—BAKHTIN (*RABELAIS AND HIS WORLD* 243)

An understanding of Roseanne Arnold's status as Domestic Goddess and queen of contemporary unruly women does not encompass the whole of her story, nor would any study of the semiotics of female unruliness, or the social structures of liminality, that did not also address the very notion of "story" itself—of how time, change, and history are represented in narrative form. In advocating the transformative potential of feminist parody, Susan Suleiman alludes to "a desire for laughter coupled with a desire for *story*," for something that takes place in time, "something that moves and changes, yet continues too" (169). Narrative has long posed difficulties for feminist critics because of its well-documented implication in the symbolic order of Oedipus. Indeed, much of Roseanne's and Miss Piggy's disruptive power arises from the fact that they resist the confines of narrative by functioning as "signs" within the realm of performance. However, narrative also satisfies that desire Suleiman refers to, because of its potential to represent the process of change—a possibility less evident in non-narrative performances of unruliness, such as Arnold's standup comedy or Miss Piggy's grotesque image. It is to this desire that the situation comedy responded when it applied principles of continuity to the sketches and jokes of vaudeville routines.

Later, I will return to Arnold's career, suggesting how its development might be understood in terms of genre. This thread cannot be picked up, however, without first considering the relation between female unruliness and narrative—especially the genres of laughter, those narrative forms most clearly linked with the liminality and inversion of carnival. In the discussion that follows, I will be using the term *comedy* to refer to a narrative structure rather than to laughter, an effect which that structure may or may not produce. As Norman Holland suggests, laughter doesn't define comedy and the comic effect so much as it "hovers in their vicinity," giving a "physical aura to the comic enterprise" (16). And rather than trying to establish a typology of genres, I will be seeking their conditions of possibility, asking, as Robin Wood advises, not their "what's" but their "why's" ("Ideology" 47). In this chapter and those that follow, I locate one of the why's of romantic comedy in the ideological tension surrounding the unruly woman. Whereas the transgressive male finds his most sympathetic home in the heroic genres of what Mikhail Bakhtin calls the "high dramatic plane," the transgressive woman finds hers in the "lower" forms of comedy, especially romantic comedy.[1]

Because genres exist not as discrete formal categories but in relation to each other and to the social formations that produce them, my discussion of romantic comedy cannot take place without considering melodrama as well. The two forms are linked by common ideologies about femininity and the limited plots they allow for narrative representations of female desire. As feminist scholarship has already shown, melodrama explores the victimization of the desiring woman, who triumphs mainly in her suffering, and with its powerful emotional appeal, it remains a potent means of curbing the feminist potential of the unruly woman. Romantic comedy, on the other hand, takes the "problem" of female desire to a different conclusion, creating space for the desiring woman's resistance to male control and rewarding her, at least temporarily, for those very qualities that in melodrama lead to her pain.

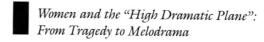

Women and the "High Dramatic Plane": From Tragedy to Melodrama

An understanding of the unruly woman's placement in romantic comedy begins with her exclusion from the genres of the high dramatic plane. That means, above all, tragedy and its related forms (the epic, the "high" drama), elements of which persist in the classical Hollywood film. Tragedy, like all genres, is not only a dramatic or narrative form but a "series of experiences and conventions and institutions" (Raymond Williams 46). It has become a critical commonplace that these conventions and institutions, which underlie the preeminent narrative forms of Western culture, are closely tied to the construction of a masculinity measured in large part by the power, and desire, to exist autonomously. Tragedy produces a male hero traditionally identified by hubris, or the principle of individuation that sets him apart from his social world. The tragic hero—outcast, warrior, prisoner, priest, or artist—undertakes an "abnormal" quest which causes him to suffer in a "normal" society (Cook 482). His fate elicits an ambivalent response commonly described as catharsis, or "pity and fear," pity drawing us to him, fear pulling us away. Tragedy ultimately affirms the order against which the hero rebels. Yet it also affirms the grandeur of the hero who seems—if only briefly—to call that order into question. In tragedy, the drive toward individuation that sets the hero "apart" also sets him "above," and so the genre reaffirms not only difference but hierarchy, and not only *sexual* difference but male authority.

Recent scholarship has demonstrated the persistence of tragedy as a conceptual and aesthetic category well into the twentieth century, where its values continue to shape contemporary theory and concepts of subjectivity.[2] Indeed, while the term *tragedy* is most often used in connection with historical periods that are centuries removed from our own, Hollywood has produced its own versions of the excessive, larger-than-life tragic hero in such figures as Charles Foster Kane in *Citizen Kane* (1941) and Michael Corleone in *The Godfather* saga (1972, 1974, 1990), heroes who suffer and struggle now not with gods or kings but with the corporate titans of capitalism. Tragedy's hold on filmmakers across the artistic and ideological spectrum can be seen in the recent work of Jean-Luc Godard, from his ironic reworking of *King Lear* (1988) to his fixation—familiar in art cinema—on the uniquely self-conscious, painfully alienated artist-hero (*Passion* [1982], *Prénom Carmen* [1984], *Soft and Hard* [1985]).

The story of a woman with heroic aspirations, however, is rarely told in tragic form. As Carolyn Heilbrun has noted, narratives of heroism cannot readily be shaped around the life of a woman because they demand that heroes display ambition or desire (often manifested in the form of a quest)—Kane's and Corleone's desire for power, Godard's for artistic sublimity. Women who display such ambition are more often portrayed as spiteful, sly, and selfish, like the monstrous career women played by Faye Dunaway in the drama *Network* (1976) and Glenn Close in the horror/thriller/melodrama *Fatal Attraction* (1987). The narrative framework of tragedy strains with a woman at its center, fracturing the ambivalence she arouses into either pity *or* fear. This separation helps explain why cinema so often portrays transgressive women as victims who evoke pity in the women's weepies, on the one hand, or as dangerous sirens and vamps in more male-oriented genres, such as film noir, on the other. In either case, the more prominent her role, the more the film shifts from the critically acclaimed "high dramatic plane" to the critically despised melodrama.[3] Melodrama is considered "debased or failed tragedy," dealing with those people—such as women, the poor, the pathetic, the weak—whose suffering matters less (Gledhill, "The Melodramatic Field" 5). As Lynette Carpenter points out,

> • *If you are watching a movie in which something terribly sad happens to a man, that is called tragedy. If you are watching a movie in which something terribly sad happens to a woman, that is called melodrama. (You may, if you like, substitute other disempowered groups for women—children, say, or the elderly.)*
> • *If the terribly sad thing takes place outdoors, then you know you are watching a tragedy, or perhaps an adventure film. If the terribly sad thing takes place indoors, then you know you are watching a melodrama.*
> • *If you cry when the sad thing happens to the man, that is called catharsis. If you cry when the sad thing happens to the woman, that is called sentimentality. (74)*

Moreover, narratives about a woman's heroism usually place her in relation to a man and, indeed, subordinate her heroism to that relationship.[4] Men's heroic quests invariably occur in the public sphere of war, politics, or empire; when they occur in more private realms, such as art, their consequences are shown to extend beyond the merely personal. In contrast, the only accepted narrative for the story of a woman's life remains in the sphere of the private—the plots of heterosexual romance, marriage, or motherhood. According to Emily Toth:

> *Narratives of women's lives in the past have emphasized their relations with men, and we've all read narratives of women's sacrifices, endless variations on "she was a success on the job, but a failure as a woman." . . . Even grocery store tabloids offer love, motherhood and loneliness as the only possible roles for women: famous stars like Linda Evans are alleged to be longing for the children they never had, and Elizabeth Taylor is always unhappy in love, for life is lonely at the top. (11)*

In other words, women's lives can be understood only in terms of "love, motherhood and loneliness." As a result, the female transgressor can rarely define herself except as a romantic heroine. Transgressive women must therefore be "emplotted," to use historian Hayden White's term, in the genres oriented toward the private—*romantic comedy*, which emphasizes love, or *melodrama*, which emphasizes loneliness and/or motherhood. According to White, historical events acquire meanings determined by the particular kinds of stories in which they are emplotted or narrated. With a few exceptions, popular fictional accounts of the life of Joan of Arc, for example—a historical figure whose actual life brings to mind tragedy—tend to emplot that life into romantic melodrama, recounting her heroism in the context of a love story with a man.[5] It would seem that a man's presence, or conspicuous absence, keeps the accomplishments and failures of a woman's life in the proper perspective.

 ### Narrative Comedy and the Feminine

If tragedy is the most masculine of genres, forcing women with "tragic" aspirations into the genres of melodrama, the implications of gender for comedy are less clear. What is the correspondence between the son who "kills and robs in the high dramatic plane" and the wife who "plays this role" in the comic tradition? Why does changing the gender of the transgressive protagonist require a change in genre? And does the movement from tragic hubris to comic unruliness tame female transgressiveness? The word *unruliness*, after all, with its quirky, less-than-grand, often misogy-

nistic connotations, would seem more appropriate to describe the misbehavior of a child or a pet than the actions of a hero.

Some feminist historians consider comedy a feminine form: "ancient,
tribal, used to celebrate family bondings like marriage . . . always moving
dramatically towards conclusions in which people are united and conflict
dissipated" (Linda Jenkins 11). Lisa Merrill asks: "If tragic form is associated with a specifically male psychological experience, might comedy be
an affirmation of female experience?" (272). The title of Linda Bamber's
study of Shakespeare, *Comic Women, Tragic Men*, suggests such a correspondence. Thomas Schatz identifies the film genres of order (the Western, the gangster film, the detective film) with male dominance and the
individual hero, and the contrasting genres of integration (musical, screwball comedy, family melodrama) with female dominance and the couple/
collective hero (*Hollywood Genres* 35). Such a characterization is surely apt.
However, the very dearth of theory and criticism about comedy in general
and the "unbearable lightness" (in Andrew Horton's words) of what does
exist (1)—in contrast to the voluminous work on tragedy—already suggest that no simple symmetry between the two forms exists.

Despite (and probably because of) its enormous and enduring popularity, comedy has never enjoyed the critical prestige of tragedy and its
descendants. Like melodrama, comedy is more often confined to the realm
of amusement than to that of art because of its popular accessibility and
its connections with gossip, intrigue, and the everyday, areas of culture
tied to the feminine. The introduction to a classic anthology of American humor notes that "the world likes humor, but treats it patronizingly.
It decorates its serious artists with laurels, and its wags with Brussels
sprouts" (White and White xvii). Even Aristotle acknowledged the difficulty in making an even-handed comparison between comedy and
tragedy: The history of tragedy is well known, but "comedy has had no
history because it was not at first treated seriously" (*Poetics* V; in Lauter
14). Overwhelmingly, films that win critical awards are serious dramas, and
it would seem that female stars are not immune to this critical preference.
When Cher won an Academy Award for her performance in *Moonstruck*
(1987), she joined only a handful of other women who have won Oscars
for comic parts—notably, Claudette Colbert as a runaway heiress in *It
Happened One Night* (1934), usually acknowledged to be the first screwball
comedy, and Judy Holliday as the dumb blonde in *Born Yesterday* (1950).[6]
In more scholarly circles, it is *Citizen Kane* that is considered to be the
"greatest movie ever made" and *The Godfather* saga the cinematic equivalent of the great American novel.

Like literary criticism, film criticism has gravitated toward genres more
aligned with tragedy than with comedy. Early genre criticism in the mid

1960s and early 1970s focused on the Western, the gangster film, the war film, the detective film, the crime film, and the horror film. More recently, film critics on the left have been wary of granting comedy any critical edge, seeing it primarily as a means of reinforcing social norms.[7] The lessons about comedy, politics, and pleasure the idealistic but naive John L. Sullivan learned in Preston Sturges's *Sullivan's Travels* (1941) seem to have remained unappreciated, or at least inadequately studied.

The consequences for film criticism of this lack of critical attention to comedy have been complex and, I believe, unfortunate. In "*The Nutty Professor*: A 'Problem' in Film Scholarship," Michael Selig ties the absence of rigorous genre analysis of comedy to the persistence of auteurism, a critical practice that has helped produce film canons based on the accomplishments of individual (male) artists. For example, the French laud Jerry Lewis as an auteur because of his originality and his use of techniques that seem modernist in comparison with the Hollywood melodrama. Yet, as Selig points out, such techniques are typical of U.S. film comedy in both the silent and sound eras:

> *In "auteurist" accounts of other comedians, especially Chaplin and Keaton, there is a similar emphasis on their creative independence and on making a case for them as social critics and/or modernists. In these cases, as well, their construction as auteurs has hindered the development of criticism of film comedy. Unlike auteur criticism of directors like Hawks and Ford, auteur criticism of comedic filmmakers generally fails to take into account the system of signification that they worked within. (55n)*

Moreover, Selig writes, auteurist studies rarely note the misogyny that characterizes the work of many comedy auteurs.

Narrative comedy is notoriously difficult to define, let alone explain, and those theories that do exist diverge widely. Emerging from them are two apparently contradictory but closely related characteristics. The first, which is often a prelude to the second, emphasizes comedy's attack on the Law of the Father—its *antiauthoritarianism*, its drive to level, disrupt, and destroy hierarchy, to comment on and contest the values tragedy affirms. Comedy breaks taboos and expresses those impulses which are always outside the social.[8] Where comedy is, so are food, sex, excrement, blasphemy—usually presented obliquely enough to be socially acceptable. Comedy, in contrast to tragedy, inflects the Oedipal story that underlies most narratives by shifting the son's guilt to his father. Youth (the small, the petty, and the powerless) triumphs over old age (authority, repression, and the law), and the "happy ending" fulfills the son's transgressive desires to murder the father and marry the mother/bride.

In this regard, comedy contests patriarchal power and so is available to women and all oppressed people as a weapon with which to express their aggression and rage at the forces of the father. But comedy can also be turned against those people in a movement of displaced abjection, when it shifts its destructive impulses from what might be considered its "proper" target—those with greater social power—toward even weaker groups. Then comedy may express the hostility to women Freud described in his analysis of the joke or the fears of what would happen if social justice were achieved and oppressed groups liberated. When comedy takes such a turn in narrative form, it emphasizes the first part of the Oedipal story—the rivalry between father and son, between forces of authority and repression and those of rebellion and release—but does not allow the son to wander far from existing structures of power. Much film comedy follows this tendency, and either excludes the feminine or subsumes it in its male figures.

Comedy's second characteristic emphasizes an impulse toward *renewal* and *social transformation*. Emphasizing the second part of the Oedipal story, the formation of the couple, this tendency finds its fullest expression in romantic comedy.[9] Male theorists, such as Northrop Frye, have often claimed too much virtue for this type of comedy, seeing its form as neutral rather than patriarchal. However, romantic comedy at least demands a place for women, or more precisely, for *a* woman, in the narrative itself and in its vision of a social order that is not only renewed but also, ideally, transformed. Romantic comedies that mock male heroism through gender inversion and female unruliness retain a strong element of antiauthoritarianism and so combine both comedic tendencies, holding sentiment and skepticism in a balance that characterizes, I believe, the most successful examples of the genre. Such is the case with a strain of romantic film comedy that emerged in the 1930s and 1940s.

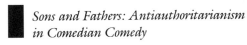

Sons and Fathers: Antiauthoritarianism in Comedian Comedy

Almost all comedic forms—from jokes to gags to slapstick routines to the most complex narrative structures—move toward a liberation from authority. Like carnival, comedy levels the lofty and erases distinctions by replacing the exalted hero of tragedy with one reduced to the level of Everyman or lower. The "son," or those characters who stand for the values of freedom, anarchy, and new life, defeats the "father," or whatever stands for tradition, authority, rigidity, and death. Traditional literary scholarship defines the comic hero by his *poneria*, or the villainy and roguishness of the picaro, and by his *polypragmosune*, the ability to land on his feet, to make a deal. Comedy favors the small and the everyday, the little person who survives at all costs. Consider, for example, the blockbuster 1990 film *Home Alone*. Like many comedies of the 1980s and early 1990s, (*Big, Pee Wee's Big Adventure, Bill and Ted's Excellent Adventure, Ferris Beuller's Day Off, Wayne's World*), *Home Alone* exaggerates the comic male hero's infantilization. Its hero is a precocious little boy, who turns his accidental abandonment by his distracted, thoughtless parents into an opportunity for an anarchic vacation from their repressive and alienating rules.

The following set of terms contrasts the attitudes or perspectives of comedy with those of tragedy:

Tragedy	*Comedy*
separation	connection
isolation	integration, community
death	sex
funeral	wedding and feast
anxiety-fulfillment (dystopian)	wish-fulfillment (utopian)
the grand	the insignificant, the everyday
aristocratic	bourgeois
superhuman	subhuman (machine, beast)
individual	social
singleness	doubleness, incongruity
finality, linearity	circularity
pity and fear	laughter and pleasure
public realm—war, law, state, empire	private realm—home, family
ethics	manners
good and evil	life and death

While male/female is notably missing from this grid (a modified version of Albert Cook's), a closer look suggests that comedy may indeed bear a relation to the cultural construct of femininity similar to tragedy's connection with masculinity. Comedy's interest in the social, as opposed to tragedy's in the individual, aligns it with values that are conventionally associated with the feminine: community over separation, and the preservation of life rather than its sacrifice for principle, power, or a Faustian knowledge that oversteps proper human limits. Comedy often mocks the masculinity that tragedy ennobles. The very centrality of sex to comedy and the comedic agenda of renewing life open up space for the feminine that doesn't exist in the more exclusively masculine world of tragedy. Because sex is to comedy as death is to tragedy, the heterosexual couple that is a mainstay of Hollywood narrative film is also one of comedy's most fundamental conventions. But in comedy, sex is not a means toward tragic knowledge or transcendence of the self (as in the Tristan and Isolde *Liebestod*) but is social—part of an overall attack on repression and celebration of bodily pleasure, a means of connection within the space of family and the time of generation.

Despite such apparent accord with the feminine, however, comedy in mainstream narrative film usually makes its case against the father with very little attention to the mother or daughter. Comedy may deflate Oedipus and show him to be a fool, but it still places him at the heart of the story. As Lucy Fischer has shown, comedy, in both theory and practice, is generally guilty of symbolic matricide, of "throwing Momma from the train," to borrow from a recent, particularly misogynist film (see "Sometimes I Feel Like a Motherless Child"). As she notes, the canon of (primarily U.S.) film comedy consists almost entirely of male directors and performers, from the Keystone Kops, Charlie Chaplin, and Buster Keaton through Woody Allen, Eddie Murphy, and many more. Mae West is the only woman regularly included among them.[10]

While some of these actors and directors have worked in romantic comedy, most of their films fall into a category commonly described as comedian comedy, or, in Stuart Kaminsky's words, comedy "in the mode of the individual." Because individual usually means individual *male*, this kind of comedy might well be described as "male-centered comedy," with male referring to an individual (Jerry Lewis, Mel Brooks), a couple (Laurel and Hardy, Bob Hope and Bing Crosby, Cheech and Chong), or an entire troupe or ensemble (the Keystone Kops, the Marx Brothers, Monty Python). Women have performed in comedian comedy since its earliest days, but until recently, their absence from the canon of comedian comedy, as well as the cultural and institutional reasons for that absence, have remained largely unacknowledged and unexamined.[11]

When comedian comedy mocks the heroic masculinity affirmed in serious drama, it often does so by appropriating in a feminized, anti-heroic male the positive, anarchic, "feminine" principles comedy affirms. From Charlie Chaplin to Harpo Marx to Woody Allen to Danny DeVito, these figures are small and feminine or androgynous in appearance, and positioned as feminine through their roles as underdogs. The films they appear in tend to emphasize their comic performance rather than a narrative trajectory to the altar: even if a bride exists in a romantic subplot, she is often a minor figure and the son remains the exclusive agent of liberation and new (social) life.[12]

Comedian comedy often concerns itself primarily with the foibles of the current society and the obstacles to its transformation—the conflict between a foolish son and an equally foolish father—rather than turning its gaze, as romantic comedy does, toward a utopian future community. It takes a satiric or ironic rather than romantic perspective, eliciting a laughter that is more corrective than festive and inclusive. If tragedy uses violence and conflict to purify, comedy uses them to make dirty or messy—to liberate from a rigidity (emotional, social, or even physical) that bears a ghostly resemblance to death. The verbal anarchy of the Marx Brothers and the parody and mayhem of Monty Python challenge formal and social restraints. Likewise, slapstick uses athletics and acrobatics to show the body seemingly out of control. In films such as *Animal House* (1978), *Porky's* (1981), and *The Naked Gun* (1988), food fights recall the forbidden, infantile desire to play with feces.

Comedian comedy often compounds its erasure of the bride by directing its corrective laughter onto the matriarch, displacing the hostility it is licensed to level at the father onto the repressive, phallic mother. In such comedy, consistent with Freud's analysis of the joke, women stand not as essential subjects in a drama of new social life but as fearsome or silly symbols of repression and obstacles to social transformation. As a result, although comedian comedy often makes use of the iconography of female unruliness, it does so misogynistically, stripping it of any positive charge. Rather than a symbol of rebelliousness and freedom, the matriarch becomes just the opposite, taking the father's place as the embodiment of all that stands between the hero and his desire and representing a dreaded domesticity and propriety, a fearful symbol of a "community" that includes women. Her ranks include spinsters, dowagers, prohibitionists, mothers-in-law, librarians, suffragettes, battle-axes, career women, "women's libbers," and lesbians.[13] Set up as the butt of laughter and occasionally the victim of physical aggression as well, these women may be old and stubbornly resistant or indifferent to male desire, fat or scrawny, shrill and "unfeminine." They serve as targets for the hatred of repression mobilized by comedy, especially by the infantile, regressive, and misogynistic hero of the comedian comedy.

Margaret Dumont played such a role, although sympathetically, in the Marx Brothers films. An early scene in *A Night at the Opera* (1935) shows her sitting alone at a table in a crowded dining room, after having waited an hour for Groucho, who is seated with his back to her at a table with a beautiful blonde woman. When he finally joins her, she plays the dowager foil to his barrage of jokes and one-liners. Margaret Hamilton as the Wicked Witch of the West in *The Wizard of Oz* (1939) plays the classic phallic mother who possesses the power to shatter the security of home when she separates Dorothy from her dog, Toto. (Polly Holliday reprises the role as the comic villain Mrs. Deagle, the widow of a real-estate tycoon, in the 1984 horror film *Gremlins*.) In *Some Like It Hot* (1959), Sweet Sue runs her All-Girl Band like a drill sergeant, terrorizing her male assistant and the vulnerable Sugar Kane, played by Marilyn Monroe. In the futurist black comedy *Brazil* (1985), the "terrible mother" is only one of many female grotesques—including an enormous secretary, an old woman who decomposes after her plastic surgery fails, and an innocent-looking little girl who asks the hero if she can "see his willy." The hero's mother, who refuses to grow old, is depicted as a hideous threat to her son's deepest desire. In *The Goonies* (1985) and *Throw Momma From the Train* (1987), Anne Ramsey plays an evil comic mother.

One of the most vicious examples of such matriarchs appears in Stanley Kramer's 1963 film *It's a Mad Mad Mad Mad World*. This film demonstrates a desire to punish female excess that is usually more evident in melodrama than comedy. Ethel Merman plays a "terrible mother-in-law"—matronly, loud, aggressive, and abrasive. The film, which attempts to recreate the silent comedies of motion, depicts a male-dominated quest for buried treasure. Throughout the pursuit, Merman's behavior as a screaming harpie encourages the audience to share the other characters' hostility to her. This hostility culminates in an act of violence when her son-in-law and another man turn her upside down and shake her to retrieve a set of keys she has hidden in her bosom. The film ends with a pratfall she takes in front of the entire cast, turning her once again into a spectacle and a target of unsympathetic laughter both within the film and outside it. The film exemplifies the hostility of much male-centered comedy toward women. While critiquing much that is repressive about the father, these films often only reinforce his subjugation of women, and ensure that after his defeat he will be replaced by a new but hardly improved version of himself.

 Sons and Brides: Renewal and Transformation in Romantic Comedy

Comedy can come close to imploding on itself when its impulse toward destruction is severed from any counter-impulse toward social renewal and transformation (as in *Dr. Strangelove, or How I Learned to Stop Worrying and Love the Bomb* [1964]). Thus, comedy celebrates excess not only as an end in itself but as a means of liberating the social world from structures grown so rigid and unyielding that they threaten its very existence. Comedy that emphasizes this principle harnesses the genre's antiauthoritarian energy and directs it toward creating a new vision of community based on the assumption that the renewal of life—biological and social—depends on connection or relation to others. In this regard, comedy insists that community does not repress individual desire but instead represents its very fulfillment.

Romantic comedy treats the social difference that impedes community as a matter of sexual difference, and so it builds the feminine into both its narrative conflict and the resolution of that conflict. The formation of the heterosexual couple, of course, powerfully reasserts the supposedly universal law of kinship. Indeed, that law extends to the very institution of what Adrienne Rich calls "compulsory heterosexuality," buttressed historically by the ideology of romantic love. But the couple's union must also be seen, I believe, as a sign of the partial suspension of conflict—the tolerance for difference—on which community depends. In the couple's victory over the obstacles between them (as well as in the child or new life implicit in their union) lie the utopian possibilities of a new social order, traditionally represented in the public ceremony of the wedding or feast. As Laura Mulvey suggests, the triumph of the Law of the Father represented in narrative isn't always absolute. Especially during times of social transformation, and especially in the genres of laughter, narratives can reabsorb "the abnormal back into a sense of an order that is altered," although still recognizably subject to the law ("Changes" 170).

Few critics have surpassed the insights of Northrop Frye into comedy's utopian dimension, its mapping of an "order that is altered." Frye, in fact, can be credited with finding in romantic comedy—and in comedy in general—a profundity that had eluded earlier generations of critics. Indeed, his project, beginning with "The Argument of Comedy" in 1948 and continuing to the present, might be seen as an attempt to reclaim comedy from its critical exclusion. For several decades, Frye's work was out of favor among critics wary of his formalism and his insistence on art's continual creation of itself out of its own conventions and histories.[14] But it was Frye whom Marxist literary critic Fredric Jameson invoked in theorizing the relation between works of the imagination and the social world. According to Frye, that relation is most fully and positively realized in the forms of comedy and romance, which express wish-fulfillment rather than anxiety-fulfillment, and so "educate" the imagination in the direction of social transformation.

For Frye, all narrative reworks a common story of community, struggle, and renewal; of birth, death, and rebirth. Comedy (and romance) emphasizes the renewal element of the cycle rather than defeat. It represents the liberation of a world wilting under repressive law by a temporary movement into a space marked by what Bakhtin would call the carnivalesque, Victor Turner the liminal, and Frye and C. L. Barber a "green world" of festivity and natural renewal set apart from the "red and white" world of politics and history. In romantic comedy, that movement follows the remarkably consistent pattern of New Comedy: "What usually happens is that a young man wants a young woman, that his desire is resisted by some opposition, usually paternal, and that near the end of the play some twist in the plot enables the hero to have his will" (Frye, *Anatomy* 163).[15] The lovers are tested and finally find themselves by retreating from the ordinary world where their union seems impossible to a "magical" place apart from everyday life, such as the moonlit island in *It Happened One Night*, the Connecticut forest in *Bringing Up Baby* (1938), the cruise ship in *The Lady Eve* (1941), and, more recently, the enchanting moments at the Metropolitan Opera and on the streets of New York in *Moonstruck*. When the couple returns, their union, in Frye's words, "causes a new society to crystallize" around them. The family gathered at the end of *Moonstruck* represents just such a crystallization. While unable to accommodate the philandering patriarch's mistress, the family has become tolerant enough to make room for the romantic hero's brother and rival, the film's buffoon.

As Frye explains, this pattern of struggle and renewal organizes most major histories and narratives, both secular and religious. Many, such as Christianity, are comedic in structure, promising the ultimate resolution of a conflict between good and evil in a triumph of the good. Marx's view of history also takes the utopian perspective of comedy, arguing that the struggle against class oppression moves toward resolution in the community or transformed social order comedy affirms. Within the overarching narrative structure of birth, death, and rebirth, every comedy contains a potential tragedy. But every tragedy can also be seen as an incomplete comedy. In the larger perspective—of history, community, or even biology—the life and death of the individual are no longer tragic. By shifting the guilt to the father and allowing the victory of the son, comedy gets the last word, just as on the Greek stage a satyr play or comedy always concluded a trilogy of tragedies. Chaplin's comment that tragedy should be filmed in close-up and comedy in long shot is suggestive here. Comedy not only requires a certain emotional detachment from the fate of the individual—ultimately death—but it makes such detachment possible by showing that fate in a broader perspective, in long shot.

There is much to fault about Frye's work. His assertions about comedy and romance as wish-fulfilling fail to ask *whose* wishes; his impulse, and it is the impulse of a liberal humanism, is to seek a common ground of shared desire rather than to investigate the divisions which make such common ground difficult if not impossible to achieve. As Frye himself recognizes, he is an *Odyssey* rather than an *Iliad* critic, drawn toward the utopian dimensions of art, to comedy and romance, rather than to tragedy and irony. Concerning romantic comedy, he assumes too readily that desire is the sole possession of the male hero: "What usually happens is that a young man desires a girl"; the woman can only be "bride to be redeemed." While this may be true of the Greek and Roman New Comedies, it is not for Shakespearean comedy or romantic film comedy, which have much in common. Frye notes that in Shakespeare's comedies, the female's passage from a kind of death to "rebirth" (often symbolized, significantly, by her disguise in male clothing followed by her return to women's clothing) often "brings about" the conclusion. However, for Frye this passage appears to happen quite apart from her own desire or will. This mistake is compounded by Stanley Cavell, who is heavily indebted to Frye.

The heightened emphasis on women in Shakespeare's romantic comedies represents an important generic shift in the tenacious pattern of New Comedy, and one which helps illuminate the film comedies of the 1930s and 1940s. Although, like the romantic film comedy, Shakespeare's comedies rarely have more than two central female characters (*As You Like It* and *Twelfth Night* are exceptions), these women function not simply as "brides to be redeemed" but as obstacles to desire, objects of desire, and subjects of desire. Characters such as Rosalind in *As You Like It* and Viola in *Twelfth Night* enjoy a dramatic weight comparable to that of male heroes in tragedy, although, of course, their transgressions are of a different order from the "killing," "robbing," and other forms of literal and symbolic violence that, as Bakhtin suggests in *Rabelais and His World*, define the male hero of the high dramatic plane. These are "women on top." If their unruliness is sufficiently disguised to make them acceptable as ideal brides, it is also sanctioned because it serves the larger goal of communal revitalization. These women avoid the fierce disciplining suffered by Kate in *The Taming of the Shrew*, who is wilder and more overtly rebellious than the heroines of Shakespeare's other comedies. But all are the forerunners to Susan Vance in *Bringing Up Baby*, Sugarpuss in *Ball of Fire* (1941), and Billie Dawn in *Born Yesterday* (1950).

Despite his shortcomings, however, Frye has much to offer feminist approaches to comedy. By asserting the priority of narrative structure over various comedic causes (such as performance) or effects (such as laughter), Frye ensures attention to the Oedipal narrative and the space, albeit limited, it ensures for the feminine. That space occurs when the narrative privileges the son's quest for a bride over his battle with the father, and even more when it places the couple—or the woman—rather than the male hero at its center. Like Jameson, Frye sees narrative as an epistemological category, a structure that provides a means of understanding those other phenomena that also contribute to comedy—performance, gags, jokes, laughter. As I have suggested above, when discussions of film comedy emphasize those factors apart from their narrative context, gender has tended to disappear. In addition, by asserting that comedy in effect contains tragedy, Frye implicitly reverses the hierarchy that has so long privileged tragedy: "The watcher of death and tragedy has nothing to do but sit and wait for the inevitable end; but something gets born at the end of comedy, and the watcher of birth is a member of a busy society" (*Anatomy* 170).

 Melodrama and Romantic Comedy

Romantic comedy exists in the same kind of generic tension with melodrama that Frye finds between comedy and tragedy (see Neale and Krutnik 133–136). Romantic comedy usually contains a potential melodrama, and melodrama a potential romantic comedy. Melodrama depends on a belief in the possibility of romantic comedy's happy ending, a belief that heightens the pathos of its loss. Similarly, romantic comedy depends on the melodramatic threat that the lovers *won't* get together and that the heroine will suffer the fate of becoming a spinster or of marrying the wrong man. But while critics have exerted considerable effort to preserve the distinctions between drama on the high plane and its "others"—melodrama or comedy—no such stakes are involved in preserving the distinction between melodrama and romantic comedy, both of which are deeply implicated in the feminine.

Both romantic comedy and melodrama are set squarely in the province of women—the private, the domestic, the home, and the heart. Even when romantic comedy takes place in the workplace, as with *His Girl Friday* (1940) and *Working Girl* (1988), that environment simply provides a backdrop for the film's real interest, the relationship between the sexes. Both narrate the stories of women with "excessive" desire which is limited to the realm of heterosexual romance and motherhood. Both use the deferral of sexual fulfillment not only as a means to create and sustain the fantasies of romance, but as plot devices to prolong narrative suspense. The narrative attention both give to women results in male characters that may be more "sensitive," even feminine, than conventionally heroic. In both forms, characters work out their conflicts more through language or conversation than through action.

Formally, each constructs a world that is meant to appear realistic—with settings, characters, and conflicts that are ordinary rather than extraordinary. Melodrama's overblown mise-en-scène externalizes emotions that are not unfamiliar but simply inarticulable by its characters. Even the glamorous couples of romantic film comedy are shown to be, at heart, "like us" in their attitudes toward sexuality and love. Both forms are also highly conventionalized, with characters that tend toward types or social masks seen from the outside, and with plots dependent on coincidences, twists, and improbable reversals. These devices not only help sustain the tension that prolongs and enhances romantic desire, but construct a world in which characters are subjected to forces beyond their control.

Important differences, of course, also define the forms. Most obviously, melodrama heightens the spectator's emotions, while romantic comedy maintains a sense of detachment, using close-ups and emotional music sparingly. Melodrama creates a landscape that is morally polarized (or "made legible," in Peter Brooks's words, as quoted in Gledhill, "The Melodramatic Field" 33), while romantic comedy affirms "life"—freedom and fertility—over "virtue," concerning itself with oddballs, eccentrics, and fools, rather than with saints and villains. That affirmation of life, of course, manages at the same time to eliminate the maternal in the symbolic matricide Fischer has described, for if romantic comedy maims the father, it kills the mother. Romantic comedy allows its heroine to participate in its utopian, symbolic rebirth only by abdicating her literal connections with maternity—her bond to her mother and eventually to her own daughters. Mothers and mother-substitutes exist in many romantic comedies (*The Philadelphia Story* [1940], *Bringing Up Baby*, *My Man Godfrey* [1936]), but the heroine usually neither has nor is a mother, and the father fills the critical parental role. Noting that the maternal missing from romantic comedy surfaces in melodrama, Stanley Cavell asks: "What is it that makes the absence of the mother a comedy, and her presence a melodrama?" ("Psychoanalysis and Cinema" 20).

One answer arises from the traditional place of the woman as a token of exchange between men, mediating the transfer of power from one generation to the other. Mothers rarely hold any power to transfer; figures like the aunt in *Bringing Up Baby* are rare exceptions.[16] A more suggestive answer concerns the genre's focus on the heroine's movement through the Oedipal passage. The formation of the couple that resolves romantic comedy also signals the heroine's successful resolution of her Oedipal struggle and her acceptance of the terms of heterosexuality—the subjugation of female by male. To do so, she must sever the most important feminine identification of her life, her mother, for an exclusive attachment to a man, a stand-in for her father.[17] In *The Philadelphia Story*, it is Tracy's relationship with her estranged father, not her mother, that is crucial; until she reconciles with him, she cannot complete her movement toward mature femininity (and accept her proper mate). It is no wonder that patriarchy writes such a story of masculine victory as comedy—or that Adrienne Rich describes this rent between mother and daughter, ignored in our culture, as "the essential female tragedy": "We acknowledge Lear (father-daughter split); Hamlet (son and mother) and Oedipus (son and mother) as embodiments of the human tragedy; but there is no presently enduring recognition of mother-daughter passion and rapture" (*Of Woman Born* 237). If melodrama offers women "guilty pleasures," then so too does romantic comedy, which covers up with laughter the costs of a woman's acceptance of her proper place in patriarchy. Romantic comedy tolerates, and even encourages, its heroine's short-lived rebellion because that rebellion ultimately serves the interest of the hero.

However, while romantic comedy and melodrama both tie a woman's rebellion to her acceptance or refusal of the terms of heterosexuality, melodrama dooms her rebellion from the start, not only teaching that a woman's lot under patriarchy is to suffer but making that suffering pleasurable. Exposing the male villainy repressed in romantic comedy—or shown as simple foolishness—melodrama takes up the story of the heroine for whom romantic comedy's happy ending never will be possible, or the story of what follows that happy ending. Melodrama, in fact, is the only cinematic genre (with the possible exception of the horror film) that has traditionally been available for that sequel.

Because melodrama concerns the heroine who fails to resolve the Oedipal passage, it leaves the pre-Oedipal mother-daughter bond intact. As Nancy Chodorow has explained, the intense love between mother and daughter, not mother and son, stands as our culture's primary taboo. Patriarchy is deeply threatened by this bond, whether it takes the form of the connections between mothers and daughters, or, more generally, the solidarity among women, or, most radically, the lesbian separatism implied at the end of *A Question of Silence*. And so it is no surprise that under patriarchy the stories of such women are told in forms that guarantee their punishment. From *Mildred Pierce* (1945) to *Terms of Endearment* (1983), mothers and daughters caught up in each other's lives can cause each other only misery. Melodrama thus insists that women's deviance from the norms of our culture can lead only to isolation and tears, their pleasures can come only in pain, and the stories of their rebellion can be the occasions only of grief.

Stella Dallas

Feminist film critics have already written extensively about the melodrama *Stella Dallas* (King Vidor, 1937), but I would like to take another brief look at the film because it exposes so clearly and movingly the structural relation between melodrama and romantic comedy and the place of the mother in each. By heightening the tension between these genres as it follows Stella and her daughter Lollie through the conventional plots of love, motherhood, and loneliness, the film exposes the often impossible contradictions of women's lives.

The film begins in the love plot, where Stella's desire to cross the boundaries of class and gender by actively pursuing the boss's son appears in the positive light of romantic comedy. (The 1990 remake of the film makes even more of Stella's unruliness by casting in the part Bette Midler, an actor more unambiguously and consistently coded with unruliness than was Barbara Stanwyck.) As the film follows Stella's story past love, it moves into melodrama, where her unruliness—initially shown in the favorable light of comedy—begins to appear less sympathetically. Stella makes the first of several disastrous spectacles of herself by behaving at a dinner party in a manner that is loud and unrestrained. After refusing in the first place to obey her husband's well-intentioned wishes that she stay home, she disobeys him further by dancing with a jolly but dissolute and unrefined man and refusing to go home. Later, she laughs uproariously on a train with the same man after he plays a practical joke on the other passengers. She constantly fights the urge to pile ruffles and bows on the more subdued dresses her husband prefers for her. Gradually, her unruliness takes on a tragic cast as it begins to signify her transgressive refusal to submerge her own identity into that of her husband, as well as the impossibility of preserving that identity and being a good mother at the same time.

Romantic comedy returns a second time in the film when the third thread of Stella's story, the motherhood plot, dovetails with her daughter Lollie's love plot. In this part of the film, Stella's unruly independence becomes a source of pathos and horror when she unwittingly makes a spectacle of herself in front of Lollie's new friends. Stella realizes that Lollie's deep attachment to her threatens her daughter's chance for the happily-ever-after ending of romantic comedy; the most dangerous expression of female unruliness, after all, is the bond between mother and daughter, which must be broken to enable the daughter's narrative to end on the note of romantic comedy. Just as Stella's unruly selfhood came between her and her husband, Steve Dallas, so it comes between her and Lollie as well. Stella has no choice but to drive Lollie away, which she does in a tour-de-force performance of the unruliness that has come to stand for a dangerous female independence from men. She puts on a masquerade of drunkenness and lust, exaggerating the most vulgar clichés of femininity. Lollie, unable to see past the masquerade, begins the painful transfer of her allegiance from her mother to her father (and his new, socially upscale wife) and the suitor who will be his successor. Lollie's story—with the important exception of her relation to her mother—remains confined to the structure of romantic comedy: a handsome and wealthy young man courts her, the obstacles to their union are overcome, and they marry. As with most romantic comedies, the film does not follow Lollie past the altar. But *Stella Dallas* does allow the viewer to experience romantic comedy from the point of view—quite literally—of the mother whose "death" is required to bring about its happy ending.

In this moment, the most wrenching of the film, the climax of Lollie's romantic comedy coincides with Stella's redemption in melodrama, after she has enacted the self-annihilation that ideology demands of mothers. Outside the house, excluded from Lollie's wedding, Stella watches Lollie while Lollie watches only her new husband. The joy of the wedding is deeply undercut by the realization of its costs—a realization which Lollie's stepmother shares in unspoken communication with Stella when she opens the drapes so that Stella can see. Both women know that the bride pays a high price for her moment of happiness. Lollie, at some point, will have to replay her own version of Stella's melodrama, as her life story moves past the confines of romantic comedy. The film concludes with the camera retreating from the scene in the window and remaining fixed on Stella's tear-stained face as she walks away, radiant in her self-denial, banished from the occasion that in comedy stands above all for inclusiveness, renewal, and festivity.

Wherever romantic comedy is, melodrama is also, if only as a structuring absence. As romantic comedy's shadow genre, melodrama remains an uneasy reminder that the unruly woman's power is fragile, subject to social and generic forces that would shift the register of her outrageousness from comedy to pathos. For the next three chapters on classical Hollywood cinema, however, melodrama will retreat into the background, where it will remain until a final chapter, which considers its impact on the post-classical romantic comedy.

Up to this point, my study has been guided more by the principles of intertextuality rather than by those of history. Now, after examining the semiotics of female unruliness and the structural components of narrative comedy, my argument takes on a more historical shape, responding, in effect, to that lure of narrative, that "desire for *story*," mentioned at the outset of this chapter. What follows is a historical account—a narrative, if you will—of a genre as it spans the period of sound cinema, responding to and evolving out of a range of social and generic forces. These forces serve more as context than cause for the changes I track, for, as Frank Krutnik has suggested in his own account of romantic comedy, films "never spring magically from their cultural context but they represent instead much more complex activities of *negotiation*, addressing cultural transformations in a highly compromised and displaced manner" ("The Faint Aroma" 57). Because my interest is not in redefining the romantic film comedy but in considering the interplay between this narrative form and the notion of female unruliness, I do not attempt to provide a survey or exhaustive account of romantic film comedy but instead look more carefully at a handful of films. My choices have been determined by several factors; most of these films are well known, and all, I believe, raise issues of gender inversion in provocative ways. Together, they document the unruly woman's status in romantic comedy as it changes from the early 1930s through the classical period to the postclassical period, in which, as Roseanne Arnold's career has suggested, television provides a more hospitable medium for female unruliness.

To begin, I would like to turn to a figure whose use of the semiotics of unruliness remains unrivaled in film history—and in fact made her uncontainable in the genre of romantic comedy. A comic embodiment of those qualities Stella Dallas enacted to such an unhappy end, a model for Miss Piggy, and an inspiration to Arnold, this unruly woman is Mae West.

Romantic Comedy and the Unruly Virgin in Classical Hollywood Cinema

A book on radical feminism that did not deal with love would be a political failure.

—SHULAMITH FIRESTONE
(*THE DIALECTIC OF SEX* 126)

Mae West's film *She Done Him Wrong* (Lowell Sherman, 1933) has many claims to fame. For one, its enormous popularity the year it was released helped save Paramount Studios from financial ruin. For another, its use of sexual innuendo fueled the drive toward censorship that culminated in the formation of the Catholic Legion of Decency and the strict implementation of the Production Code. And while the film has little in common with the romantic comedies of the 1930s and 1940s, it helped launch the career of Cary Grant, who played opposite West and would become the male actor most strongly identified with the genre during the classical Hollywood period.[1]

The film, based on West's Broadway hit *Diamond Lil*, also provided a national showcase for one of the most influential examples of the unruly woman in this century. At a time when actresses such as Greta Garbo were playing romantic heroines embodying traditional notions of femininity— women suffering for love—West offered something quite different. She was not alone, of course. Other women at the time were making their own contributions to early sound comedy, most notably Jean Harlow, whose career as a blonde bombshell was cut off by her death in 1937, at the age of 26. But none of them had a more enduring impact than West, both on screen and off, from the controversies in the 1920s surrounding her plays *Sex* and *Drag* to her performance in *Myra Breckinridge* (1970) at the age of 78. Her brazen, comic attack on Puritan attitudes toward sexuality under-mined sentimentalized ideals about "true womanhood." And, as she aged, the spectacle she made of herself became even more outrageous because of our culture's difficulty in seeing sexual forwardness in older women as anything but grotesque.

Few unruly women who followed West in U.S. popular culture have been untouched by her influence. With her campy performance of femi-ninity, she provided the model for Miss Piggy, the Muppet femme fatale in a comic key. As a writer and creator of her own star persona, she in-spired comedian and television star Roseanne Arnold, who acknowledges her debt to her and whose Domestic Goddess shares the bravura, if not the campiness, of West's "Twentieth Century Sex Goddess" (West 163). Finally, by de-romanticizing romance and exposing the relation between sexuality and a woman's financial security, West's role in *She Done Him Wrong* anticipated Marilyn Monroe's in *Gentlemen Prefer Blondes* (1953) twenty years later. Important changes occurred, of course, in the meta-morphosis of the unruly woman from West to Monroe, and, in fact, female unruliness was to follow a course in classical Hollywood cinema quite different from the one set by West. But the images of the two women stand as a pair of diamond-studded blonde bookends to a period of history during which the topos of the unruly woman served a range of generic and historical needs.

That period, from the early 1930s into the 1950s, coincided with the height of the classical Hollywood cinema style, and it is also often consid-ered something of a golden age of romantic film comedy. The genre has been identified by a wide range of characteristics, from its "screwball" or "zany" characters, usually women, to its populist themes. These perspec-tives are illuminating in important ways, and indeed the eclectic collection of films that can loosely be considered romantic comedy warrants such critical diversity.[2] One commonplace about these films, however, is that they are "comedies of equality," which challenge patriarchal power relations to the extent that they put men and women on an equal footing, and the films in fact *do* center on the relationship between the sexes, establishing conflict along a male/female line. For such conflict to be dramatic, the sides must be well matched, at least temporarily. Women must be allowed more power, or men less, than they are allowed in conventional forms of representation. In other words, these films are guided by the principal of gender inversion and are sympathetic to the presence of women on top.

It is true, of course, that the progressive potential of any structure that remains within the category of binary oppositions and simple inversions of power relationships is limited. When used most conservatively, gender inversion harnesses the unruly woman's disruptive potential only to create a new and not-very-improved male hero. Like film noir, romantic comedy often subjects a weak male to a predatory woman, but within a comedic frame that mutes the threat of male chastisement.[3] The genre can thus be seen as a benign male fantasy in which men surrender rational control only to have their social and sexual power restored. Furthermore, when gender inversion is layered on to the narrative structure of New Comedy, it enables a displacement of class issues onto gender. Social class is often used as a marker of the heroine's unruliness: she is either an outlaw or an heiress, outside the conventional middle class, while the hero has the "invisible" signs of the middle class, the makings of the All-American Everyman who needs only to submit to the tutelage of the unruly woman to overcome the suspicious effeteness of his occupation, often as a man of letters. The couple's cross-class union thus affirms U.S. ideology that class doesn't matter.

However, gender inversion can also set in motion a destabilization of the binary categories of gender, opening the way to more fluid forms of sexuality before the hero and heroine are reinscribed into the norms of a more conventionally figured heterosexuality. Its negotiation of power between the sexes can be seen as a preliminary, imaginary step toward dismantling the structures of masculine dominance. That first step is especially intriguing because romantic comedy often makes it sexy, undoing traditional heterosexuality's eroticization of masculine dominance and feminine submission.

Despite Mae West's impact as an unruly woman, however, the heroine of the classical Hollywood romantic comedy assumed a shape quite different from hers, one that was less voluptuous and more boyish, more consistent with Katharine Hepburn's in *Sylvia Scarlett* (1935), another early generic misfit that coincidentally stars Grant. The reasons for that morphological shift can be found in a third film, *It Happened One Night* (1934), which establishes the appeal and adaptability of the New Comedy plot during the Depression. *It Happened One Night* initiates a film genre that requires its female leads to be coded not with the experienced sexuality of a Mae West but with chasteness or virginity. *Sylvia Scarlett*, in turn, extends the heroine's virginity into the more liminal area of androgyny. Together, these films lay the groundwork for the later professor-hero comedies, such as *Bringing Up Baby* (1938), *Ball of Fire* (1941), and *The Lady Eve* (1941), that more fully realize the potential of the woman on top before she is stripped of her intelligence, resexualized, and domesticated into the dumb blondes played by Judy Holliday and Marilyn Monroe at the end of the classical Hollywood period in the 1950s, when female unruliness is more likely to surface in the new medium of television and the new genre of the domestic sitcom.

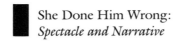

She Done Him Wrong:
Spectacle and Narrative

She Done Him Wrong is set in a Bowery saloon during the Gay Nineties and tells the story of Lou, a singer of great beauty and sexual allure who enjoys the attention and gifts of many male admirers. Cummins, an undercover cop played by Cary Grant, disguises himself as a mission worker to investigate a crime ring involving Lou's current beau. By the end of the film, he cracks the case. He also convinces Lou to settle down and marry him. The plot isn't the major interest in the film, however, but merely a backdrop for West's performance—as "Lou" and as actress/author/unruly woman "Mae West." That performance displays a number of motifs traditionally associated with the unruly woman: a carnivalesque openness toward sexuality; an ironic attitude toward romance; the presentation of her self, especially her gendered self, as visual construct or image, created through a performance of femininity that exaggerates its attributes and thus denaturalizes it; and a comic gender inversion that reduces men to interchangeable sexual objects while acknowledging, as Lou does, that men make the rules of the game ("I'm just smart enough to play it their way," she says). West's famous invitation—"Why don't you come up and see me?"—mocks not only Puritan attitudes toward sex but Victorian ideals of female delicacy and sentimentality.

These themes are evident from the earliest moments of the film. While Lou's admirers become fools for love, she remains supremely detached from sentiment about men, using them only for her own pleasure and for gifts that secure her independence. During the film, five past or present lovers move in and out of Lou's life, and when she strolls by a row of jail cells, one abject prisoner after another greets her fondly, even though love for her has brought many of them there. But Lou doesn't waste time grieving for them. "I ain't the sentimental kind," she says. As she tells a young woman who tried to kill herself after losing her virtue, men are all alike, whether they're married or single, and they are good for only two things: money and sex. "Diamonds is my career," she tells Cummins, who knows that as long as she has her diamonds, she remains out of his control.

Lou eludes male control by controlling men herself, which she does by creating and manipulating herself as spectacle. For Lou, as for West, being a spectacle doesn't make her vulnerable to men but ensures her power over them. Even before we see Lou, she is introduced as a spectacle. The film begins with a montage of street scenes then moves into a saloon filled with men who are drinking, brawling, and making business deals. In the foreground men at the bar discuss a prize fight, while another man gazes at an object concealed from our view. His comments soon reveal it to be a painting of Lou. Another man, Gus, boasts of his plans to wrest control of the saloon from Dan, its current owner, and to take Lou as his prize. Other men discuss a dispute between calendar companies fighting over the right to use Lou's image on their New Year calendars. In the meantime, the camera gives its first glimpse of the painting, which depicts a nude Lou in a reclining position.

The scene recalls John Berger's analysis of sexual representation and social power. According to Berger, business in early capitalism was often conducted in rooms lined with paintings of passive female nudes, whose display of sexual difference and availability reassured the businessmen of their own power. In this case, however, West turns the tables on the men, asserting both her power over—and desire for—them. She draws on what Gaylyn Studlar describes as the masochistic pleasure men may experience in giving themselves over to the image of a female who evokes the all-powerful mother.[4] Lou displays her savvy manipulation of her image and her ability to actively control the male gaze in an early scene with Dan and the crooked couple, Serge and Rita. After passing around a series of photographs of herself—with all her "rocks," the signifiers of her power—she fixes her own provocative gaze on Serge, invites him to come up and see her, then saunters up the stairs. The camera and the gaze of the men follow her until she poses on the balcony, back-lit to display her corseted figure. She positions herself in front of her bedroom door, with one hand resting suggestively on a pillar. For several lingering moments, she leers provocatively at the men below her and offers her image to their gaze.

West, of course, didn't create her persona out of a cultural vacuum. The unruly woman flourished in other popular traditions of the late nineteenth

Mae West exerts her power by presenting herself as spectacle and manipulating the gazes of her male admirers. As Diamond Lil in She Done Him Wrong, *she asserts her dominance by posing herself above Serge (Gilbert Roland).*

and early twentieth centuries. As Henry Jenkins has shown, a popular figure in early sound film was the "wild woman." While not the comic sex goddess West portrayed, the wild woman disrupted gender norms about feminine restraint and humiliated male characters to comic effect. This figure, he argues, provided an alternative to the dominant comic paradigm of the time, which centered on male suffering from domestic power (as in the films of W. C. Fields). In *So Long Letty* (1929), Charlotte Greenwood overturns ladylike decorum with her "ear-piercing voice and thrashing movements," disrespect for authority, and vulgar use of language (Henry Jenkins, "Don't Become Too Intimate" 3). However, unlike West, who exaggerates her apparent allure, many of these women derived their comedy from their *failure* to meet traditional standards of feminine beauty. Winnie Lightner, for example, offers her own unfeminine appearance as a "grotesque parody" of femininity, "an unfit object for male desire" (Henry Jenkins 22).

A more suggestive context for West's explicit celebration of female power and sexuality can be found in the tradition of burlesque. As Robert C. Allen argues, burlesque created an "upside-down world of enormous, powerful women and powerless, victimized men."[5] The burlesque queen, epitomized by the exoticized stripper, enacted a range of sexual transgressions, from impersonating men to aggressively returning the male gaze. In her own career, West brought elements of burlesque into the more middle-class performance form of vaudeville. She alludes to the connection in *She Done Him Wrong*, when a chorus line of bare-legged women introduces Lou's singing act. The film, in fact, is set during the heyday of burlesque, when, as its opening titles remind us, "legs were confidential."

West was unique, however, both in her control of her image and in its impact. As she explains in her autobiography, *Goodness Had Nothing to Do With It*, "I became a writer by the accident of needing material and having no place to get it. At least not the kind of writing I wanted for my stage appearance. . . . Yes, I had to create myself, and to create the fully mature image, I had to write it out to begin with" (72). That image took on a life of its own, she noted:

> *Few people knew that I didn't always walk around with a hand on one hip, or pushing at my hairdress and talking low and husky. I had created a kind of Twentieth Century Sex Goddess that mocked and delighted all victims and soldiers of the great war between men and women. I was their banner, their figurehead, an articulate image, and I certainly enjoyed the work. (163)*

Furthermore, the image she did create was multivalent and powerful, consistent with the topos of female unruliness. While some reviewers praised her skills as a comedian and her appeal as an entertainer, *Variety* reviewed her act in terms of the grotesque: "She is one of the many freak persons on the vaudeville stage where freakishness often carries more weight than talent."[6] The ambiguity of her sexual image is well known. From the outset of her career, as she notes in her autobiography, she had special appeal to gay men as a female female impersonator, presenting sex largely as a matter of style—a theme that would be taken up, though more conventionally, in the stylish, playful couples of the classical romantic comedy. The element of camp about West points to a strain of female unruliness that exists, like her own work, outside conventional romantic comedy, in the figures of Joan Crawford and Carmen Miranda, for example (see Robertson), as well as in Jack Lemmon's female impersonation in *Some Like It Hot* (1959). Parker Tyler opens *Screening the Sexes* with a lengthy tribute to her as "The Mother Superior of the Faggots" (1). As film reviewer Stark Young observes, it is the "abstraction" of her image that most fully accounts for the "howling, diverting mythology" that clings to her. He compares her to Harlequin, Pierrot, Chaplin, and Sarah Bernhardt, "as abstract as . . . a song, good or bad; or as the circus." That abstraction, he writes, comes to a single conclusion affirming the power of the woman on top: "that every woman has the lure and that every man can be had" (91–92).

This abstraction—or more precisely, fetishization—largely accounts for West's success as an image of female unruliness based on sexuality.[7] Because the "real" sexuality of any woman presented as image or spectacle is always hidden, that image heightens desire for what is missing while at the same time defusing the potential threat of unruly and unmediated female sexuality. West's image, like Dietrich's, is fetishized—redolent with signs (the phallic attire, the husky voice) that reassure male viewers that femininity is not so different from masculinity. In *She Done Him Wrong*, West heightens the irony surrounding her image by reinforcing distance through both setting and style. The film is a period piece. Despite its musical numbers and its dependence on West's delivery of her lines, it has the feel less of the sound film than of silent cinema, with its opening montage of street scenes and intertitles. West's parodic tone further puts her in the realm of excess, "freakishness," or the "horrible prettiness" (in Allen's words) of the burlesque queen, removing any real erotic charge—and therefore danger—from her persona.

She Done Him Wrong concludes with Cummins making Lou his personal "prisoner," taking from her fingers her many diamond rings and replacing them with a small solitaire. The ending is entirely conventional;

leading ladies are paired up with the right man at the end of almost all comedies and indeed most other films, and the arbitrariness of such endings is usually overlooked or accepted as an inevitable part of narrative.[8] That is hard to do in the case of this film, however. The power of West's personality, the independent and cynical character she plays, and her age at the time of the film (she was 40, compared with Grant's 29) make Lou's willing surrender laughable, even to a man as suave as Cummins. Cummins must be given all the authority of the Law—from his masquerade as a mission worker to his job as a police officer—to give his character sufficient weight to bring Lou/West into the social fabric of marriage, family, and bourgeois respectability.

The film's ending illustrates the difficulty of emplotting the unruly woman in a traditional narrative. The Chaplin Tramp as Everyman can be himself—perform himself—in virtually any narrative, since narrative is built around the activity or agency of a male hero. Chaplin simply uses those narratives of male action—whether prospecting for gold in *The Gold Rush* (1925), or working on an assembly line in *Modern Times* (1936), or taking his place in the front lines of history in *The Great Dictator* (1940)— as fuel for his comic performances. Chaplin's performances indeed dominate the narratives of his films, as West's do hers, but, for Chaplin, narrative generates an abundant storehouse of material for performance. (This is true whether he is working entirely in mime and physical comedy, as in the silent films, or using verbal humor as well, as in the less successful sound films, although silent comedy's dependence on "activity" may well contribute to its effectiveness in undercutting the heroic "man of action.") In contrast, West is limited to the single narrative of a woman's life: that of her relation to men. West's persona bursts out of the narrative of the whore with a heart of gold, which is the only narrative that would make her acceptable to a mainstream audience. And yet, that narrative confines her to a single-note performance. There are few narrative options for strong examples of female unruliness.

At the same time, the appetite *for* narrative is tremendous, as the history of Hollywood film has proved. The pull of narrative over simple performance is evident in another film released a year after *She Done Him Wrong*—Frank Capra's *It Happened One Night*—which was equally popular and ultimately more influential than *She Done Him Wrong*. *It Happened One Night* set the pattern for a kind of comedy that had unique appeal to a country finding its way out of the social crises of the 1930s. Much of the appeal of this genre depended on its use of female unruliness. That unruliness, however, was associated no longer with sexual experience, as in West's case, but with something quite different: virginity. The unruly virgin retained much of the essence of the West persona—its foregrounding of gender, resonances of sexual ambiguity, dominance of men—but tempered into a form more amenable to traditional narrative.

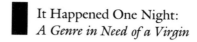

It Happened One Night: A Genre in Need of a Virgin

It Happened One Night tells the story of Ellie (Claudette Colbert), a runaway heiress, and Peter (Clark Gable), an out-of-work newspaper reporter, whose rocky journey to the altar takes them through the landscape of a nation struggling to restore its economic well-being and its belief that success results from hard work and character, not from social class or other forces beyond an individual's control. During their journey, a blanket strung over a rope—the "wall of Jericho"—stands for the social and sexual barriers between them. A strong populism and unabashed sentimentalism infuse this film, as they do Capra's others. What the later romantic comedies borrow from the film, however, are not its images of a working-class America on the road, in auto camps, on the bus, and out of work; instead, they adopt a narrative *structure* that allows a more complex negotiation of class anxieties, a shifting of one set of social contradictions—the slippery issue of class in Depression America—onto the more readily managed ones of gender and generation.[9] In the later films the dynamics of class are less apparent, and those of gender inversion more so, but the essential elements of the genre emerge in *It Happened One Night*.

The genre resurrects the familiar structure of New Comedy, the comedic Oedipal story ending in the victory of the son over the father and the constitution of the heterosexual couple, and it is easy to see why such a structure would be appealing during the 1930s, when the country placed its faith in a New Deal and a new hero, a new "son," to bring it out of a crisis of its own. However, as it took its shape in the 1930s, the form worked in historically specific ways reflecting the era's social turmoil regarding both gender and class. By focusing on the couple, it validated marriage at a time when the institution was threatened by a rising divorce rate, increasing numbers of women in the work force, and other changes following women's suffrage.[10] These films evolved along with production practices that were ideal for developing and refining the genre film; the consolidation of the producer-unit system throughout the decade encouraged stylistic similarities across the industry while maintaining the tension between uniformity and innovation that characterized classical Hollywood cinema.[11] The couple also made use of the tendency of sound to demystify the romantic heroine. Silence has long been considered a virtue in women, something that enhances a notion of beauty dependent on passivity and mystery, and Garbo's allure might be attributed in some degree to her silence. When a woman's image is accompanied by the sound of her voice, that image is less readily reduced to a screen for the projection of male fantasy.

With such attention to gender, the genre enabled a displacement of social contradictions in a move similar to the one Claude Lévi-Strauss describes in his analysis of myth, whereby cultures unable to resolve one set of contradictions shift them onto another set that is more readily managed (see Eckert). At a time (1932) when twenty million people were on public assistance and J. P. Morgan paid no income taxes, these contradictions were indeed enormous. The New Comedy structure that reenacts an inevitable resolution of gender and generational conflict proved eminently adaptable to class. In *It Happened One Night* and the romantic comedies that followed, the familiar union of man and woman also bridges the gap between social class, asserting that the differences between social classes are as illusory as those between the sexes. What matters, these films tell us, is a certain set of virtues, among them spunk, the ability to work hard, a sense of principled independence, and sexual vitality. With these virtues, a person can achieve perfect happiness. The inequities of the class system and the oppression of women cease to matter.

It Happened One Night's dependence on this structure can be seen in some of its differences from *She Done Him Wrong*. Whereas Lou's marriage to Cummins is perfunctory, a tipping of the hat to convention, the entire narrative momentum in *It Happened One Night* moves toward establishing the couple, toward removing the obstacles between Ellie and Peter and bringing down the wall of Jericho. And while Lou stands monumentally alone, an "abstraction" out of time, each of the central characters in *It Happened One Night* is anchored in generation by a father or father figure—Peter by his boss, the newspaper editor who fires him, and Ellie by her father, Mr. Andrews. The importance of these fathers is evident from the film's opening scenes, which show both Ellie and Peter fighting with their respective fathers. Mothers are absent because they hold no social power to transfer; moreover, the Oedipal struggles to bring the couple to heterosexuality require the mother's symbolic erasure.[12] By the end of the film, the generational and gender battles are over. Ellie's voice has been silenced and she has accepted her place. Peter's rival, the rich, effete King Westley, has receded into the background, having been bought off by a "pot of money." And not only is Peter back in the good graces of his editor but he has been recognized by his "true father," Mr. Andrews. The middle-class editor may represent the future power of the country, but

Ellie's father holds the keys to the kingdom at present, and to ensure that his successor be Peter, he actively intervenes to save Ellie and Peter from their youthful stubbornness.

It is through Mr. Andrews's choice of Peter that much of the film's ideological work occurs. By establishing a bond between Mr. Andrews and Peter, the film suggests a smooth transfer of power not only from father to son but also from the upper class to the class represented by Peter—the hardworking, tough, cynical, streetwise people who are the real Americans, who, like Lincoln, know how to give piggyback rides. His choice is dramatized in two ways: through the contrasting character of King Westley, and through the emerging qualities of Peter as ideal hero. Peter does not demonstrate his worthiness, however, until a certain transformation has occurred in his character. As in the old quest myths, he must prove his worthiness to win the hand of the princess. With both King Westley and Peter, the film disguises the issue of class by confusing social power with sexual power. It defines the worthiness of the new hero in terms of sexuality—his masculinity and virility.

The Westley character, played by Jameson Thomas, enables the film to displace the negative qualities of the rich onto one character and the positive qualities onto another. Because Mr. Andrews represents the self-made man—the American success story, the man Peter can become—his success is removed from the taint of social class and represents an innocent fantasy of material abundance consistent with the film's comedic perspective. In contrast, King Westley is associated with a class that is "less American" than Mr. Andrews and certainly than Peter. His name suggests a titled aristocracy. It is not his wealth, however, but other qualities coded through gender that make him less attractive than his rival. If the fathers are played as buffoons—fat and balding like the men on the burlesque posters Robert Allen describes—that is appropriate for fathers. It is not for romantic heroes. Westley is foolish and foppish, less masculine and sexually attractive than Peter. Peter would never display such vanity or make a spectacle of himself as Westley does with his grand entrance to his wedding by autogyro. Most important, Westley is not sincere. "He's a fake, Ellie," Mr. Andrews tells her, which Peter echoes when he tells her he's a "phony." Sincerity is a virtue Americans associate with the national character—with rural life, the middle class, and masculinity. Urbanity and irony are the marks of the European sophisticate, and dissembling a mark of the feminine. Peter, on the other hand, is the real thing. Or he becomes the real thing by the end of the film.

Early in the film, however, despite the casting of the "rugged" Clark Gable in the role, Peter's suitability to be such a hero is not certain. Like

In It Happened One Night, *Ellie (Claudette Colbert) and Peter (Clark Gable) converse in a motel room through a blanket strung over a rope. The "wall of Jericho," as Peter calls it, protects Ellie's virtue. It also preserves her independence on a journey during which she is not attached to any man.*

David in *Bringing Up Baby,* who has lost his bone, Peter assures Ellie that she is safe because he has no "trumpet" to blow down the walls. In fact, it takes Ellie, a virgin, to restore his trumpet to him. Few films offer such insistent metaphors for the hymen as the wall of Jericho, the fragile but powerful barrier Peter strings up each night between himself and Ellie. The female virgin—or rather, the bride, with its attendant mythology of virginity—is central to romantic comedy. So, too, is the prohibition against sex between the lovers, which is always implied but does not happen until after the plot concludes and the credits roll.

Because of these conventions, the rise of romantic comedy during the 1930s is often tied to the decade's heightened censorship, and the Production Code has generally been derided as the triumph of puritanism and philistinism over more open explorations of sexual and political issues.

However, to overplay the regulatory power of the Hays Office and the Legion of Decency is to underestimate the complexity with which these films explore the relations between the sexes. As Leonard Leff has argued, drawing on Foucault, the Production Code functioned—especially in regard to sex—by *regulating* rather than repressing discourse under a regime of internal surveillance: "Instead of hiding sex, the Production Code . . . invents countless devices 'for speaking about it, for having it be spoken about, for inducing it to speak for itself' "; rather than censorship, "what was involved was a regulated and polymorphous incitement to discourse" which flourished particularly in "smart features" like the romantic comedy. Regulation thus forced sex to become "more concentrated, more verbal, even more intense" with such stars as Hepburn and Grant than it was with Mae West (436).

The prominence of the female virgin and the sanctions against sex in the classical romantic comedies are better understood by considering the general meaning of sex and gender within the genre. Neither convention should be taken literally. Virginity in the woman is often less a matter of "physics than metaphysics," in Stanley Cavell's words, and the fact that many of these films are indeed comedies of "remarriage" suggests that what is at issue is the degree of intimacy between the couple (*Pursuits of Happiness* 54).[13] On the most obvious level, the lovers remain sexually apart because they are often unaware of their attraction to each other. The drive of the comedy is to bring them to such an awareness. In addition, because all other contradictions are contained within the couple, Peter and Ellie cannot be united sexually until those contradictions are resolved—until the gap between their social classes has been bridged by Peter's alliance with Mr. Andrews. At that point, the resolution of social difference paves the way for the resolution of private difference, traditionally represented by marriage, the joining of sexual and social. And in this way, romantic comedy uses romantic love to absorb all other needs, desires, and contradictions, to promise the fulfillment not only of sexual desire but of *all* desire. As such, that fulfillment is not representable. In *It Happened One Night*, it is mediated by language and metaphor, by words of trumpets and walls.

The obstacle to such consummation, then, becomes the central issue of the comedy, the primary narrative conflict. Because the goal is to bring the characters together sexually, that obstacle can be constructed most readily in terms of sex; the couple's blindness to their desire for their "one true love" is easily translated into a generalized sexual repression or denial by either character. Locating it in the character of the woman follows from a range of cultural beliefs, beginning with the traditional valuation of female virginity and modesty. Peter taunts Ellie by singing, "Who's afraid of the big bad wolf?" when she expresses skepticism about her safety behind the barrier, although it is Ellie who first breaks the sanctity of the wall and Peter who retreats in fear. Locating that resistance in the male, in a kind of *male* virginity, however, is potentially more radical and more comical. While this reversal occurs in the later films—and accounts for the uniqueness of many of the romantic comedies during this period—it is latent even in the macho Peter, whose dislike of Ellie for her social class, it turns out, is not the whole story of what keeps them apart. That dislike conceals a deeper resistance to his own needs, which he must acknowledge for the resolution to occur.

What is often presented as sexual repression is actually an issue of gender, however, and it is not sex so much as gender which the films explore—the maturing into an acceptance of our culture's ideology of heterosexuality, of what it means to be a man or a woman. The persistence of films which posit the romantic couple as the source of all happiness and reinscribe women into traditional notions of femininity—long after the sexual changes of the sixties—indicates that sexual mores often change faster than do patterns of either gender or genre.[14] This sense of the cultural and social dimension of sexuality is what is missing in Cavell's readings of the films. For Cavell, the classical romantic comedy centers on a woman like Ellie who is not fully a woman because she has not yet acknowledged her own sexuality by choosing the right man over his sexless rival. Indeed, Ellie is usually read as embodying many of the stereotypes of the female virgin: inexperienced, helpless, childlike, and in need of protection, a holdover from the Victorian notion of woman as child. Ellie loses her bus ticket, she doesn't know about traveling on buses or sharing a shower. She is a woman in need of an education, or an education about certain things, and the film is usually read as dramatizing Ellie's growth from being a spoiled "brat" into a mature person, from an heiress to the wife of a middle-class man. Cavell writes:

> *In the genre of remarriage the man's lecturing indicates that an essential goal of the narrative is the education of the woman, where her education turns out to mean her acknowledgment of her desire, and this in turn will be conceived of as her creation, her emergence, at any rate, as an autonomous human being.* (Pursuits of Happiness 84)

It is the man's business to create her, he writes, which Ellie acknowledges with her "Thanks, Professor" when Peter corrects her about how to dunk a doughnut.

However, the female virgin is a more complex figure than Cavell acknowledges, and the notion of "creating" a woman more entangled in the social realities of gender and sexual politics. When Cavell writes that the comedies of remarriage differ from the classical New Comedy in that the obstacles to the couple are within them, not social, he fails to see the degree to which what is "within" is shaped by what is outside—in other words, the extent to which the self is also a subject.[15] "Creating" the bride also means domesticating her, bringing her in line with social expectations and standards. Peter's spanking of Ellie becomes both more and less than a playful erotic gesture when he tells her father that she became a brat because she lacked proper discipline—being hit every day whether she needed it or not. Peter "tames" the out-of-bounds eroticism of the gesture by bringing it into the discourse of "woman's proper place." To Mr. Andrews, this is a sign that Peter is the right husband for Ellie and the right son for him, for, after all, it was his blow that sent Ellie overboard and on her way to Peter in the first place. If Peter teaches her to become an "autonomous human being," in Cavell's words, it is one who fulfills *his* needs—someone to become part of his fantasy about a "moonlit island" rather than to have a fantasy of her own. Ellie learns, and the film teaches, two lessons about femininity. First, a woman's happiness comes from becoming a wife, and a good wife—someone who becomes the fulfillment of a man's dream rather than a dreamer herself. Second, her happiness has nothing to do with money or economic security. Eating raw carrots on the road with Peter is more fun than anything her old life could offer. Unlike *Gentlemen Prefer Blondes* (the 1953 film based on Anita Loos's 1925 novel), *It Happened One Night* doesn't allow for the possibility that, as Lorelei explains, it is as easy to fall in love with a rich man as with a poor one.

At the same time, by neglecting to consider why the *woman* alone needs creation, Cavell overlooks the man's similar need. In a curious way, these comedies reverse the fairy-tale plot of the sexually unawakened princess who sleeps until the first kiss of true love by, of course, the true prince. In these films, it is the prince who is in something of a daze, sleepwalking until touched by the unruly virgin princess. This becomes clearer in later comedies but is evident even in *It Happened One Night*. Peter possesses the raw material of the hero, but he too is in need of education, from trivial matters such as how to hitch a ride to the most essential business of recognizing the fulfillment of his own dream when it is right before his eyes. Two things impede Peter's growth: his failure to see past the blinders of class, and his retreat from emotion, a closing down of his feelings after one unhappy experience with love ("I was sucker enough to make plans," he tells Ellie). What "happened one night" was the realization of Peter's dream, when he and Ellie sleep under the stars on an island that is rendered, through expressionist lighting, as close to an enchanted dreamscape as the realistic visual style of the film allows. Yet Peter is too caught up in his grumbling and ill temper to see that. He tells Ellie later that he dreams of someone who is "alive," a "real person," but the abstractions that absorb Peter—images, dreams, prejudices, and principles—blind him from seeing Ellie as just that person and keep him from being fully alive himself.

Ironically, the power to restore Peter to life is in the hands of a virgin, Ellie, who is responsible for the "creation" of a new Peter, the transformation of a cynical, opportunistic, and powerless man without trumpet or job into the hero who grabs his secretary, kisses her, and says, "All women are beautiful." Romantic comedy allows the woman to look at the castrated man, but with a gaze that restores his potency. The film depends on her ability to make Peter realize what she knows well before he does and what we know all along. Once again displacing class onto gender, the film makes *Peter's* self-discovery the critical issue, although Ellie's choice of an unemployed Peter over King Westley has vastly more important social consequences than does Peter's decision about whether to marry Ellie or remain a bachelor.

It is this power, more than her rebellious flight from her father, that identifies Ellie with gender inversion and female unruliness and that prefigures Claudette Colbert's more overtly unruly roles in such later films as *Palm Beach Story* (1942). Despite Ellie's apparent innocence and helplessness, she is wiser than Peter in the fundamental truths affirmed by romantic comedy. While Peter instructs Ellie on how to hitchhike or give a piggyback ride, Ellie becomes his unacknowledged tutor in the areas of self-awareness, generosity, the pragmatic, and the erotic. Her behavior constantly exposes the error of his naming her "Brat." She recognizes the nature of their relationship before he does. Her instincts are more generous—she gives away their money to the hungry family. She's a good sport about her hardships on the road and knows how to have fun. She is in tune with her adventure, willing to take a chance, the first to venture past the wall and expose her feelings for Peter. The film grants her a degree of subjectivity it doesn't give Peter, in long close-ups of her eyes which show her to be reflecting on the changes within herself and her feelings for Peter. Her flaws are shown to be a product of her social class, which she can discard as easily as jumping off her father's yacht. Her "Thanks, Professor" is thus also ironic, a gentle jab at Peter's pompousness about such a trivial matter as a doughnut, while at the same time indicating her willingness to accede to the rules of the game between the sexes, which require a wife to submit cheerfully to her husband's instruction.

The Ellie character is built out of a tradition of virginity that encompasses independence and strength as well as vulnerability, and in fact is the key to her control over the expansion or "fatness" of the narrative itself. In the strictest sense, virginity is the key to a woman's value as a token of exchange among men, and the film acknowledges that female virginity is a cultural construct by and for men. Peter, not Ellie, rigs up the wall of Jericho, and Peter—along with Mr. Andrews and the law—determines when it comes down. Peter's remaining on his side of the wall has less to do with his respect for Ellie, or lack of desire for her, than with his own principles and respect for an understanding among men about property: on paper, Ellie belongs to King Westley. Virginity can also be understood as the sign of a prohibition against maternity rather than against sex, for the classical romantic comedy, like comedy in general, makes little room for mothers or motherhood. Yet the hymen also serves as a barrier that preserves a kind of independence in the romantic heroine. Ellie is in a liminal state. She has escaped the control of her father and not yet come under the control of King Westley or Peter. She is no longer a child, and not yet either a wife or a mother, or that other form of virgin, the old spinster. That liminality is protected by her hymen.

Traditionally, according to Nancy Huston, women who remain outside the social and symbolic matrix of marriage and motherhood have been allowed to partake in certain kinds of power usually reserved for men. Thus female virginity serves as a kind of "invisible armor" and the hymen a "shield designed to protect both the body and soul of the young girl."[16] Examples of female figures from history and myth who have derived strength from their virginity include Athena the goddess of war, Artemis the hunter, the warrior Amazons, the Virgin Mary, the feisty nun (the seventeenth-century poet Sor Juana Inés de la Cruz), and the spiritually virginal loner (the hero of Agnes Varda's film *Vagabond* [1985]). Brunhilde loses her fierce power, in a reversal of the Samson story, when she sleeps with Gunther. Susan, in *Bringing Up Baby*, is an Artemis-like predator stalking her prey, which includes David, in a forest that re-creates more demonically the island of *It Happened One Night*.

Such freedom from the social law that would bring her under the control of a husband and the natural law that would subject her to the biological fate of motherhood allows the virgin a unique kind of laughter, the kind of laughter implicit in Ellie's "Thanks, Professor," or in her grin during the hitchhiking scene, or in Susan's laughter at David's silliness and Eve's indulgent teasing of Hopsy in *The Lady Eve*. This "laughter of maidens," in Judith Wilt's words, stands in opposition to the "cackle of matriarchs" that has long dominated women's humor. Matriarchal laughter, such as Erma Bombeck's, is "of this world," a carrier of anger and protection against pain. Wilt argues instead for the laughter of "the virgin-mocker, the girl-hunter of folly with the feasting smile—Artemis, Diana":

> *She expresses, rather than represses; she piles no sandbags on the dike of the collapsing world; she exposes and deflates, in fundamental comic style, finding no role in the world which totally satisfies her. She hesitates, laughing, at the edge, withholding fertility, humility, community. (179–180)*

By holding out against "fertility, humility, community," this laughter resists the very qualities women are socialized into accepting in marriage and motherhood (and also the qualities that Frye identifies so strongly with comedy). Wilt finds this laughter in Shakespeare's comedies and in the novels of Jane Austen, George Eliot, and George Meredith. It also rings in the classical Hollywood romantic comedy.

The virgin's hesitation on the edge of the cliff requires what Wilt calls embroidery and invention and what Patricia Parker identifies with textual deferral, a resistance to closure identified with the genre of romance and the figure of the "literary fat lady." In romantic comedy, the virgin assumes the expansiveness of the fat female body in other texts and mythologies. The hymen allows the expansion of the narrative—the story expands as long as the virgin is unvanquished and the hymen intact, and the celebration that ends festive comedy is hymeneal. This deferral of narrative closure also creates the gap necessary for romantic love. The gap is an Imaginary of sorts, which heightens the curiosity and strangeness that fuel the desire of romantic love. As Parker notes, the association of the romance narrative with the figure of a female enchantress extends to the genre of romance itself as a Circean, bewitching form that saps masculine energy (10). Such an association continues in the disparagement of many forms of popular culture, including the soap opera, which has often been feminized by critics who find its form flawed by its endless deferral of resolution. In films popular with women, from *Celine and Julie Go Boating* (1974) to *Daughter Rite* (1978), language or speech often allows the text to meander outside the constraints of more rigorously controlled narrative.

In *It Happened One Night*, the duration of Ellie's virginity is linked, like the film itself, to the journey to New York. When that ends, Ellie's liminal period of freedom will also end, so she insists that she and Peter spend one more night together. She wants to preserve the power she still has and put off what she knows would be the end of *her* story if she marries Westley. The wall of Jericho stands as an obstacle to the film's closure, and as long as reasons can be found to keep it up—the multiple misunderstandings of comedy, the coincidence that awakens the motel owners and thus awakens Ellie too early, Peter's delay before the train, Mr. Andrews's misunderstanding about Peter's "financial matter"—the narrative can continue. Here, as in other early sound films, the narrative makes use of storytelling and language to prolong itself. The most intimate moments of Ellie and Peter's courtship occur in conversation through a blanket, and Peter's desire to "get the story" for his editor gives him a rational excuse to stay with Ellie and follow a desire of which he is not yet aware. "Getting the story" means getting money in his pocket, which means he can then marry Ellie.

The presence of money at the end of the film seals Peter's alliance with Mr. Andrews and the film's collapsing of class onto gender. Ellie's transfer from Mr. Andrews to Peter requires a financial transaction, which becomes yet another assertion of the irrelevance of class divisions and yet another means of affirming Peter's masculinity and value as a middle-class hero. Peter cannot consider asking Ellie to marry him (or accept her proposal) until he has some money of his own. His insistence on a payment of thirty-four dollars to put an heiress in her place—while having no interest whatsoever in the large reward—becomes the crucial contrast with King Westley who, despite the money he already has, can be bought for more.

With the joining of Ellie and Peter, the film succeeds in reaffirming middle-class ideology about social class and about that most middle class of institutions—marriage. The image of the couple presented in this film and the other classical romantic comedies is neither so glamorous nor so intense as to seem out of reach or beyond the comfort zone of middle America. These films suggest that sexuality should be taken neither too lightly nor too seriously and that heterosexual love can provide all happiness, overcome all difference, in a "partnership" which offers friendship and sex, but in moderate amounts. Despite Peter's capacity to imagine an enchanting life, and Ellie's ability to bring it about, Peter and Ellie must be seen as capable of becoming Ward and June Cleaver, if not Dan and Roseanne Conner, and the ease of their masquerade of domestic married life suggests that they will. Ellie will not move from conquest to conquest, like Lou or the devastating heroines played by Marlene Dietrich in Joseph von Sternberg's films. Nor will she and Peter play the sophisticated marital games of a Lubitsch comedy. Instead, they will find their enchantment, as they did from the beginning, in ordinary America.

 Sylvia Scarlett: *The Virgin as Androgyne*

That hesitation of the virgin on the brink of "fertility, humility, community," her "finding no role *in* the world which totally satisfies her," is nowhere more evident than in George Cukor's *Sylvia Scarlett* which, like *She Done Him Wrong*, is an anomaly of sorts. *Sylvia Scarlett* pushes the notion of female virginity into the more ambiguous area of androgyny, and the virgin's resistance to full femininity into male impersonation. The film is part of a tradition of male impersonation in drama and film that includes Shakespeare's comedies and romances (*Twelfth Night, As You Like It*, and *All's Well That Ends Well*) and such films as *Queen Christina* (1933), *Sullivan's Travels* (1941), *Victor/Victoria* (1982), and *Yentl* (1983) (see Straayer; Kuhn). *Sylvia Scarlett* establishes Cukor's affinity for the romantic comedy of gender inversion and his sensitivity for directing women who would figure strongly in the genre, such as Katharine Hepburn and Judy Holliday. *Holiday* (1938), *The Philadelphia Story* (1940), *Adam's Rib* (1949), *Born Yesterday* (1950), *Pat and Mike* (1952), and *It Should Happen To You* (1954) all examine the tensions created by the disruptive and desiring woman on top.

Although *Sylvia Scarlett* has long been a favorite among certain audiences, especially lesbians, the film was not a popular success (see Bernardoni). Perhaps too forward looking in some aspects of its treatment of gender, too backward regarding class, and generically too much of a puzzle, the film was ideologically and formally out of step with the times. However, the options for female behavior it presents as extremes and as a temporal problem to be solved by the passage of the heroine from one state to another became incorporated in the *character* of the more fully realized unruly woman. And, like the physical strength and toughness associated with Sigourney Weaver after her performance in *Alien* (1979), the qualities Katharine Hepburn displays in her portrayal of the boy "Sylvester" became attached to her emerging star persona and helped define the unruly romantic heroine.

The film opens in France, with young Sylvia lamenting the death of her mother and disguising herself as a boy so she can accompany her father Henry, a con man, to England. She, as Sylvester, and her father meet

Monkley, another con man, played by Cary Grant. After several unsuccessful scams, the group takes up theater as "The Pink Pierrots," a traveling troupe of clowns. When Sylvia meets and falls in love with Michael, an artist, she abandons her disguise, but she despairs of competing with her rival Olga, an exotic Russian femme fatale. Her father kills himself after an unhappy love affair with Maudie, and Sylvia resigns herself to staying with Monk. After several misunderstandings, she and Michael are united.

The film is marked by contradictions and instability, with its shifts of genre and tone mirroring the extreme transformations of gender Sylvia undergoes. The film is not a classical romantic comedy, first because it relies so little on humor, but even more importantly because the central couple is not central enough; in fact, Michael doesn't even appear until the second half. At certain points, when the group performs musical numbers accompanied by nondiegetic music, the film appears to be a musical. At other moments, its physical comedy suggests broad farce. Most of all, it recalls a version of romance rooted in theater and the novel. In the first half the romance is picaresque and episodic, as the trio moves from one adventure to another. Later, the film recalls Shakespeare's romances, from its bucolic settings, starlit feasts, male impersonation, and echoes of the fool figure and commedia dell'arte to the madness and suicide of the father, which briefly darken its tone from the comic to the melodramatic.

If class creates the underlying tension of *It Happened One Night*, gender does so in *Sylvia Scarlett*, and in fact defines the structure of the film. In the first half, Sylvia must become a boy to fulfill her desire to stay with her father, and this part of the film centers on "Sylvester's" adventures with her father and Monk. In the second half, she must become not only a girl but a woman to fulfill her desire for Michael, and this half centers on Sylvia and Michael. Sylvia's problems begin with an initial rupture in the Oedipal triangle. The first spoken words of the film are Sylvia's, when she weeps, "Poor Mama" over her mother's death. The symbolic death of the mother is the first step in a girl's passage into heterosexuality, and, in this regard, the film highlights the mother's absence that is more typically unspoken in romantic comedy. Sylvia makes the requisite transfer of her love from mother to father when, without hesitation, she hands him the money her mother gave her for a dowry and vows that she'll never marry. It is her father's weakness, however, that sends her into a gender detour and prevents her smooth passage to femininity. His trouble with the law forces him to flee France, and to stay with him she must disguise herself as a boy. Later, his suicide confirms his inadequacy as a figure of masculinity, especially since he kills himself over love, something men just aren't supposed to do (cf. Wilt 193).

"I won't be a girl, I won't be weak and I won't be silly," Sylvia says early in the film, when she looks in the mirror and cuts off her braids. "I'll be a boy and rough and hard." The first half of the film demonstrates how readily she adapts to being rough and hard, although "radiant" more aptly describes her, suggesting that "Sylvester" is not a disguise falsely layered over a natural and true femininity but an expression of her deepest nature. Her movements become athletic: she leaps over gates, scrambles out windows, and swims through heavy surf. Her high-pitched voice becomes deeper and more expressive. She laughs exuberantly when she accidentally ruins an extended scam on the street. Being a boy allows her to play and laugh, to move freely in the public world. It gives her a freedom from seriousness. It allows her to be the "adventurer" of the film's opening inscription, which addresses itself "to all who stray from the beaten path." It also allows her to follow her highest moral instincts. She strikes Olga for toying cruelly with her father, prevents Monk and her father from overstepping her standards of fairness, and halts the Pierrot show to lecture Michael and his crowd for their rudeness. Liberating her body liberates her imagination as well, and she becomes an artist herself. Her performance as Sylvester generates other performances, from the homeless French boy on the London streets, to "Mr. Sylvester Scarletto" with a penciled-on Ronald Colman mustache, to the Pierrot. The idea that the group leave petty crime for theater is hers. She becomes so attached to Sylvester that she refuses to give up her masquerade even when her father says she'd be more help to him as a girl.

However, Sylvia *does* become weak and silly in the second half of the film. With her first glance at Michael, she becomes self-conscious, and we begin to watch a second, more painful transformation of Sylvia. Once her femininity asserts itself, she assumes a tone of abjection and self-blame: "You were right to throw me out," she tells Michael when, still as Sylvester, she apologizes for disrupting his feast by striking Olga. "Everything was so lovely, and I made it horrible. I'm cheap and I'm loudmouthed, and I can't control myself." This abjection becomes only worse when she abandons her disguise and discovers that she was more charming to Michael as Sylvester: "I'm rude and rough and clumsy. I should have stayed as a boy." And still later, she sobs, "I'm sorry, I'm just a fool." Sylvia has good reason to weep. The man she adores responds to her revelation of her sexual identity with disbelief and then uproarious laughter. "Sit down, you oddity, sit down, you crowing hen, you freak of nature," he tells her.

In Sylvia Scarlett, *"Sylvester" (Katharine Hepburn in drag) falls in love with artist Michael (Brian Aherne), whose femininity contributes to the film's play with sexual ambiguity.*

For Sylvia, becoming a woman means learning another masquerade—one of coy gestures and poses that Michael teaches her. Becoming a woman is more painful than becoming a boy.

For the remainder of the film, Sylvia moves toward womanhood, although her progress is uneven. The contrast between the active masculinity she abandons and the passive femininity she acquires is clear in her despondent consent to stay with Monk although she has no desire to do so. In a far more extreme way than Ellie does, she learns to adapt herself to the wishes and needs of the men around her. This contrast is even clearer when her decisive behavior returns once she puts on men's clothing again. In her exuberance, she accidentally slams the car door on Michael's hand. Her full accession to femininity is apparent, however, when we last see her gazing up at Michael with adoration and telling him, "I worship you."

While the film's pairing of Sylvia and Michael fulfills certain Cinderella fantasies of romance, the match is not successful for both dramatic and ideological reasons. The film seems torn by two impulses—a sentimental one favoring the retrograde romantic hero Michael, and a more ironic one favoring the charismatic and offbeat Monk. Michael gets the woman, but Monk the greater dramatic interest. Monk is present from the earliest moments of the film, when he gazes with interest at Sylvester. His relationship with Sylvester/Sylvia is charged with tension, and the wariness between them brings to mind *It Happened One Night* and the other romantic comedies in which hostility masks erotic interest. That tension is increased by casting Hepburn, with her aristocratic, well-bred aura, in a lower-class role. Class becomes an overt issue when Monk discusses his working-class roots with her. When he tells Sylvia, "You and me, we suit," he is referring to their common class background. He warns her, "It don't do to step out of your class." While the plot of the film disproves Monk, he is still given the privileged narrative point of view. His laughter is the last sound we hear. It separates him from Olga, who remains unaware of Michael's leaving her for Sylvia, and from the romantic couple, already swallowed up in the trees.

By pairing Sylvia with Michael, the film attempts to deny Monk's insight about class and to insist, as does *It Happened One Night*, that romantic love is all that matters. In *It Happened One Night* that insistence is borne out in the figure of a robust new middle-class male hero who subdues his heiress bride. *Sylvia Scarlett*, on the other hand, tries to make a hero out of a King Westley and offers to a middle-class audience the spectacle of a working-class girl worshipping her aristocratic beloved. As played by Brian Aherne, often cast as a pipe-smoking British gentleman, Michael is entirely too aristocratic and too cosmopolitan to appeal to the same audiences that responded so favorably to *It Happened One Night*. With his blond curls, he lacks the rugged masculinity of Clark Gable and the cockiness of the "handsome bad Pierrot" Grant plays. For much of the film, he is dressed in a floor-length, hooded robe—artistic to the point of effeminacy, by middle-American standards. In fact, short of the rakish Monk, the film offers no fully satisfactory male characters.

Sylvia is as problematic a figure as Michael, although a far more interesting one. Here a contrast between Mae West and Katharine Hepburn is suggestive. Both convey unconventional images of a femininity which is "performed" and thus destabilized. But the two women have very different body types, personal styles, and class associations. Each makes use of those differences to create her own version of female unruliness. Consider the following oppositions loosely derived from their star personae and their roles in *She Done Him Wrong* and *Sylvia Scarlett*:

West	*Hepburn*
irony	romance
age: 40; "matron plays maid"	age: early 20s; "maiden plays boy"
blonde	dark hair
rounded figure	angular
corseted body exaggerates shape	loose clothing conceals shape
aggressively sexual	sexually innocent; "pre-sexual"
"female impersonation"	male impersonation
slow, restrained movement	free, athletic movement; abrupt gestures
fetishized attire; jewels	simple attire
vulgarity	refinement; upper class
no family	father, mother
presentation of self as spectacle	desire for invisibility
mask—abstraction	mask—masquerade

Hepburn's coding as upper class extends beyond her aristocratic appearance and body type (her leanness and refined bone structure) to her personal background—the Yankee family, the early stage and screen roles in literary or high art productions, the eccentricity and independence of style (wearing pants, eschewing conventional signs of feminine glamour). Indeed, this class coding makes the wealthy or independent characters she plays vulnerable to hostile readings from middle-class and working-class audiences. The restraint and lack of excessive display associated with the upper class help desexualize her image, whereas the opposite holds true of West, who enhances her sexual "vulgarity" by playing roles connected with characters far removed from the upper class. The voice and elocution of each actress bears this out; each appears to affect an accent, Hepburn's suggesting aristocracy and West's a certain "looseness."

Both West and Hepburn can participate in unruly scenarios of gender inversion because they successfully defuse the threat of sexual difference, although West invoked indignation from censors and at a certain point in her career Hepburn was considered "box office poison" for her portrait of strong women.[17] Whereas West presents herself as an image of mature female sexuality, Hepburn conceals her sexuality behind an appearance not only of youth but of youthful boyishness, and that very boyishness distances her from the spectacle that is so closely associated with femininity.

Parker Tyler notes, "Nature formed Mae's mature figure to look not only reassuringly maternal but reassuringly Victorian, suggesting old-fashioned times when sex in women was a simpler proposition. . . . Mae's well-packed curves made men think of their mothers, not in particular but in general" (Introduction 15). Hepburn's body, on the other hand, recalls both that of the wealthy woman—who can never be too thin or too rich—and that of the athletic adolescent boy. Writing on current fashion, Judith Williamson describes that body as our culture's ideal for women. Leggy, slim, curveless and hairless, minus the markers of adult female sexuality, such a body dismantles men's fears of sexual difference.[18]

Hepburn in this film recalls the figure of the androgyne, a figure well suited for narratives of romantic love, with its quest for a union of opposites across the divide of sexual difference. Psychoanalysis locates the androgyne in the Imaginary, the place of wish-fulfillment, before the resolution of sexual identity in the Symbolic. When an individual is assigned to one sex, he or she is deprived of the powers of the other. The position men and women adopt upon resolution of the Oedipal passage is always precarious, so, as Francette Pacteau writes, "the post-Oedipal subject carves statues in the shape of sleeping hermaphrodites, . . . paints curvaceous, hairless Endymions, watches movies about Victorias who pose as Victors and enormously enjoys the confusion s/he creates by dressing up in the codes of the opposite sex" (69).

As a figure in film, the androgyne positions the spectator in a place where identity as male and female oscillates, undermining not only gender but any fixed subjectivity (Kuhn).[19] The essence of the masculine hovers about Sylvia, and that of the feminine about Sylvester, suggesting that sexuality is a matter of fluidity, of easy slippage from male to female and back again. "Are you a girl playing a boy, or a boy playing a girl?" asks Maudie, and characters repeatedly exhibit "inappropriate" desire for Sylvia/Sylvester. Maudie tries to seduce Sylvester, Olga plants a very friendly kiss instead of a slap on Sylvia's face, and Michael seems to find Sylvester more desirable than Sylvia. For female spectators, the androgyne becomes a site of fantasy about what it would be like to assume the activity and social potency of the male, as Sylvia does as Sylvester. For men, the figure of a "not-yet-fully sexual, a boyish, never manly" woman such as Hepburn offers a safe object on which to displace their own sexual ambivalence (Pacteau 82). Hepburn's androgyny is further heightened by the film's use of the fool figure from social history and literature. As one of the Pink Pierrots, Sylvia draws on a figure who is usually played by a male but bound to the feminine by his sexual indeterminacy and position on the social margins. The fool's role as "detached ironist" about love and marriage—and about the entire social vision of comedy—aligns him, in turn, with the unruly romantic heroine, from Ganymede/Rosalind in *As You Like It*, to Mae West, to Barbara Stanwyck's role in *The Lady Eve*.[20]

Yet there is a darker side to the androgyne as well. The androgyne must be a shadow figure, dwelling in distance, because, as Pacteau has written, it is an "impossible referent" that collapses upon closer scrutiny and is then safely contained within the frame of the masculine or feminine, a site of condensation for all those instances when "the certainty in our identity wavers under the constant pressure of something hidden but not forgotten" (79). That something is the uncanny, which so unsettles Michael and returns us to his laughter at the sight of Sylvester as Sylvia.

On one level, Michael's laughter can be explained by the tendency in our culture to view femininity as intrinsically more comical than masculinity. Male impersonation is rarely, if ever, played for the degree of comic effect that female impersonation is: as Judith Williamson observes, false breasts and fannies on a man are perceived as funny, but "we have yet to see a female comic stuff a sock in her trousers and waggle it at crowded studio audiences to roars of laughter" (48).[21] More suggestively, however, Michael's laughter wards off fear. He recoils from Sylvia because she draws him into the Imaginary, where all boundaries dissolve. Michael calls her a "freak," an "oddity," and speaks of the "queer feeling" he had when he looked at Sylvester and responded to "something in you that I've painted." In that pointed remark, Michael betrays his own sense of Sylvester as containing "something hidden but not forgotten"—something hidden not only in Sylvester but in himself. That something is the feminine, which *presents* itself, even when most concealed, as something to be abstracted or sublimated, something that requires representation. It is his desire to paint the irrepressible femininity in Sylvester that first brings the lovers together, and later he draws Sylvia's face—when she is dressed again as Sylvester— in the jail cell. By painting Sylvester/Sylvia, he represses the masculine in her and the feminine in himself.

Sylvia's awkwardness during her domestication is poignant. Yet even though the plot of *Sylvia Scarlett* "kills off" Sylvester, his qualities remain a part of both the Sylvia character and Hepburn's star persona and help determine the shape of the unruly romantic heroine. Such actresses as Barbara Stanwyck, Carole Lombard, Irene Dunne, and Jean Arthur bring together in the characters they play the extremes that Sylvia negotiates. While not as explicitly androgynous as Hepburn in this film, they convey a kind of femininity that is decidedly more active, more aggressive, more physical, and indeed more masculine than anything modeled on Mae West would allow. Yet they avoid the threat of castration embodied in more mature, masculine stars such as Bette Davis and Joan Crawford (see Robertson). The lingering sense of the boyish about the unruly virgins these romantic heroines play enables the masculine superstars of their era, from Clark Gable to Gary Cooper, to explore with them their own sexual ambivalence.

Professor-Heroes and Brides on Top

In the last scene of Howard Hawks's *Bringing Up Baby* (1938), David, a scientist played by Cary Grant, runs up the scaffold on one side of an enormous skeleton of a brontosaurus. He is trying to escape from Susan, a young woman played by Katharine Hepburn, who has pursued him throughout the film. Susan follows him up another ladder propped against the other side of the skeleton. She asks why he is running away from her. "If you must know," he answers, "I'm afraid of you." He has good reason to be. He has just endured an extraordinary series of humiliations. But at the same time, he has had the best day of his life, and he tells her so. Susan begins to sway on her ladder in pleasure. David begins to sway on his, and by mirroring her motion he expresses a bond with her that he is only now beginning to perceive. As Susan's ladder totters more and more wildly, David climbs across the spine of the skeleton that separates them. He grabs her, but the skeleton collapses beneath them, literally undermining the embrace that conventionally concludes a romantic comedy. What also crumbles is a notion of masculinity that is shown to be as fossilized and laughable as the skeleton and that is demolished by the efforts of the couple working according to some unconscious imperative, at the initiative of the woman on top.

The paradox Grant alludes to underlies the film. In *Bringing Up Baby* the path to the male hero's happiness requires serious chastisement. The source of that chastisement—and the payoff for it—is the unruly woman, who corrects his complacency and liberates the energy he has alienated by burying himself in his intellectual pursuits.[1] *Bringing Up Baby*—noisy, chaotic, its energy bordering on the demonic—is the first of three romantic comedies unrivaled in classical Hollywood cinema for their dependence on gender inversion. The others are *Ball of Fire*, directed by Hawks in 1941, and Preston Sturges's *The Lady Eve* of the same year. All three sustain the delicate balance of tone achieved in *It Happened One Night*, which combines the irony of *She Done Him Wrong* with the romance of *Sylvia Scarlett*. Such a balance allows these films to avoid sentimentality by, on the one hand, teasing the spectator with the promise of a utopian fulfillment of desire and, on the other, skeptically reining that fantasy in.

With the qualities of the unruly romantic heroine well established, all three films turn to an investigation of masculinity centering on the figure of the male professor. This investigation, tentatively begun with the poetry-writing newspaper reporter Peter in *It Happened One Night*, requires a dismantling of the very foundations of masculine identity. *Bringing Up Baby* extends the project of *Sylvia Scarlett* in two important ways: The sense of a venture into the Imaginary, which is fleeting and magical in *Sylvia Scarlett*, encompasses the entire film and takes on a tone that is more ambivalent; and the androgyny of the female hero is extended to the male. However, where Sylvia undergoes a disciplining into a mature heterosexuality that drives her masculinity underground, David undergoes a kind of reverse disciplining that releases the femininity already latent within him.

That disciplining, accomplished through moments of male humiliation, is often accompanied by the sound of the unruly woman's laughter, which halts the forward motion of narrative in much the same way as moments of spectacle organized around the female body do in other films. It also lays the groundwork for the ideal couple implied at the end of each film. If the union between an unruly heroine such as Susan and a befuddled hero such as David strains credibility, that is entirely the point, an indication less of a weakness in the genre than of the ideological contradictions it attempts to negotiate. Indeed, the ideal U.S. couple is one of "quite staggering incompatibility," in Robin Wood's words ("Ideology" 47). It is made up of two figures who occur across a range of genres and in variations suited to those genres: the "virile adventurer, potent, untrammeled man of action" and the "wife and mother, perfect companion, endlessly dependable, mainstay of hearth and home." Because these types are so poorly matched, each has its "shadow figure"—the "settled husband/father, dependable but dull" and "the erotic woman (adventuress, gambling lady, saloon entertainer)" (47).

I believe that comedy, concerned less with the ideal than with what falls short of it, is the home of the shadow figures: The "erotic woman" becomes the unruly woman and the "settled husband/father" the pedant, the professor, or the man of letters. They form a "Shadow Couple" of parallel incompatibility, which comedy exploits to produce its comic effect. The more conservative the comedy, the more its resolution paves the way for the Shadow Couple to become the Ideal Couple. The pedant's encounter with the unruly woman points him toward becoming the adventurous and virile Ideal Male. The unruly woman, her job done, can then settle into the domesticity of the Ideal Woman.

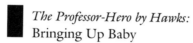

The Professor-Hero by Hawks: Bringing Up Baby

The plot of *Bringing Up Baby* repeats the familiar patterns of romantic comedy. A woman and man of different temperament and class must endure a series of struggles and transformations before acknowledging and fulfilling their mutual love. Susan, a wealthy young woman, decides she wants to marry David, a staid paleontologist she meets on the eve of his wedding to Miss Alice Swallow. David, meanwhile, has two things on his mind: a million-dollar gift to the museum and a bone—an "intercostal clavicle"—he needs to complete a skeleton of a dinosaur that has been his life's work. Susan involves David in a scheme to bring "Baby," a tame leopard, to Connecticut. The trip takes them into a "green world" of mistaken identity, masquerade, and inversion, where they lose Baby and the bone, find a wild leopard, and end up in jail. David's misbehavior costs him the gift and his bride. Susan, meanwhile, finds the missing bone and receives the bequest. She turns them both over to David, and he admits he loves her.

More fully than *She Done Him Wrong, It Happened One Night,* or *Sylvia Scarlett, Bringing Up Baby* realizes the potential of the topos of female unruliness in romantic comedy to challenge existing structures of gender and social authority. First, the film gives greater presence to the feminine. It builds its love triangle around an extra woman, Miss Swallow, rather than an extra man. And the father figure associated with social power and a gift of money is also a woman, Susan's aunt. Thus the important stakes must be fought for between women—Susan must defeat Miss Swallow, and she must appease her aunt. She succeeds in both, and the money passes matrilineally from the aunt to Susan, and then to David. Second, the chaotic tone of the entire film reproduces the male hero's loss of control when the unruly woman enters his life. Indeed, *Bringing Up Baby* has been criticized for an "extremeness" which leaves the spectator "uneasy," a criticism I will return to later.

Bringing Up Baby is organized around two symbols, Susan's leopard and David's bone. The bone, which David carries with him for much of the film until Susan's dog steals it, bears several levels of meaning: as fossil, as sexual symbol, and as social symbol. First, as a fossil, the bone is related to David's occupation as scientist. The philosopher, or pedant, is a comic type with a tradition that extends at least as far back as Aristophanes, who lambasted Socrates in *The Clouds*. In the classical Hollywood film, the motif draws further on the broad current of anti-intellectualism in U.S. culture, which expresses its suspicion of artistic or literary pursuits by gendering them feminine. The newspaper reporter is perhaps the only man of letters to escape the suggestion of effeminacy, and that is because of a masculine ideology cultivated around the newsroom. No such ideology clings to the occupation of philosopher, scientist, or professor, however. David is shown at the outset in the pose of Rodin's statue *The Thinker*, rigidly emulating a lifeless object. That removal from social power and from a world of action links him, like all "thinkers," with the feminine. Already emasculated, the male professor is a safer target for critiques of masculinity than more macho figures, such as the gangster, the cowboy, the soldier, or the private eye, might be.[2]

At the same time, the professor's class position enables him to be recuperated as an ideal American hero, for such a hero must support the belief in a classless society by bearing no extreme traces of class himself. The professor or philosopher is of indeterminate social class, high in cultural capital but rarely seen as wealthy or holding power in the social world. The stereotype of absent-mindedness presents him as absorbed in matters far removed from, and of little consequence to, practical everyday life. Despite his supposed brainpower, however, he is shown to be just an average fellow, if that, in terms of the issues that matter in romantic comedy—self-knowledge, the ability to play, and a fitness for romance.

Moreover, the unruly woman's intensity or energy only heightens his comfortable ordinariness.

As fossil, the bone represents all that the film opposes: David's avoidance of the chaos of life—of live animals rather than dead ones, and of lively women rather than women like Miss Swallow. David prefers the morgue-like quiet of a museum of natural history, where he pursues his work as a paleontologist, studying the remains of extinct reptiles. "I like peace and quiet," he tells Susan. The fossil's rigidity corresponds to the sense that David himself is not fully awake or alive. The film is thus another example of an inversion of the Sleeping Beauty story. Susan recognizes him as Prince Charming ("You're so good-looking without your glasses," she tells him), but he is hard to awaken. With every pratfall and intrusion of a body too inflexible to adapt to its surroundings, he gives evidence of Henri Bergson's insight that laughter often arises from the mechanical encrusted on the organic. In this, David recalls Grant's earlier role in *She Done Him Wrong* as Cummins, who was told by West to "loosen up, you'll have more fun."

Miss Swallow is an even more extreme example of the same kind of rigidity. With her spectacles, prim suit, and insistence on a marriage without "domestic entanglements" or sex (no "swallowing"), she is one of the masculinized battle-axes more common in comedian comedy than in romantic comedy. The couple in a romantic comedy often begins as a triangle, in which the third person represents the misguided temptations of one of the lovers. The presence of King Westley helps define Peter Warne and clarify Ellie's options in *It Happened One Night*. The competition of two men for a woman has behind it the considerable mythological and psychic weight of the Oedipal triangle. The competition of two women over a man, on the other hand, has no comparable structure, and so when a female rival appears, as in *Bringing Up Baby* and *Ball of Fire*, she often becomes a stand-in for the real temptation or threat internal to the hero. *Bringing Up Baby* displaces onto Miss Swallow all that threatens David from within: sexual repression concealed as devotion to "higher" matters, an overinvolvement in *work* and overinvestment in a Puritan ethic of self-denial. Her presence shows that the effort to make a compatible couple by crossing the "Ideal" and "Shadow" lines—by matching the settled Shadow Male with a phallic version of the settled Ideal Female—just doesn't work. Sparks don't fly until David meets a proper Shadow partner, the unruly Susan.

David, however, must also be shown from the outset as having the raw materials of the Ideal Male, and so it matters what he is thinking about in his contemplative pose, and that is the bone. He is wondering where to put it—maybe in the tail? The bone, of course, is not only fossil but penis, and Susan calls him "Mr. Bone." David must learn in the course of the film about what that name means. One of the first signs that there's more to him than first appears is when he uses slang to express his enthusiasm ("I'll wow him, I'll knock him for a loop") until Miss Swallow scolds him for it. (Three years later, Hawks was to build *Ball of Fire* around the motif of slang.)

Finally, the bone is also a manifestation of the phallus, or symbol of social power, and the skeleton a sign of bourgeois patriarchy. It has meanings related not only to sexuality but to gender and to the organization of property and language, all of which undergo a massive assault at the hands of Susan. As Andrew Britton suggests, the phallus is the quintessential commodity, which David acknowledges when he says, "It's rare! It's precious!" To Susan, more oriented to use-value, "it's just an old bone." Her job is to bring about a reorganization of sexuality around something other than the phallus. It is a job that requires a systematic destruction of a kind of masculinity bound up in power, order, and dignity.

Susan's disregard for property—for who owns a golf ball or a car—can be seen as a function of her own class privilege, but it is also a marker of her unruliness, and in fact she brings to both property and language a sense of play hostile to the spirit of capitalism. In the romantic comedies of the 1930s and 1940s, which invariably invoke class difference, the unruly woman's class primarily identifies her as "other," outside the middle class and free from its conventionality. Combining Sylvester's boyishness with Sylvia's femininity, Susan as unruly virgin extends Ellie's tentative transgressiveness to new limits. She plays golf, takes innumerable pratfalls, slides into water over her head. David recognizes her as a figure of inversion when he tells her, "You look at everything upside down." Like David, she is associated with animals, but with two leopards that are very much alive. When we first discover Baby, Susan too is wearing spots, on a negligee, and she wears them again, on the veil of her hat, at the end of the film. The leopard is as unsubtle a symbol as the bone, but effectively establishes what Susan represents—the "live animal" repressed within the ossifying David. While Baby is tame and gentle, there's also the other leopard, the dangerous double. The film acknowledges the latent danger in the sexuality David has repressed and through Susan links it with women. Women, it suggests, can be gentle like Baby or dangerous like Baby's double, and their appearances are deceiving. Yet the alternative is worse, and life without the danger Susan brings to it resembles something like death.

For Susan, words function similarly to property, but with greater consequence, and her mercurial use of language breaks down the foundations of rational discourse. It also is her means of initiating, advancing, and controlling the movement of the plot. This film, more so than *It Happened One Night*, brings to mind Patricia Parker's argument about the connection between female speech and textual expansion. Here, Susan's speech enhances narrative pleasure and romantic desire by deferring the closure of both. Through wordplay, storytelling, misunderstandings, and lies, Susan entangles David in a script she is authoring, which is also the script of the film—her hunt for David and her demolition of all that stands in her way. Her lies and storytelling culminate in her performance in the jail, when she pretends to be a gangster's moll, "Swinging Door Susie," who anticipates Barbara Stanwyck's role in *Ball of Fire*. On the surface, Susan disavows any sense of control over the events of the film. Her actions, and the transparency of her facial expressions, suggest a total lack of self-consciousness. She lives in the moment, responding with alarm when George runs off with the bone or with hilarity when she sees David snagged, with a butterfly net over his head. However, it is her desire for David that initiates the action and awakens his desire for her. She tells her aunt, "I'm going to marry David. He doesn't know it yet but I am."

To catch David, Susan must destroy the kind of masculinity that impedes their union: the dignity and sense of conscious control over his life that sets David on the course to becoming a fossil himself. Once Susan enters his life, David's preoccupation is replaced by another kind of altered consciousness resembling sleepwalking, hypnosis, or paralysis. "I know we ought to go now but somehow I can't move," he says when Susan throws pebbles at the bedroom window of the man he hopes will help him get the bequest. Susan strips him of his identity as easily as she steals his clothes. She guides him through a series of identities that move him down the ladder of social privilege and biological evolution. He loses his dignity as a scientist who plays golf and dines at the Ritz, and becomes a buffoon dressed in a crumpled top hat and covered with feathers. When Susan steals his clothes and leaves him only a woman's robe, he loses the outward signs of his masculinity ("I went gay!" he yells).[3] Later, he parodies a big-game hunter, and finally he is mistaken for a member of a criminal gang and locked up in jail. Biologically he moves from maturity to childhood to infancy, and even to a lower form of life when he chases George around a tree on all fours and digs for a bone. When he follows Susan and repeatedly, mechanically echoes her calls for George, he recalls a child's mimicking of the mother. More important, like the mirrored swaying on the skeleton, the behavior shows an unconscious connection between the two. All the while, Susan increases each humiliation by laughing at him.

In Bringing Up Baby, *Susan (Katharine Hepburn) displays a level of energy that often disarms David (Cary Grant) but finally liberates him from his repressive masculinity. Pretending to be the outlaw "Swinging Door Susie," Susan escapes from jail, leaving a powerless David behind. Copyright 1941, RKO Radio Pictures, Inc.*

To understand this humiliation, it is worth taking a look at *Bringing Up Baby* in the context of Hawks's other films, for he is as well known for his adventure dramas as for his romantic comedies.[4] According to Robin Wood (*Howard Hawks*), Hawks's comedies invert the dynamics of his adventure films by subjecting the male hero to sexual reversal, humiliation, and "loss of mastery." While the comedies generally affirm the "*resilience* of the male, his ability to live through extremes of humiliation retaining an innate dignity" (68), the effect of *Bringing Up Baby* is ultimately unsettling: "One can only feel uneasy," he writes (71), seeing the film as advocating a kind of "irresponsibility." He doesn't ask, however, if the film advocates a responsibility to some other set of values associated with comedy or even with the Hawks oeuvre itself. Peter Wollen, who takes a closer look at gender in Hawks's films, views the comedies more sympathetically. For him, they don't merely invert the adventure films but complement them, adding a complexity to Hawks's recurring interest in male solidarity and in the "danger" and "fun" that give "pungency" to life (84–94). In Hawks's world, according to Wollen, woman is not fully human. Often associated with predatory animals, she poses the greatest threat to the male group.

In the comedies, Hawks confronts the contradiction that occurs when that threat is also the source of "danger" and "fun." Susan represents those very values of danger (the wild leopard) and fun (Baby) that Hawks so prizes, the "pungency" that has David reeling on the scaffold over his prized brontosaurus. For Wood, the danger overwhelms the fun. Indeed, the film seems to tread a fine line for some viewers between pleasure and pain. David's symbolic castration and the spectator's unrelenting immersion in a world of the Imaginary where the phallus seems largely irrelevant evoke a laughter that is ambivalent. It is also likely that gender influences the kind of laughter a film like *Bringing Up Baby* produces. Mastering the threat posed by David's symbolic castration might well be a different matter for the female spectator than it is for the male.

Wood's response to the film recalls Michael's laughter in *Sylvia Scarlett*, the unease and fear at returning to something "hidden but not forgotten," familiar and strange, something similar to Freud's "uncanny." For Ernst Kris, the fear associated with the uncanny adds another "insufficiently appreciated" element to Freud's analysis of wit. Kris's theory of laughter, in fact, has more in common with Freud's notion of the uncanny: both emphasize ambivalence and cast important light on the relation between gender and laughter. According to Freud, the essence of the uncanny is ambivalence, a sensation—specifically associated with the maternal body— that oscillates between "homelike" (*heimliche*) and its opposite, "not of the home" (*unheimliche*).[5] For Kris, laughter has less to do with the pleasure of released aggression, which Freud describes in his account of jokes, than with warding off a fear arising from past threats to the ego. Laughter, Kris argues, often aids the ego in "repeating its victory" over fears only partially mastered. Because laughter is so closely bound to fear, comedy is "doubleedged," readily passing from pleasurable success to unpleasurable failure (446–447).[6] From such a perspective, the world of *Bringing Up Baby* can be understood as returning the spectator to the site of those fears. The humiliations David undergoes repeat the ones we have experienced, and we laugh to reassure ourselves that they no longer frighten us.

However, neither Kris, nor Freud on the uncanny, fully acknowledges the place of woman in these scenarios of ambivalence. In a critique of Freud's essay on the uncanny, Jane Marie Todd shows how Freud unintentionally reveals his own ambivalence or "partially mastered fears." Much of Freud's essay is based on a story from Hoffmann concerning a man,

Nathanael, who falls in love with Olympia, a mechanical doll he believes is alive. His love for her arouses his fears of the Sandman, a frightening figure who tears out children's eyes. For Freud, the eyes are linked to the penis, and the Sandman to the threat of castration. However, Freud writes Olympia out of his account, making her merely a projection of Nathanael's mind, a double, having nothing to do with real women. He fails to see how the ideal *real* woman is a mechanical doll, robbed of her own eyes, docile, silent, and powerless. Olympia, Todd argues, is a sign of the social meaning of castration for women.

By interpreting castration in the context of the Oedipal rivalry between father and son rather than that of the love story between Olympia and Nathanael, Freud "veils" a real fear of female power. (And he in fact begins an early version of his essay with a parapraxis that substitutes *Schleiermacher*, a word that means *veilmaster*, for *Schelling*, the name of a German philosopher.) At the end of his discussion of the Sandman story, Freud briefly recounts the following: "I have occasionally heard a woman patient declare that even at the age of eight she had still been convinced that her dolls would be certain to come to life if she were to look at them in a particular way, with as concentrated a gaze as possible" ("The Uncanny" 235). As Todd notes, the eyes, previously associated with castration, now suggest the female power to give life—the exact opposite of castration. However, the power to give life is also tied to the power to take it away.[7] Thus, Todd writes, the *woman's gaze* "is quite simply unnerving" (526). Later in the essay, Freud describes the dread of the "evil eye" as one of the most widespread forms of superstition: "There never seems to have been any doubt about the source of this dread. Whoever possesses something at once valuable and fragile is afraid of the envy of others, in that he projects on them the envy he would have felt in their place. A feeling like this betrays itself in a look even though it is not put into words" ("The Uncanny" 242). Yet, as Todd notes, Freud could not name what that "valuable and fragile" thing is, and he denies in a number of places that "penis envy" could be a male projection of castration fear. Freud, she concludes, thus veils from himself the truth that it is women who are *unheimliche*.

I believe that this fear of the woman's gaze underlies much of the anxiety aroused by the unruly woman. In these comedies, the woman gazes upon the castrated man—or even castrates him, much as Susan's laughter furthers David's humiliation and Wood's uneasiness. Yet her gaze is ambivalent. Like the grotesque realism of Bakhtin's carnivalesque, it is bound up in life and death, with the process of becoming. When viewed as a group or a genre, these films show the unruly woman giving as she takes away, making a hero of the man (or a man of the hero) at the same time as she destroys much about him.

A more suggestive context for understanding the relationship between the unruly woman and the male hero lies in the aesthetic of masochism. Gaylyn Studlar's work on the Marlene Dietrich/Josef von Sternberg collaboration has opened up new avenues for feminist film theory by turning from Freud and Lacan to Gilles Deleuze. Deleuze identifies masochism with the pre-Oedipal phase of the subject, who willingly submits to an idealized, all-powerful mother. Such a notion of masochism differs from the Freudian dynamic of sadomasochism, which arises out of Oedipal sexuality.

Deleuze's masochistic aesthetic, I believe, bears remarkable parallels to the structure of comedy—in particular, the comedies of gender inversion. As Studlar notes, Deleuze turns Freud's Oedipal theory upside down by laying guilt on the father rather than the son. Just as masochism expresses the desire to exclude the father from the symbiotic relationship between mother and child, so in comedy the son ultimately triumphs and the father retreats. The circus's abject clown is the defeated, guilty father, with a floppy tie that signifies his loss of sexual power (Grotjahn 92). Masochism also inverts the power relations of patriarchy by making the woman dominant and the male willingly subordinate. The masochist endures castration because it results in a nonphallic sexuality that permits a union with the plenitude of the mother. That symbiotic union, however, also conjures up fears of being overwhelmed, and so masochism—like much laughter, like the uncanny, and like the carnivalesque—is also ambivalent, marked by a movement toward and retreat from the idealized object. Fetishism, as with Mae West and Marlene Dietrich, helps preserve a distance from that object. So does masquerade or "erotic metamorphosis," which often takes the form of cross-dressing, producing a suspended movement between concealment and revelation and holding off the regime of Oedipus. Studlar writes: "The male masochist wants to be led in a round robin of pretense, misunderstanding and sexual disguise in order to prolong the pleasure of desire unfulfilled" (237). In other words, the male masochist is like David, and like any number of other male heroes who find themselves in such a relationship of mixed attraction and anxiety with an unruly woman.

One question remains about *Bringing Up Baby*, and that concerns how much David's loss of phallic power restores another kind of power to him. In some regards, it appears not to. *Bringing Up Baby* may be unsettling as a romantic comedy because it does so little to recuperate the male hero or curb Susan's anarchic, amoral energy. The collapse of the skeleton barrier between them is hardly the resolution provided by the tumbling wall of Jericho, and David hardly the reborn hero Peter Warne is. His final words, "Oh dear, oh my," suggest that he is as distressed as ever.

However, because romantic comedy rests on a narrative that is social and utopian (unlike the more tragic narrative of psychoanalysis), the release of the unconscious in the film is not monstrous or fearful but liberating. Susan guides David into an infantilism that restores to him something he has lost, and it is not only his bone, but his repressed femininity. While most of the male stars of the period played similar roles, these roles were especially well suited to Cary Grant, whose femininity complemented Hepburn's androgyny. He was able to retain his sexual charm and glamour despite the comic humiliations he endured, and the expression of his femininity did not detract from his masculinity. When Miss Swallow calls him "Butterfly," the insult directs more laughter at her than at him. The very openness of the ending—the resistance to a closure that would domesticate Susan, recuperate David, and restore the rightful order of the man on top—is a strength. If the film ends with a pile of rubble, at least it has made a major step toward that freer and more pleasurable world romantic comedy takes as its ideal.

 Ball of Fire

In *Ball of Fire*, Hawks appears to be trying to short-circuit those qualities that left Wood so unsettled and to lift his hero out of that rubble. The film seems to be an effort at reassurance and at dispelling the nervousness of *Bringing Up Baby*.[8] That shift in tone can be explained in part by the film's production in 1941, when the country was on the brink of World War II. Between 1941 and 1945, Hollywood joined the war effort by producing movies intended to retain their entertainment value while also supporting government programs to boost morale. Indeed, with the war came a desire to turn from such "frivolous" subjects as romance and the battle of the sexes to the more serious matters at hand.[9] As its unruly heroine, *Ball of Fire* featured Barbara Stanwyck, a star much associated with the war and as at home in comedies as in melodramas, such as *Stella Dallas*. Born in Brooklyn, she began her career as a chorus girl and by 1944 was the highest-paid woman in the United States. Her film career faltered in the 1950s but then revived on television, where she starred in *The Barbara Stanwyck Theatre* (1960–1961) and won an Emmy for her role in *Big Valley* (1965–1969). Despite the tough women she played in her earlier work with Frank Capra (and would continue to play, as in Billy Wilder's *Double In-*

In Ball of Fire, *Barbara Stanwyck as Sugarpuss O'Shea plays Snow White to a group of seven professor dwarfs; unlike Snow White, however, she brings disorder to their tidy lives. The eighth dwarf towering above the others in this advertising poster for the film is Professor Gerald Potts (Gary Gooper), who seeks her out to teach him about slang and eventually becomes the prince.*

demnity [1944]), Stanwyck in the 1940s brought a softer, less threatening, and more middle-class aura than did Hepburn to the unruly woman.

The film tells a whimsical version of the Snow White story, but with eight dwarfs instead of seven. The eighth is Prince Charming, the grammarian Professor Gerald Potts, played by Gary Cooper. By placing the prince among dwarfs, Hawks can pursue the thematics of gender inversion, making an unruly Snow White the means of "awakening" the prince from his slumber among the dwarfs. At the same time, Hawks ensures that the hero will have an opportunity to distinguish himself from the dwarfs, unlike David in *Bringing Up Baby*. In *Ball of Fire*, the dwarfs are a collegial group of celibate, mostly elderly professors writing an encyclopedia commissioned by the family of a deceased industrialist. They live a quiet life until Potts recruits Snow White, the nightclub performer Sugarpuss O'Shea, to help him with his research for his entry on slang. Sugarpuss, who is also the girlfriend of gangster Joe Lilac (Dana Andrews), moves in with the professors and disrupts their orderly lives. Potts and Sugarpuss fall in love, but they cannot marry until after a showdown in which the professors fight the gangsters and Potts beats up Lilac.

Clearly the film has much in common with *Bringing Up Baby*, beginning with the professor-hero. Potts makes the same mistake as David, but with language rather than biology. Sequestered from the world since his childhood days as a prodigy, Potts has come to view language as a fossil. When he hears people from the streets speaking, he realizes that his article on slang is out of date: "That man talked a living language," he says. "I embalmed some dead phrases." Here, the dinosaur/leopard opposition becomes linguistic—"dead phrases" versus "a living language," especially slang. In *Ball of Fire*, language itself is not aligned with a repressive Symbolic, but is a material living phenomenon that is the means of social intercourse and, eventually, sexual intercourse. It brings Potts back to his body and attracts him to Sugarpuss; he can't remember what color her hair was, but she spoke with "words so bizarre they made my mouth water," he says.

Pott's ignorance of current slang is a sign of his refusal to acknowledge time. His "corny" boiled cuffs are funny not because style itself is intrinsically important but because an awareness of style, whether in language or clothing, indicates a connection with a world that changes. What the film critiques is the scholarly attempt to impose an artificial stasis on language, to render something living into something abstract, and to sever it from its relation to the world. That separation of signifier from signified is what Professor Oddly was guilty of when he allowed his respect for the image of a flower—the fragile "anemone nemorosa"—to stand between himself and Genevieve, the woman who was his wife. The danger comes from failing to recognize when "words cease to be of use," as Potts says at the end of the film, when he finally convinces Sugarpuss to stay with him by taking her in his arms, kissing her, and in fact showing her that he has learned the lesson she has taught him.

Sugarpuss is as clearly marked with unruliness as Susan is in *Bringing Up Baby*. As a dancer, a singer, and a "gal who came up the hard way," she is also something of a gold digger who sparkles at the sight of the ring Joe Lilac gives her. Whereas heiresses like Susan and Ellie make use of their social privilege to free them from middle-class convention and the need to worry about money, women like Sugarpuss (and the characters played by Mae West) draw on a playful vulgarity associated with show business, gangsters, and the wrong side of the tracks. In romantic comedy, that vulgarity is sexy, fun, and the essential antidote to the male hero's repression. What matters most about Sugarpuss is that she is a rule-breaker. Her speech violates the rules of an "embalmed" language. Her behavior disrupts the dusty order of the Totten Foundation. "Look at me as an apple, just another apple," she tells Potts after reminding him of that man "who learned so much from watching an apple drop." Miss Bragg confirms Sugarpuss's comparison of herself with Eve when she says, "*That* is the kind of woman who makes civilizations topple."

Despite *Ball of Fire*'s similarities with *Bringing Up Baby*, the films differ in important ways, beginning with the former's gentleness of tone. Rather than the stark opposition between male and female, *Ball of Fire* creates a more complex environment for its hero by returning him to the traditional Hawksian fellowship of men. The unruly woman is more a source of "fun" than of "danger," softened, more vulnerable and self-aware. This film locates danger back among men. By allowing the hero to confront that danger, it rejects one aspect of conventional masculinity while redeeming another. As in *Bringing Up Baby*, women carry much power in the world of *Ball of Fire*. Miss Bragg manages the professors' lives like a strict mother scolding small children. The plain Miss Totten, a more vulnerable version of Miss Swallow, manages the Totten endowment and the future of the scholarly enterprise. However, two male groups dominate the action of the film—the professors and Joe Lilac's gang. Each represents an imperfect version of masculinity.

The professors are infantilized and emasculated, yet despite their extreme silliness, they are sympathetic characters, innocents more than fools. In the most lyrical moments of the film, their voices render in music the harmony of the ideal male group. They sing "Genevieve" to share Professor Oddly's memories of his wife, and then "*Gaudeamus Igitur*" to recall the ideals of male fellowship associated with the tradition of the academy. The target of our laughter isn't so much a masculinity in need of chastisement for its arrogance and rigidity as the professors' very absence of masculinity, their pre-sexual innocence. By not knowing when "words no longer suffice," the professors are excluded from a masculinity defined by the ability to take vigorous—and even violent—action when necessary.

The gangsters, on the other hand, represent a masculinity untempered by the feminine. In the gangsters, Hawks extends the phallic bone of *Bringing Up Baby* to the gun. The film locates violence and danger not in a wild leopard—in Sugarpuss, or some generalized sexuality—but in a masculinity distorted by its excessive affection for the bone as phallus, or social power. As is often true in Hawks's films, that affection is vaguely linked with the homoerotic, as suggested by Joe Lilac's name and jokes about missing pajamas. At one point the struggle between the two male groups includes a comical and childish taunt about size of equipment. A professor/child/dwarf says: "You're under the impression that you're big because you have those firearms, know how to load them and pull the trigger." More to the point, the film gives dramatic evidence of the excess of that masculinity when Joe Lilac slaps Potts's face and punches him in the stomach.

Out of this confrontation between two imperfect male groups Potts emerges as a hero. When Potts throws away the boxing manual and simply pounds Joe Lilac out of the frame of the filmic image and into a garbage truck, Potts demonstrates that it isn't enough for a man to be intelligent, tender, and passionate—he must also be brawny and tough. He must know what to do with the gun in all of its dimensions. Sugarpuss tells him he's "big and cute and pretty," alluding to the femininity about him she finds appealing. Yet, in contrast to David in *Bringing Up Baby*, Potts counters much of that feminine aura with his ease in becoming a romantic hero. His distance from the professors is evident from the start. Not only is he considerably younger, he stands a full head above most of the others, and much of the film's humor about the infantilized professors comes from the irony of including such a giant among them. Potts orders up an engagement ring with a moving inscription. He speaks with an authority that is not silly or cruel but full of dignity when he discovers Sugarpuss has used him. More passionately than David, he insists that honeymoons are for "domestic entanglements," not for painting watercolors, as Professor Oddly's Genevieve did on hers. In the end, Potts turns out to be a nearly perfect romantic hero, an idealized version of the average fellow, only with an overdeveloped brain.

By locating danger so clearly in abuses of masculinity, the film diminishes the threat of the unruly woman. Indeed, Sugarpuss is both more self-aware than Susan and more vulnerable. The film tracks her discovery that Potts—the man who could barely keep her in manicures—offers what she really wants. Her pain in discovering the depth of Potts's feelings for her, and hers for him, is clear in a scene that recalls the final conversation across the wall of Jericho in *It Happened One Night*. Potts reveals his feelings for her in a darkened motel room, although he thinks he's speaking to Professor Oddly. Sugarpuss's eyes shine with tears just as Ellie's do, although Sugarpuss hasn't yet reached the point where she is ready to act on her own desires, and she doesn't reveal herself to him.

The festivity that ends *Ball of Fire* is almost classical in its inclusiveness. Miss Bragg, the battle-ax mother, has already shown that she will never leave the household but will accommodate its coming changes. Even prim Miss Totten, clinging to the speeding car filled with the triumphant professors, announces, like David, that the topsy-turvy adventure has given her the most fun of her life. Her conversion is a rare instance of a romantic rival being incorporated into a comedic resolution. (Another one occurs in *Moonstruck*, as Chapter 7 will show.) Pott's final embrace of Sugarpuss takes place within the familial embrace of the professors. A new household is established, and it remains a feminized one. However, this ending is as closed as the ending of *Bringing Up Baby* is open. Sugarpuss, the ball of fire, has come to rest. Potts has earned his place, and takes it, as patriarch.

 The Professor-Hero by Sturges: The Lady Eve

The nervousness of *Bringing Up Baby*, as well as *Ball of Fire*'s efforts to dispel it, are entirely missing from Preston Sturges's *The Lady Eve* (1941). The film conveys absolute ease with the premise of gender inversion, which it sustains through its conclusion. That ease is consistent with the gift for scathing social satire that Sturges displayed in his writing for both stage and screen, which included *Strictly Dishonorable*, the most popular comedy of the 1929–1930 Broadway season. He achieved his greatest success as a film director in the early 1940s, with a series of works, including *The Great McGinty* (1940) and *Hail the Conquering Hero* (1944), that gave full expression to comedy's antiauthoritarian impulse. And when he expressed that impulse through the conventions of romantic comedy, as in *The Palm Beach Story* (1942) and *Unfaithfully Yours* (1948), as well as in *The Lady Eve*, he demolished the traditional male hero and ideology of romantic love with unrivaled energy and wit.

Hopsy (Henry Fonda), the hero of *The Lady Eve*, is not only an innocent, like David and Potts, hiding behind his work from an encounter with his sexuality, but he is guilty of a greater moral error. And Jean, or Eve (Barbara Stanwyck), the unruly woman, not only gets her way, but her desire dominates the film. There is little sense of the struggle between equals that characterizes many romantic comedies, or even of Hopsy providing much of a challenge to Jean, until the dark moment when she realizes the real nature of her desire for him. The film bears many signs of what Thomas Schatz in *Hollywood Genres* has described as a genre in its maturity, winking at the conventions of romantic comedy, and at those of melodrama as well. But while countering every one of its utopian implausibilities with irony, it preserves the balance between belief and disbelief so essential to the genre. In fact, it heightens the pleasure of its fairy-tale ending by giving its last shot and last word to Muggsy, the hero's skeptical bodyguard, who has skulked around the periphery of the action throughout the film. Slipping out the cabin door Jean has just closed behind the couple, he insists once again, this time directly to the camera, that *he* won't be fooled by such romantic nonsense, even if the hero, and the heroine as well, may be.

The Lady Eve is located squarely in the tradition of romantic comedy. Hopsy, the son of a wealthy brewer, is pursued by Jean, a "card sharp." They meet on a cruise ship and fall in love. When he learns that she is not who he thought she was, he bitterly leaves her. Later, with the help of "Sir Alfred," another con artist, Jean gets even with him by pretending to be the Lady Eve Sidwick, a noblewoman from England. He does not recognize her, falls in love with her again, and marries her after a whirlwind courtship. On their wedding night, she tells him of all the other men she has eloped with, and he leaves her once more. Soon she regrets what she has done and wants to see him again. Despite his father's advice, he refuses to meet her. Jean learns he's leaving on another cruise, discards her masquerade, and beats him to the ship. They meet again, embrace, and this time forgo any explanations of her past.

The Lady Eve expands *Ball of Fire*'s brief allusion to the Garden of Eden into a full-blown comic revision of the tragic myth. The film depicts the "fall of man" repeatedly and in many variations, from Hopsy's first pratfall when Jean trips him, to their "falling" for each other, to their subsequent falling—in differing degrees—from innocence. As in the myth, Jean's desire is largely responsible for these falls. But instead of being linked to sin and loss, that desire redeems Hopsy and leads him from an Eden "up the Amazon" that consists *only* of snakes to another one behind the closed cabin door at the end of the film. The debonair serpent of the opening credits signals the obvious themes of sexuality and gender associated with the myth. But while the discovery of sexuality leads to death and exile in the original story, in the film it leads to the opposite—the "homecoming" and renewed life the couple finds in each other. The snake's top hat and castanets are a reminder that romantic comedy often treats sexuality and gender in relation to social class, and the film's two major characters, through casting and plot, absorb extremes of social class, emerging in the end as a new American Adam who retains most of his innocence and an American Eve in whom experience does not equal guilt.

Such an American Adam must ring true to the deepest aspects of American ideology. The film retains the structure of the cross-class marriage by making Hopsy the son of a wealthy brewer. Yet his class is undercut in various ways, beginning with the casting of Henry Fonda. The male actor most closely associated with romantic comedy is Cary Grant, and, to a U.S. audience, his urbanity, smoothness, and British roots conveyed a certain degree of "cultivation," despite the actor's actual working-class background. Such was not the case with Fonda, whose face reads sincerity rather than sophistication. In the 1930s Fonda had already established himself as an international star for his "characteristically 'American' personality" (Katz 430–431). In the two years before *The Lady Eve*, he played the sharecropper Tom Joad in *The Grapes of Wrath*, Abraham Lincoln in *Young Mr. Lincoln*, and Frank James, Jesse's brother, in *Jesse James*, roles which identified him with the plain-spoken, down-to-earth American hero. In *The Lady Eve*, Fonda plays the son of a man who appears to be self-made, like Ellie's father in *It Happened One Night*. Mr. Pike is indifferent to aristocratic decorum. He doesn't know or care whether the correct attire for a party is black tie or white tie. He bangs his plates for his breakfast. The film even undercuts the source of his fortune. Despite Hopsy's treatise on the varieties of his family brew, "Pike's Pale—The Ale that Won for Yale" *is* just beer.

Yet Hopsy has no interest in beer or in his fortune. He considers himself a scientist, an "ophiologist." "Snakes are my life, sort of," he says. As a result, he has the professor-hero's aura of indeterminate class and (despite the sexual connotations of snakes) undeveloped masculinity. When the film opens, he is preparing to return home after a year up the Amazon, removed from women and from the masculine world of public power. He leaves reluctantly. "That is how I'd like to spend all of my time—in the company of men like yourselves, in pursuit of knowledge," he says. When Sir Alfred later recalls him as "that tall backward boy who was toying with toads and things," Jean corrects him by telling him that Hopsy isn't backward, he's a scientist. Sir Alfred replies, "Well, I knew he was peculiar." Hopsy tries to preserve his detachment from women after he boards the ship by burying his nose in a book (*Are Snakes Necessary?*) to avoid their attention. Even before she's met him, Jean recognizes that other women pose no competition to her. "It's a shame he doesn't care for the flesh," she says when he appears immune to blatant flirtation by the other women on board. There is no love triangle in the film, no rivals such as Miss Totten or Miss Swallow, and in fact no maternal figures either, such as the dowager aunt in *Bringing Up Baby* and Miss Bragg in *Ball of Fire*. Hopsy has always loved only Jean/Eve and snakes, and his devotion to his work seems to be the only obstacle between the lovers.

That devotion, however, is only part of the problem. Hopsy has to overcome an even more insidious aspect of what is represented by the dinosaur in *Bringing Up Baby* and embalmed language in *Ball of Fire*. First, he must learn the familiar lesson about trusting his senses. Had he done so, he would have kept the essential truth about Jean clearly in mind when the photograph unmasked her. He would also have recognized her in her masquerade as the Lady Eve. Like Peter Warne in *It Happened One Night*, he lets an ideal obscure the reality before his eyes. "Why didn't you take me in your arms that day?" Jean asks at the end. He didn't because of an error, a rigidity, that is more serious than his estrangement from his own body. Like Adam, his fall is brought about by pride. But unlike Adam, who chose to stay with Eve when confronted with her sin, Hopsy cannot forgive. He is not only innocent but self-righteous. He is guilty of the most ancient tendency to idealize women or vilify them, and, when in doubt, to judge them as patriarchy has always judged Eve—with arrogance and self-righteousness. Jean tells him, "You see, you don't know much about girls. The best ones aren't as good as you think they are. The bad ones aren't as bad, not nearly as bad."

Hopsy takes a moral fall the first time he rejects Jean. He falls again when he struggles to overcome his horror at the Lady Eve's first confession on the train. He makes a tortuous speech that suggests that he has learned some humility: "If there is one thing that distinguishes a man from a beast, it is the ability to understand, and understanding, to forgive." Yet, with each new "confession," the gap between what he knows he should aspire to and his own capabilities becomes greater and he falls again and again. Just as he rushed to judge Jean, so he cannot bring himself to forgive the Lady Eve her admittedly prodigious indiscretions. His jump from the train and slide down a muddy slope take him to a new low.

In the same way that the film diminishes the stature of its Adam, it also reverses the weakness traditionally associated with Eve. The character of Jean draws on the strengths of both common types of unruly romantic heroine—the heiress and the outlaw—and she plays both in the film. In her, female unruliness is a matter not only of anarchic energy, vitality, or playfulness, but also of power. Moreover, that power is a source not of fear or sin, as in the Eden story, but of a kind of comic redemption.

One source of Jean's power lies in her ability to perform and to use herself as a spectacle toward her own ends. She earns her livelihood as a con artist, charming wealthy men to trick them out of their money. When she begins to fall in love with Hopsy, she plays the woman he wants her to be. Finally, she plays the Lady Eve Sidwick to even the score with him. Her initial contact with Hopsy, and ours with her, establishes the dynamics of their relationship. A long tracking shot moves along a row of passengers lined up on a deck then up to a higher deck where it rests on her.

Henry Fonda, as Hopsy, begins to lose his composure—a regular occurence in The Lady Eve—*when Barbara Stanwyck as the Lady Eve exacts her revenge for his lack of trust by sweetly confessing to a series of infidelities, each one more outrageous than the last. Copyright 1941, Paramount Pictures Inc.*

From above, she looks down on Hopsy in a point-of-view shot as he boards the ship. She drops an apple on his head, replacing Eve's seduction with a direct blow. Her assault continues when she trips him in the dining room, and he falls from that point right into her hands. When Jean does use more seductive means to lure Hopsy, her embraces of him often place him beneath her. When she takes him to her room to replace her broken shoe, she tells him to kneel before her and help her with her shoe. She smothers him with her arms and knocks him off the chair. Like David in *Bringing Up Baby*, he is powerless to move. By the second half of the film, when he sees her disguised as the Lady Eve, the very sight of her sends him into a paroxysm of pratfalls and escalating catastrophes. Her appearance to him then is uncanny and disorienting, and he crashes over furniture, into drapes, under trays of food. He has to change his clothes three times, mirroring in his own comic metamorphoses his inability to fix her appearance in his mind.

Like Susan and Sugarpuss, Jean also derives power from language and storytelling, extending that control to the widest reaches of narrative. Not only can she script a story around herself, like Susan's "Swinging Door Susie," she can tell other people's stories, predicting their actions and speaking what is in their minds. "'I wonder if my tie's on straight,'" she says while watching Hopsy in a mirror, before he straightens his tie. Jean chooses her man and builds a story around him that is driven by her own desire. This is most obvious in the "Lady Eve" segment of the film, when she creates a new identity for herself and predicts the precise course of her second romance with Hopsy. As she describes what will happen—"One day about six weeks from now—no, about two weeks from now, we'll be riding"—the film dissolves to just such a scene. She uses her facility for storytelling most dramatically on their wedding night, when she concocts a series of stories that exploit the male premium on female virginity. Each story gives Hopsy another chance to fail. He still wants a "virgin," a woman without a past, whose only history is in his imagination. He wants the image from his memory of the "little girl in pigtails." Jean's stories have the additional effect of producing the narrative pleasure of delayed gratification. Her very success in her revenge plot introduces the film's final complication, which is her discovery that hurting Hopsy actually gave her little real satisfaction.

Jean has an additional source of power that bears directly on the cinematic, and that is through her gaze. In this film, the gaze, typically associated with the male's objectification of the female, is linked with a female's power over the male, recalling the "staring eyes" that accompany Medusa's laughter. Jean's gaze, ambivalent and "quite simply unnerving," activates the uncanny. Hopsy, like Peter Warne, cannot see past the image of Jean in the photograph, or even past the Lady Eve disguise. His vision of her blurs and he nearly swoons when he comes too close to her the night they first meet. Jean, on the other hand, fixes Hopsy constantly in her gaze, watching him, sizing up her prey, making a spectacle of *him*. Jean violates the cultural taboo against the female gaze, beginning with the first shot of her on the deck of the ship searching him out with her eyes. Another episode early in the film demonstrates her narrative and visual power. Jean is seated in the dining room some distance from Hopsy with her back to him. She looks over her shoulder at him by framing his image in a small mirror. Then she gives a blow-by-blow account of a mini-movie (Cavell, *Pursuits of Happiness* 66), in which "every Jane in the room" tries to get his attention: "Watch his head when that kid goes by. It won't do you any good, dear, he's a bookworm, but swing them anyway. . . . She's up, she's down, she can't make up her mind. She's up again. The suspense is killing me," she says, although it really isn't, because she knows the outcome all along.

Jean enacts a symbolic castration of Hopsy much as Susan does of David, and it is no surprise that her power to castrate is associated with her gaze.[10] Yet Jean's gaze is not ultimately threatening because its object, as in the other films of gender inversion, is already castrated to a certain degree, or in need of discovering his own potency. Her gaze is what eventually *restores* that potency, and so she is allowed its ambivalent power.

Another reason her power is tolerated arises from the film's casting. Just as Fonda's dignity not only provides humor but helps make Hopsy an acceptable hero despite his foolishness, so Barbara Stanwyck moderates the unruly excesses of Jean. Stanwyck brings an Americanness to Jean and a melancholy shading to her character, which soften her power and defuse its threat. Her star image is middle class, in contrast to the more aristocratic Hepburn, whose independence in such films as *The Philadelphia Story* (1940) and *Woman of the Year* (1942) demands to be reined in. Stanwyck's diction and manner, especially during her masquerade as the Lady Eve, help the film convey the notion that the trappings of social class are as superficial as those of gender in *Sylvia Scarlett*. Stanwyck's style of femininity also is more conventional than that of the androgynous Hepburn. While her body is as slender as Hepburn's, she moves in ways that are less boyish, more consciously feminine and even seductive, as when Jean presents her leg to Hopsy to put on her shoe.

Jean endures two moments of defeat herself, adding an element of vulnerability to her unruliness. The first occurs when Hopsy leaves her of his own accord, and the second when she deliberately drives him away, during the "Lady Eve" segment. It is during this segment that the film explores the contradictions in Jean's desire, using comedy and melodrama to undercut with great irony the tropes of romantic love. Hopsy's second proposal to Jean follows her prediction of exactly how it will occur, with a romantic ride into the country and a stop to admire a flaming sunset. Hopsy's first declaration of love was comical but credible when Jean wanted to believe it on the deck of the ship. The second time around, it is shown as part of a laughable courtship ritual, especially when Hopsy repeats word for word his story about how he has always loved her. The horse's persistent intrusion into the scene heightens its absurdity. The film then moves to a comic mini-melodrama to exaggerate and make fun of Hopsy's suffering when Jean gets her revenge on their wedding night. She embroiders the "gaslight melodrama" of the coachman and two babies Sir Alfred began, and as her stories continue, the train roars through the rainy night like a scene out of a melodrama, passing over bridges and through tunnels and blasting its whistle, while the music on the soundtrack reaches a dramatic pitch. But melodrama is also the generic home of female suffering, and the mini-melodrama of the confession scene doesn't end when Hopsy steps off the train. Jean finds that her story has temporarily escaped her control when she realizes that she didn't need Hopsy *only* "like the ax needs the turkey." She wants Hopsy to know her as she is and still love her as his ideal.

Jean's period of chastisement is brief, however. It lasts only long enough to permit her a remarkable final victory. The film completes its comic revision of the tragic story of Adam and Eve by restoring the original balance—or imbalance—of power between Hopsy and Jean. When Jean rushes to the ship and trips Hopsy once again, Hopsy gets a third chance. This time it works. He takes her in his arms and, with a past of his own now, he refuses to hear any further explanations. Even with Jean's face before his eyes, however, he still doesn't seem to know that she was the Lady Eve. Hopsy's sin is absolved and his innocence restored, but this American Adam remains in the dark, recuperated only enough to fulfill Jean's desire. Jean, meanwhile, regains her original power. While the myth condemns Eve to obey Adam, the new Eden this comedy creates keeps her on top, undermining the ideology of gender sustained by the myth. Jean as the American Eve, once again casually dressed and coiffed, remains a figure of experience, a detached ironist in the tradition of the heroines of Shakespeare's comedies and Jane Austen's novels. Like the film itself, she is poised between the skepticism of Muggsy, who knows that she and the Lady Eve are "positively the same dame," and Hopsy's belief (cf. James Harvey 582). The film tells us, with Jean's and Hopsy's joy, that we are impoverished without our utopian desires for new Edens in which the real merges with the ideal. At the same time, we are foolish to expect too much of them.

6

Dumb Blondes

By the late 1940s and early 1950s, the expansive assurance of a woman on top like the Lady Eve was no longer possible. The elation that immediately followed the war was soon followed by a period of paranoia and unease, and containment became the watchword in both the film industry and the culture at large. In 1948, the antitrust suit against Paramount was resolved and the breakup of the studios began. Studios economized by slashing production costs and looking for scripts that were high in quality and low in risk. As the Cold War heated up the rhetoric of patriotism and anti-communism, the House Un-American Activities Committee witch-hunt further threatened Hollywood's sense of security. At the same time, a series of court cases in the mid 1950s eroded and then overturned the Production Code, contributing to a "representational instability in the figuration of sexual relations" (Krutnik, "The Faint Aroma" 59). Alfred Hitchcock tapped into the terror produced by that instability in *Psycho* (1960). And while Elvis was causing wild reactions on both sides of the generational divide, Hollywood made the most of new markets for exploitation films and teen pics.

During this period, the threat of communism and the atom bomb became linked with the threat of women out of control, and taming women was seen as an essential element in taming the dangers of the atomic age.[1] The decade accompanied its heightened interest in sexuality (both the Kinsey report on female sexuality and the first issue of *Playboy* appeared in 1953) with an increasing fear of sexual degeneracy, which it saw as a key indicator of moral weakness. The resulting call for traditional values urged women to retreat from the workplace to the home, where they could resume their proper roles as guardians of morality. Those women who did not were seen as threats to the national security, weakening the country's moral fiber and the masculine authority needed to combat communism. Not surprisingly, popular magazines cultivated a new image of femininity far removed from unruliness: "Listen to your laughter. . . . And if you hear your laugh sound hysterical, giddy or loud, tone it down. . . . Serenity is the well-spring of the romantic look" (from a 1946 issue of *Photoplay*, quoted in May 66).

While the culture was promoting an ideal that sentimentalized marriage, motherhood, and homemaking, however, the reality for women was quite different: between 1940 and 1960, the number of working wives doubled and that of working mothers quadrupled (French xiv). This contradiction, a massive denial of wide-ranging social changes, lay the groundwork for what would become the second wave of feminism in the 1960s. It also contributed to the instability Krutnik alluded to in popular representations of gender, sexuality, and domestic life. The new medium of television courted female viewers with shows that tapped into their ambivalence about domestic life by creating the beginnings of a sitcom tradition that would ultimately lead to *Roseanne*. *I Love Lucy*, the best known of these early shows, reenacted every week the frustration of women confined to the home, reworking Lucy's buried anger into humor and channeling her uptapped energy into dazzlingly out-of-bounds performance.

In film, gender inversion took on a new and more dangerous tone. With an ebbing of the confidence that had allowed the most popular male stars to experiment with role reversals and sexual ambiguity, gender ideals became increasingly polarized, and the unruly woman was stripped of her intelligence, often reduced to a purely sexual creature, and either domesticated or made a source of fear. The irony with which Sturges had held romantic comedy together in *The Lady Eve* gave way to something darker, as in his 1948 film *Unfaithfully Yours*, where anarchic energy becomes demonic and the female hero a target of rage. The woman on top who had been smart, classy, and good for the hero in the romantic comedies of the 1930s and early 1940s was more likely to appear as the evil femme fatale of film noir, the genre which perhaps best captured the paranoia of the period. In *Gilda* (1946), Rita Hayworth—who would later, in fact, be linked to the bomb—offered herself up in the song "Put the Blame on Mame" as a sizzling but ironic scapegoat for catastrophes that spanned the continent.

Two figures, Judy Holliday and Marilyn Monroe, stand out as models of the unruly woman in the post-war period through the 1950s. Both had supporting roles in other late comedies of inversion—Holliday in *Adam's Rib* (1949) and Monroe in *Monkey Business* (1952). But it is in *Born Yesterday* (1950), *Gentlemen Prefer Blondes* (1953), and *Some Like It Hot* (1959) that their own variations of unruliness stand out most clearly. Both stars were blonde comedians who died young, and both complicated the image of the unruly romantic heroine in new ways. Monroe added an element of pathos rooted in her private life, from her tragic childhood to her unhappy romances to her death in 1962 at the age of 36 from a drug overdose. Holliday added ethnicity. Harry Cohn, who described her as "that fat Jewish broad" (quoted in Rosen 295), considered her too Jewish and too unglamorous to be very popular (see Stephen Harvey 132). Subpoenaed by the House Un-American Activities Committee, she mystified her questioners by answering with the voice and illogical language of Billie Dawn, the dumb blonde she played in the stage play and film *Born Yesterday*. But her refusal to cooperate cost her her career. While she was a shrewd businesswoman and became very rich, she made few films afterward and died of cancer in 1965 at the age of 43. No mystique clung to her after her death, as it so often does to stars who die prematurely.

Both stars cultivated the dumb-blonde image. While the popularity of blonde sex goddesses such as Mamie Van Doren, Jayne Mansfield, and Monroe herself suggested that female unruliness had returned to the kind of overt sexuality represented by Mae West in the 1930s, the resemblance was largely superficial. Rather than using sexuality self-consciously for their own pleasure and power, as West did, these women, especially Monroe, replaced power with vulnerability and offered up their own sexuality for male pleasure.[2] Attempts to sustain the dynamics of gender inversion, as in *Gentlemen Prefer Blondes*, could only push the motif toward the grotesque. And experimentation with gender took on a cynical tone, as in *Some Like It Hot*, where the place of the unruly woman is taken over by a man. The "sex comedies" of the time, in Molly Haskell's words, were "about sex, without sex" (235), simplifying the relationship between the sexes to a matter of the male sex drive and female virginity, rather than a complex struggle over the meaning of heterosexual identity and intimacy. By the end of the decade, Doris Day, sunny and sexless, typified the new heroine of romantic comedy.[3]

 Born Yesterday: *Education as Domestication*

Born Yesterday, directed by George Cukor, highlights the transition from the strong heroine of the 1940s to the more submissive ones of the 1950s (see Thumim). Like his earlier *Sylvia Scarlett*, *Born Yesterday* depicts the "birth" of a mature woman from an earlier unruly one. Both births are brought about by men, Pygmalion-like. Both films show the woman "before" and "after," and the charm of both films lies in the vividness of the "before." In *Sylvia Scarlett*, the passage is a matter of gender, and the setting is magical and intimate. In *Born Yesterday*, the passage has to do with social class, morality, and nothing less than the fate of the nation, gravely threatened by corruption. Paul Verrall, the professor-hero, is an investigative reporter who also writes learned treatises ("The Yellowing Democratic Manifesto") about democracy. Reversing the dynamics of the earlier films, however, *Born Yesterday* shows the unruly woman, not the professor-hero, in need of an education. When Susan takes off David's glasses in *Bringing Up Baby*, David accedes to his own liberation. In *Born Yesterday*, Billie Dawn learns to wear glasses herself.

Billie Dawn is a former chorus girl who lives with Harry (Broderick Crawford), a boorish "junkman" who is also a multimillionaire. The two come to Washington, D.C. so that Harry can bribe a congressman. When Billie's ignorance embarrasses Harry, he hires Paul (William Holden) to smooth her "rough edges," and Paul gives Billie a crash course in Western civilization. As a result of her new knowledge, Billie exposes Harry's crooked business dealings and leaves him for Paul. Along with its character types, the film shares structural similarities with the romantic comedy—the love triangle, the absence of the mother (who died before Billie knew her), and the importance of the father. Like *Sylvia Scarlett*, however, the film fits uneasily into the genre. It is more a comic morality tale, and Holliday's brilliance lies more in her performance as a comedian than as a romantic heroine. Furthermore, the narrative drive to bring the couple together is overshadowed by a larger issue that absorbs the film—an anxiety about a moral decay that deeply threatens the culture.

This issue is evident from the film's opening shot of the Capitol, and later Billie's education (or "birth") is placed literally against a backdrop of

Born Yesterday reverses the pattern of earlier comedies in which a bookish male hero learns to give up his glasses. Here, Billie Dawn (Judy Holliday) is educated out of her unruliness and learns to wear glasses herself.

the monuments of the nation—art galleries, the Library of Congress, the Jefferson memorial. This framing establishes what is at stake in the romance. The film gives Billie the choice of Harry, who represents a corruption that threatens the entire democratic order, or Paul, who guards it. Paul appears to offer her a liberation from the interior scenes, where she is shown imprisoned by her own ignorance, into the larger world of history and culture. The film's real concern, however, is to tame Billie's unruliness and teach her middle-class virtue and restraint.

One of the most interesting aspects of the film is its efforts to untangle the abuses of capitalism from the ideals of democracy by opposing the two romantic rivals, Harry and Paul. Indeed, *Born Yesterday* signals a shift in interest from women to men that becomes even more pronounced in *Some Like It Hot*. This trend, which began in the early 1940s (with Abbott and Costello, Clark Gable and Spencer Tracy, and Bob Hope and Bing Crosby) and accelerated through the 1950s and 1960s, contributed to the disappearance of strong roles for women. Harry is a corrupt working-class brute, and the film displaces onto him the excesses of both capitalism and masculinity. He appears to have much in common with the father figures of some of the earlier films—the self-made men, such as Ellie's father in *It Happened One Night* and Eve's father in *The Lady Eve*. However, as romantic rival, he is more central to both the film's narrative and its comic effects. Billie establishes her unruliness during the first part of the film in tandem with his, for he is guilty of what she will later call a lack of "couth." Billie and Harry represent the working-class couple Ellie and Peter play-acted in *It Happened One Night*. They communicate by screeching at each other. He takes his shoes off in company and walks around with his shirt-tails hanging out.

Whereas the self-made men in the other films are eccentrics, however, and are redeemed from their wealth by the pluck and eccentricity that produced it, Harry is a comic monster, an emblem of a capitalism gone morally amuck. "I'm a junkman, I ain't ashamed to admit it," he boasts, or, as another character calls him, "King Junk." But he should be ashamed. The junk business is a metaphor for a capitalism cut off from the principles Paul preaches. Harry's life story, which he tells to Paul, would in another context be a textbook case of the successful entrepreneur who combines an enterprising spirit with hard work. (It is also the story of several Hollywood moguls.) Harry worked since he was twelve. While the other kids picked up junk in the alleys and kept it, Harry sold it and started a business. But he didn't get to be so rich without brute force and dishonesty as well. As a kid, he gave his competitors a "kick in the keister" whenever they stood in his way, and soon he was stealing merchandise from his customers at night and selling it back to them the next day. Now he believes he can muscle the U.S. government to get his way. That abuse of "muscle" ties Harry's moral corruption, like that of the gangsters in *Ball of Fire*, to his masculinity. Harry treats Billie brutishly. He won't let her speak, he bullies her, he won't marry her. He admits he loves her, but he doesn't know how to show her his feelings. Finally, when she refuses to cooperate in his business schemes, he strikes her, an irrevocable blow that "kills" the old Billie and produces the new one.

Paul, on the other hand, is a curious case of an unregenerate intellectual as romantic hero. In Paul, the film shows that knowledge leads to moral virtue and social ascendency. Where Harry is ignorant, Paul is educated. Where Harry is brutish, Paul is gentle. Where Harry is slovenly, Paul has tweedy good looks. At times, Holliday's performance of the dumb blonde exposes Paul's romantic naiveté. When he says, "Harry's a menace. Has he ever thought about anyone but himself?" she answers, "Who does?" Yet apart from that, the film does little else to undercut its professor-hero. He is not endearingly absent-minded, and his sanctimoniousness and preachiness go uncorrected. Where the earlier professor-heroes learn humility and spontaneity from their encounters with the unruly woman, Paul learns little or nothing from his. Billie "gets a yen" for Paul "right off," and tries to shift the dynamics of the relationship from one in which he is the teacher to one in which they are equals—or she his teacher. "It's only fair, we'll educate each other," she says. But he resists, his immunity testifying to a moral superiority that in the 1950s was associated with sexual restraint outside of marriage. The types are the same as those in the earlier films— the male rigidly caught up in abstraction, the female ready to educate him. But the reverse occurs. Billie, hardly licentious, learns restraint—along with a heavy dose of patriotism—from Paul. In Paul, the film valorizes a kind of masculinity defined by invulnerability, self-control, and moral righteousness.

Billie's real name is Emma, and when Paul asks her why she changed it, she asks him, rhetorically, if she looks like an Emma. He doesn't answer her directly, replying only that she doesn't look like a Billie. That Billie "look" is the look of the unruly woman, and Billie Dawn is an unruly heroine more out of the tradition of carnivalesque performance than romantic narrative. Her portrait of unruliness depends largely on the character's working-class background, with its motifs of the impropriety and bad taste that so often cause women to make spectacles of themselves. Billie is a gold digger like the Lady Eve and Sugarpuss, but whereas Stanwyck underplays the class backgrounds of those characters, Holliday exaggerates Billie Dawn's through the character's body language, her voice, and her "dumbness." Billie chews gum, smokes cigarettes, and drinks. She disrupts Harry's efforts to make a proper impression on the congressman by dancing to jazzy music when she becomes bored. As a "kept woman," Billie Dawn adds an element of sexual experience to the unruly woman that was missing in the more chaste romantic heroines. She is tough, and when she walks out on Harry the first time, no one really fears for her safety because, as one character notes, Billie doesn't get attacked—"it's more likely the other way around." Billie's voice is unruly in both tone and language. Her conspicuous silence in the first two scenes heightens the impact of her voice when we first hear it and she replies to Harry's bellow with a screech of her own. She must be warned to avoid "rough language."

Billie's dumbness represents an important shift in the representation of female unruliness. The dumb blonde domesticates the earlier unruly heroine by tying her out-of-bounds behavior to dimness rather than to a liberating eccentricity or disregard for convention. When Susan misunderstands language in *Bringing Up Baby*, it is a sign of a mind working rapidly, but in its own direction. When Billie Dawn does, it's a sign of a mind that isn't working at all. There is no question, of course, of Billie's intelligence. Any doubts about that are put to rest during her card game with Harry, when the film in fact alludes to *Bringing Up Baby*; Billie responds to Harry's efforts to shut her up by humming the tune to "I Can't Bring You Anything but Love, Baby," the song Susan sang to her leopard. Billie demonstrates her intelligence most significantly in her scheme to keep Harry straight when, at the end of the film, she beats him at his own game. Holliday doesn't play this dumbness as a joke against women, however, but as a defense against a world of limited options for a chorus girl, a means of getting what she wants, like two mink coats (a theme that is taken up more fully in *Gentlemen Prefer Blondes*). "I like being dumb," Billie says. Like the fool figure, the dumb blonde can enjoy a supreme detachment from the world. Dumbness insulates Billie from Harry's demands that she play the role of the good wife, or "fiancey." However, by showing that women need instruction from men, the dumb-blonde character-type also bolsters traditional gender roles.

Moreover, Billie's unruly dumbness does not provide the means of removing an obstacle to the couple, located in the male hero, but is the very obstacle itself. Paul will not allow their romance to unfold until she has learned what he has to teach her. That is because her dumbness is not innocent but a sign of her moral complicity in Harry's guilt. "I never thought of anything," she says ruefully, about the years she spent with Harry. Billie's dumbness may be only a veneer, but it also represents refusal to examine what she wants. While she never says as much, it is clear that her desire to drink isn't a sign of looseness or abandon, but an escape from the pain of having sold out—and for a couple of mink coats, at that. For Paul, ignorance such as Billie's contributes to the "yellowing" of the democratic manifesto. In his opinion, ignorance is dangerous because it allows people to turn their eyes from moral corruption. "I want everyone to be smart," he says, believing that if people would only open their eyes to what is around them, justice would prevail. "Think about it, Billie. The whole history of the world is about a struggle between selfishness and unselfishness. Selfishness can get to be a cause. Then it becomes fascism." Once Paul opens Billie's eyes, she gets the moral strength to take part in the fight against fascism by seeing to it that Harry gets put away. Billie, the prodigal daughter of a former meter man, becomes Emma.

Billie's father is the moral touchstone of the film, although we never see him, and a bond must be formed between him and Paul. Billie has been estranged from her father since taking up with Harry, and so the shift in her affection from Harry toward Paul also reorients her toward her father. She shows her increasing awareness that principles matter more than money when she tells Harry that her father is a "bigger" man than he, even if he only makes twenty-five dollars a week. Through her father, the film salvages its comic indictment of the working class. His presence counters the mutation of the Horatio Alger myth represented by Harry with a populist faith in the virtue of the common man who carries a small burner to work because he believes "everybody should have a hot lunch." When Billie reclaims the name her father gave her and "Emma" appears on the wedding license, the film connects the father to Paul, putting the common man back into the democratic manifesto and giving a common touch to the suspiciously literate hero Paul. Yet Billie's education also causes her to shed her class along with her unruliness. Despite Paul's assurances that being educated doesn't mean that she must give up her old tastes (for jazz instead of classical music, for example), clearly her movement toward Paul is a also movement up in class. And in Paul an undercurrent of the earlier films I have discussed comes to the surface. The unruly woman's excesses, rather than diminishing the hero, provide a point of contrast that heightens his stolid, all-American averageness.

With the rebirth of Emma, the story ends, and her marriage to Paul is meant to be seen as her liberation. However, that liberation substitutes the character's narrative empowerment with a performative loss, for the transformation of Billie into Emma diminishes the comedic pleasure of the film. Moreover, the degree of Emma's empowerment isn't entirely clear. There was an easy equality between Harry and Billie that does not exist between Emma and Paul, even if Emma has now reached the point where she can tell others to look up the big words she is using. The world Emma has entered is what the film represented earlier in its real moments of romance, when the couple appear in long shot as tiny figures against the massive monuments of the nation. This configuration locates the couple in its proper place as the bulwark of the nation, and the once-unruly woman in her proper place beneath the man.

Gentlemen Prefer Blondes: *Into the Grotesque*

Marilyn Monroe is perhaps the most elusive and resonant of American female stars. She has been reexamined and reappropriated in the years since her death by figures as diverse as Norman Mailer, Gloria Steinem, and Madonna. While *vulnerability* may be the word most often associated with her, she also represents a revision of the unruly blonde sex goddess Mae West embodied. That unruliness can be seen most clearly in her performance as Lorelei Lee in *Gentlemen Prefer Blondes*, where Howard Hawks adapts the premise of gender inversion that had interested him throughout his career to changing conditions in the film industry and culture. By testing the limits of that premise, the film ventures into the grotesque and depicts a version of female unruliness that in some ways both exceeds and falls short of those that preceded it. Generally, the film points to the demise of a certain figure of female unruliness and the genre that served that figure so well.

The film follows the romances of two former "little girls from Little Rock" who have grown up to become nightclub performers. Lorelei, who has become engaged to the rich Gus, is a gold digger. Dorothy, played by Jane Russell, is more interested in love than money. On a voyage to France, Dorothy falls in love with Malone, a private detective hired to watch Lorelei. When Dorothy catches Malone spying on Lorelei, and Malone catches Lorelei flirting with a rich old man named Sir Francis Beekman, or "Piggy" (Charles Coburn), both romances fall apart, and Lorelei and Dorothy return to the stage. Later, Dorothy settles a misunderstanding about a diamond tiara by impersonating Lorelei in court. Lorelei explains herself to Gus's father, the lovers are reconciled, and the film ends in a double wedding.

The film is based on Anita Loos's 1925 novel, which was remade a number of times for stage and screen. By the 1950s, the small black-and-white romantic comedy was beginning to appear dated, and Hawks turned Loos's story into a wide-screen technicolor musical. His choice of this genre reflects a number of developments during the period, including the threat of television to the film industry and an intensified interest in marketing consumer goods. The film makes its statement about the relation between a woman's sex appeal and her financial security in part by celebrating the delights money can buy—at "Tiffany's! Cartiers! Black Star!"

Its use of spectacle also taps into the sexual fantasies and obsessions of the decade. If the development of sound in the late 1920s helped demystify the female star, the popularity of wide-screen color fostered a return to the female body as spectacle. As Richard Dyer explains, Monroe's star image became the culture's fantasy site of female sexuality, conceived as natural, "oceanic," total, like the normative vaginal orgasm touted by a popularized Freudianism.[4] The image of the blonde sex goddess also played on racial tensions at a time when the civil rights movement was gaining momentum, for color photography set off her skin tones and made her whiteness an essential component of her desirability.

Like Monroe herself, *Gentlemen Prefer Blondes* elicits strong and conflicting responses.[5] Viewed critically, the film demonstrates the cost of re-sexualizing the unruly woman, especially in the context of the ideology of sex that prevailed in the 1950s. For the earlier unruly woman, chastity or virginity was a sign of an *autonomy* that she guarded until she found the right man and established the right relationship with him. It represented her desire to defer her inevitable surrender to marriage and motherhood and her ambivalence toward that surrender, although she actively pursued the right man once she found him. Lorelei's virginity, on the other hand, is a commodity in a very serious business, something to be traded to the highest bidder. It is a sign of her value to men, rather than to herself.

Monroe and Mae West are antithetical versions of the blonde sex goddess. Both control men through their sexual allure, but each represents a radically different conception of sexuality and the power relations between the sexes. West presents her sex appeal as something she is acutely aware of. Monroe's sex appeal, on the other hand, is tied to its apparent artlessness and innocence. As a result, her exercise of sexual power is shown to be largely unconscious. The term *natural*, used so often to describe Monroe, calls to mind its Renaissance meaning—an innocent, a simpleton or fool. When West—or Stanwyck—dispenses a sexual favor, she carefully observes its effect. Lorelei does not. When she kisses Gus, he's "zinged." He knows it, and so do we, because of the noise we hear on the sound track. But she doesn't, and so she is made the object of not only our gaze but our laughter, the victim of a joke on her. In this film, she reveals only gradually—and ambiguously—that she is really the *subject* of a joke on all men who are vulnerable to their own foolishness and lust, and it is never entirely clear how much her performance of the dumb blonde actually is a masquerade.

In Monroe, "natural" female sexuality, in contrast to West's more stylized sexuality, appears entirely oriented toward male pleasure. In this film, at least on the level of the Lorelei plot, female sexual pleasure is a matter to be dealt with *after* the important business—that of catching a rich husband—is taken care of. Lorelei plays on the dumb-blonde image by suggesting that Dorothy, who likes sex for itself, needs to be educated by her. Most important, Monroe, unlike West, derives her sex appeal from weakness rather than strength. That weakness reinforces the ideology of traditional heterosexuality, which eroticizes an imbalance of power based on feminine submissiveness and masculine dominance.[6] Lorelei attempts to turn her weakness into strength by exaggerating it, with her "little girl" style, when she calls her fiancé "Daddy" in gratitude for a diamond bracelet. This style draws on Monroe's own life and the stories of her victimization that were part of her star persona. In contrast, West eluded any hint of the victim throughout her career until its end, when her parodies of her own image opened her to ridicule.

Despite this constriction of Lorelei's power, female unruliness erupts quite forcefully in other aspects of the film, beginning with the opening number, which introduces us to *two* sex goddesses. Even as Monroe's straight woman, Jane Russell brings a formidable degree of unruliness to the film in her own right. In addition, an unruliness that cannot be contained by the ideology of the sex goddess escapes into the film's mise-en-scène, its production numbers, and its mode of address (Arbuthnot and Seneca 18, 20–21). Lurid colors—clashing reds and pinks—draw attention to the spectacle as spectacle, inviting the spectator to watch what will follow not as voyeurs, but as observers of voyeurism. This move is borne out by the director's avoidance of exploitative silhouette shots of Monroe and Russell and by the film's comic tone, which produces distance from, rather than identification with, its characters and events.

Lorelei's blatant performance of the sexy dumb broad is an unruly exposure of the economic rationale behind the "tropes of femininity." In two production numbers, the film makes parallel comments on the relation between spectacle, female beauty, and the erotic, and their very excessiveness indicates the strain within the contradiction they attempt to negotiate—that female weakness and submissiveness are actually strength. In Russell's "Is There Anyone Here for Love?" with the Olympic athletes, the men's passive display of their bodies, blank expressions, and nude-colored swimsuits parody the ways women's bodies, including Monroe's, are typically objectified and eroticized. Later, Monroe's performance of "Diamonds are a Girl's Best Friend" in the Paris nightclub complicates the pleasure a viewer might take in the spectacle of her body by overtly displaying the sadomasochism of female submission and male dominance in the chorus. Some women are bound to chandeliers by black leather, while others are costumed in girlish pink, but with their faces concealed by sinister black net veils. The number's ballet sequences, Lorelei's mock operatic voice in the opening bars of her song, and the silver temples and black tuxedoes of the male dancers layer the issue of high culture and social class on the scene, suggesting the stakes involved in the quest for diamonds by the two "little girls" from "the wrong side of the tracks."

Lorelei most explicitly exposes the tropes of femininity in her conversation with Mr. Esmond, Gus's father, when she explains the reasons for making the most of her beauty while she can, playing dumb, and trying to catch a rich husband. In effect, she casts a new light on Billie Dawn that is both more cold-eyed and more sympathetic. From the outset of the film, Mr. Esmond poses the greatest obstacle to Lorelei's desire, and he becomes her most difficult and most important conquest. Unlike the fathers in the earlier films, he is not a benign buffoon, impotent and marginal, but is actively hostile to the couple. In this film the comic reversal of the Oedipal plot, like much else, is on the edge—the son's victory over the father doesn't have a ring of inevitability because the father is simply too potent, and the son too infantile. The father's intransigence, however, testifies to the power of Lorelei's irresistible "dumbness," and when she explains herself—and all women—to him, she wins him over. "Say, they told me you were stupid, but you don't sound stupid to me," he says, and she answers: "I can be smart when it's important, but most men don't like it."

It is important that Lorelei's self-awareness is ultimately undecidable; too much self-awareness makes her use of power too cynical; too little makes her a victim, the butt of a joke. If Lorelei is necessarily ambiguous as a woman on top, however, there is no such ambiguity about the male figures in the film. They are extreme parodies of masculinity and the romantic male hero. Here, there is no Cary Grant, Henry Fonda, Clark Gable, or Gary Cooper to bring a strong sense of masculine sex appeal to a feminized role. The Olympic team is a nameless collection of fine bodies, sex objects for Dorothy. Sir Francis Beekman is a lecherous old fool. "Mr. William Spafford and valet" is a precocious little boy. Malone, played by Elliot Reid, is a morally righteous Paul Verrall without William Holden's sex appeal. And Gus, while undeniably sweet, is hopelessly ineffectual and infantile. He is all that's left of the professor-hero, retaining only his spectacles and his goofiness, and he enjoys no recuperation whatsoever. Throughout the film, these men endure comic humiliations similar to the ones inflicted on earlier male heroes. Malone is paid back for his duplicity when Dorothy and Lorelei drug him, spill water on him, strip him, put him in a woman's robe, and send him on his way.

The film's faithfulness to the structure of gender inversion is most evident in the dominance of the female couple, at a time when a female star could rarely carry a film alone.[7] Hawks's interest in "female buddies" is similar to that shown in his earlier *His Girl Friday* (1940), a revision of *The Front Page* (1931) in which he turns the male buddies into a heterosexual couple by making one of them, Hildy, a woman. The buddy mystique clings to Dorothy and Lorelei, who have been described as strutting their wares like a couple of gunslingers (Haskell 258). They know what their weapons are, they know how good they are, and they're loyal to each other, above all. Dorothy is Lorelei's straightwoman and sidekick, her shadow and chaperone. Her unruliness both complements and sets off Lorelei's, representing the more familiar version of the romantic heroine, a bit world-weary but still a believer in love. The real love story, however, is between Lorelei and Dorothy. Not only does the film reserve its most spectacular visual effects for them, it also begins and ends with the two women dressed alike, performing together.

Such a bond between women is dangerous, and the degree of its threat most vividly indicated by Dorothy's disruptive masquerade of Lorelei in the French court. Courtrooms offer ideal sites for unruly challenges to patriarchy and the authority of the law, and this one is no exception. The darkness of the surroundings, meant to convey tradition, and the old male judges in wigs and black robes heighten the impact of Dorothy's blonde wig and silver spangles. In this scene, Dorothy's multiple masquerade—of Lorelei playing the dumb blonde—shows the easy identification between the two women. "Life is sometimes hard for a girl like I, especially when she happens to be pretty, like I, and have blonde hair," Dorothy whispers in a voice mimicking Lorelei's. Mr. Pritchard, one of the old lawyers, is suspicious, but like Hopsy and the other "mugs" of the earlier comedies, he cannot see past the surface—the wig, the exposed leg, the simpering voice. A close-up of her face under the wig, however, shows Dorothy as a drag queen, suggesting that the dumb blonde is only a more exaggerated masquerade of a femininity constructed to please, and appease, men. In a reprise of "Diamonds are a Girl's Best Friend," Dorothy stages her own version of the song by abruptly throwing off her fur coat to expose her body dressed in a skimpy black costume with silver fringes on her breasts and hips. She performs the number with the bumps and grinds of burlesque, and a voice that growls rather than purrs like Lorelei's. The performance draws on the camp elements of Mae West that linger about Dorothy, with her blunt interest in men for sex, her manipulation of her Olympic musclemen, and the masculinity suggested by Russell's broad shoulders and deep voice. Mr. Esmond later expresses the danger of that image during his conversation with Gus and the real Lorelei. He describes the woman he saw in the courtroom as "That monster, Lorelei," and the fact that there now appears to be more than one opens up the frightening possibility to him of an all-engulfing swarm of them—"How do you think I feel, with thousands of Loreleis coming at me from everywhere?"

Dorothy's performance sends the courtroom into turmoil. When the judge restores order, however, it is a new order that has been brought about by Dorothy and that accommodates the desires of both women. In one blow she has cleared the way for the double wedding that concludes the film. Rather than doubly affirming the heterosexual couple, however, the ceremony is filmed to subvert it. Dorothy and Lorelei walk down the aisle together, dressed identically as they were in the opening scene, and singing a final reprise of their song. Briefly, the two bridegrooms are shown standing by their sides, but then the camera moves closer in on Lorelei and Dorothy, excluding the bridegrooms and framing the two brides together in a celebration of the female couple.

 Some Like It Hot: *Men as Unruly Women*

In many ways, the impulses of the romantic comedy of gender inversion, so strongly suggested in the last shot of *Gentlemen Prefer Blondes*, culminate in Billy Wilder's 1959 film *Some Like It Hot*. The film's use of transvestism and its famous last line (Joe E. Brown's reply, "Nobody's perfect," to the disclosure that the "woman" he loves is really a man) can be seen as tolerant glimpses into a restructuring of sexuality and gender that is fluid, playful, and even carnivalesque.

Indeed, the film is a retrospective of sorts on the classical romantic comedy of gender inversion, recalling Mae West's masquerade of femininity in *She Done Him Wrong*. Both films use comedy to present sexual issues somewhat daringly for their times. Both are period pieces, returning to the past—the Gay Nineties, the Roaring Twenties—for a setting of greater license than the present. Both make heavy use of the ambience of a fringe culture on the edge of respectability—the crooks of *She Done Him Wrong*, the gangsters of *Some Like It Hot*. *Some Like It Hot* pushes even farther West's ironic stance toward sexuality, and it parodies many of the motifs that had become conventionalized in the previous twenty-five years of romantic comedies. While West shows femininity as a masquerade women can wear for power over men, this film shows femininity to be readily available to men as well, and it takes gender fluidity to new limits in mainstream Hollywood cinema—limits made permissible largely because of the comic framework of the film. *Some Like It Hot* also returns full circle to Cary Grant. Masquerading on the beach and in a later seduction scene as the heir to the Shell oil fortune, Tony Curtis sends up the romantic lead Grant had come to typify since his roles in *She Done Him Wrong* and *Sylvia Scarlett*. When Curtis puts on his glasses and glamorous nautical attire and Grant's clipped accent, and Jack Lemmon protests that no one talks that way, the film brings the spectator in on a joke that wouldn't be possible without the shared knowledge of a quarter of a century of romantic film comedy.

At the same time, however, *Some Like It Hot* also represents a full scale retreat from the liberation the genre had earlier offered to *women*. Its investigation of gender—and embrace of femininity—occur within an overwhelmingly masculine perspective. In this film, women are reduced to passivity—and Mae West's power replaced by Marilyn Monroe's pathos and victimization. Curtis masquerades not only as romantic-lead-Grant, but as the professor-hero played by other actors in the comedies of gender inversion, and eyeglasses are a crucial element of the Curtis character's masquerade. But in contrast to the earlier films, where glasses are a sign of the hero's repression and lack of self-awareness, in this film they are important for how *he* uses them to catch *his* prey. That shift in the direction of sexual pursuit, and in the dynamics of sexual power, indicates the most important difference between West's film and this one, as well as how completely the inversion of power she represented has become righted again. The place of "woman" is now relegated to that of the sad victim and object of a male quest. The female buddies of *Gentlemen Prefer Blondes* have become male buddies. And those male buddies, by taking up female masquerade and colonizing the topos of the unruly woman, have become the agents of a social and sexual liberation that is limited to men.

The film tells the story of two out-of-work musicians, bass player Gerald (Jack Lemmon) and saxophonist Joseph (Tony Curtis), who accidentally witness the St. Valentine's Day massacre in Chicago. They escape by disguising themselves as women so they can play in an "all-girl" band traveling by train to Florida. On the trip they meet Sugar Kane (Marilyn Monroe), the lead singer, who has sought refuge in the band from men who take advantage of her. In Florida, Joseph exchanges his female disguise as "Josephine" for that of the Shell heir so he can seduce Sugar. Osgood (Joe E. Brown), a real millionaire, proposes to "Geraldine," or "Daphne," as Gerald later calls himself. When the gangsters reappear, the two men drop their disguises and make a final escape, this time with Sugar and Osgood.

Some Like It Hot's investigation of gender begins with its use of genre. Like *Gentlemen Prefer Blondes*, the film is a sign that the classical romantic comedy no longer offered a compelling means of examining the social anxieties of its time. As the contradictions of social class receded, so did the drive to mediate them through the form of the New Comedy plot. Class is present in *Some Like It Hot*, as in *Gentlemen Prefer Blondes*, but as a vestige of the earlier form, seen through the lens of gender; millionaires such as Gus, Piggy, and Osgood are important primarily for what they reveal about women as gold diggers. In fact, the film's pastiche of genres— the backstage musical, the buddy film, the comedian comedy, the gangster film, and the romantic comedy—points to the end of the genre film itself, as it existed under the studio system.

The genres that most inform *Some Like It Hot*, however, are the gangster film and the romantic comedy. The film begins as the former, in the extended sequences of the speakeasy and the St. Valentine's Day massacre, and ends as the latter, moving from one kind of lawbreaking to another. The gangster plot functions both narratively—by motivating the initial escape and disguise and forcing the resolution—and thematically—by providing the central point of reference, a picture of a kind of world the rest of the film tries to escape. The violence it depicts—the gratuitous execution of the gas pumper in the garage, the prolonged shooting of Spats Malone—exceeds the tone of a romantic comedy. The evil Spats, played by George Raft as the only noncomic figure in the film, gives a weight to the element of danger represented by the gangster film—the danger of abusive authority, corrupt law, and violent masculinity that also exists, but less threateningly, in *Ball of Fire*. This masculinity is part of a strict heterosexuality that widens the gap between male and female, with femininity present only as the legs on the chorus line in a speakeasy. It is this heterosexuality that Jerry and Joe resist when they first put on women's clothes. Its danger remains behind the scenes until it self-destructs in the second explosion of violence at the Florida banquet, which obliterates Spats Malone and releases Joe and Jerry into the romantic comedy their lives are moving toward.

Joe and Jerry's escape from such masculinity entails a detour through femininity initiated by their masquerade as women. This role-playing is well within the tradition of romantic comedy, as the earlier films have shown. Here, however, it becomes more ambiguous because it works against the more common tradition in romantic comedy of female-to-male cross-dressing (as in *Sylvia Scarlett* and indeed many Shakespearean comedies). Where male impersonation is usually played as romance, however, female impersonation is played, as in this film, as farce. Joe and Jerry's female masquerade is their first step toward appropriating the license of the unruly woman, and on the simplest level it exploits the comic possibilities of the woman on top. Curtis and Lemmon are both cast against men who appear smaller—the little bellhop who propositions Josephine

("That's the way I like 'em, big and sassy," he says) and Joe E. Brown in the role of Osgood Fielding, whose "zowies" indicate his relish at the size of Daphne, with her bull fiddle. Sexual role-playing in romantic comedy, however, is less an end in itself or a source of humor than a means of producing the romantic couple by moving its primary players toward heterosexuality. In this film, sexual role-playing breaks down the male couple that opens the film and hastens the move toward two new couples: the traditional heterosexual couple of Sugar and Joe; and the more indeterminate, potentially gay couple of Osgood and Jerry, whose sexual orientation remains deliberately unresolved.[8]

The motivations of the male buddies to disguise themselves as women show an important progression from self-interest to a kind of self-fulfillment through redefined sexuality. First, the masquerade is a crazy idea to make some money. Next, it becomes a means of escape for their lives. Then it leads to the unexpected sexual pleasure of two men who are still little more than escapees from the blighted masculinity of the gangster film—men who express their sexuality by ogling women and abusing them. Finally, it makes a "new man" of Joe, and becomes an end in itself for Jerry. This parallel production of two new couples is clear in the sequence that flash-pans back and forth between Osgood's yacht, where Sugar is attempting to arouse a supposedly "defective" (impotent or gay) "Junior," and the roadhouse where Daphne and Osgood are dancing the tango. In that second location, Jerry/Daphne gradually relinquishes his desire to lead while dancing with Osgood and surrenders to the femininity that he has been so comfortable with from the beginning of his masquerade.

For Joe, his feminine disguise is always superficial, a liminal period he passes through, with predictable results. It allows him to become the romantic hero he only impersonated on the beach. By coming close to Sugar's pain, he learns to abandon his earlier ways, earning his escape from the gangsters and the boat ride into the night with Sugar. For Jerry, on the other hand, femininity becomes something quite different. Jerry's masquerade penetrates his identity and shakes the stability of his gender. Joe warns him that he cannot pass himself off as a woman to marry Osgood: "Listen to me, Jerry. There are laws, and conventions. It's just not being done." Those "laws and conventions"—from vague ideologies about gender to precise laws prohibiting sodomy—are less about preventing trickery and dishonesty than about preserving the sexual difference Jerry is undermining.

The character of Jerry speaks to several desires rarely represented so directly in mainstream cinema—the male desire to become a woman, the

By Some Like It Hot, *the space of female unruliness has been taken over by men. Gerald (Jack Lemmon) comes to prefer being Geraldine/Daphne, especially after he falls in love with Osgood (Joe E. Brown). The film limits its destabilizing of gender to its male characters, however. Copyright 1959, United Artists Corp.*

desire to renounce a masculinity represented by types like Spats Malone and Sugar's sleazy saxophone players, the desire for the license to shift from one identification to another, to be liberated from either/or choices. Jerry's situation remains unresolved at the end of the film. From the start he has shown his openness to abandoning his masculinity and his "naturalness" as a woman. He was eager to try the masquerade from the first and his control over his sexual identity is precarious. At first, he is carried away with voyeuristic masculine pleasure of being in a "dream," locked up in a "pastry room." Joe urges him to remember who he is pretending to be, and he repeats "I'm a girl, I'm a girl, I'm a girl (get a load of that rhythm section), I'm a girl." However, he is almost immediately caught up in the pleasure of *being* "a girl"—the gossip, the jokes, the girl talk, the slumber party in which he participates, not as a male voyeur but as one of the girls.

The crucial change comes the night he goes dancing with Osgood. When the two exchange endearments ("You're dynamite," and "You're a little firecracker"), it is already evident that Daphne is sincerely falling in love not only with Osgood, but with being a woman. He still forgets—"Daphne, you're leading again," Osgood tells him—but by the end he's following, and the two succeed in a credible, if comical, performance of the tango, a dance that exaggerates the poses of heterosexual romance. Later, we see Jerry/Daphne alone on his bed, barely able to contain himself, the picture of a bride-to-be. When he later tells Joe he's engaged, Joe asks who's the lucky girl and he answers, "I am." The transformation is almost complete, and Jerry returns to his masculinity only with great difficulty. His claim that his masquerade is only a means of tricking Osgood out of his alimony is not convincing, and he reverses only half-heartedly his earlier mantra to: "I'm a boy, I'm a boy (I wish I were dead)." Jerry's rebellion transforms him not only into a woman, but into a simulated unruly woman, outrageous and "monstrous," like Miss Piggy, because of his blatant mixture of male and female attributes—the exaggerated femininity of his behavior and the unconcealed masculinity (the broad shoulders, the hairy, muscular legs) of his body.

By the end of the film, the gangster movie has been put to rest and romantic comedy prevails. The traditional couple embraces in the backseat of the boat against the sunset. Yet that embrace is merely a backdrop for the more outrageous, and partial, resolution of difference represented by the "odd couple" in the foreground. When Jerry/Daphne takes off his wig, he appears confused and disturbed. It is Osgood who represents, in fact, the ideal the film seems to argue for, and he is given the last word. One by one, he shrugs off the excuses men traditionally have given to avoid marrying women. He dismisses Daphne's claims of vanity and trickery (she's not a natural blonde), a "past" (she's lived with a saxophone player), her revelations that she can't have children and that she'll come between him and his mother. When none of these matters, Osgood's sanguine acceptance of Daphne's being a man seems almost believable as well. This is a union that does not put the unruly "woman" in her place. Osgood enables the film to end on a note of instability—to escape the resolution of sexual ambiguity that almost invariably accompanies the stripping away of sexual disguise. When Hepburn takes off her male attire in *Sylvia Scarlett*, biological difference is confirmed. When Lemmon takes off his wig, we learn that biological difference doesn't matter.

The cost of achieving this ending, however, severely diminishes its utopianism. While the film chastises masculinity by rejecting the gangster genre, and undermines strict heterosexuality, the liberating options it offers are available only to men. Sugar cannot free herself from a restrictive femininity. Furthermore, these options are made possible only by marginalizing the film's one "real" woman, Sugar Kane, victimizing her in the plot and exploiting her as spectacle. The final scene—in contrast to the last scene of *Gentlemen Prefer Blondes*—affirms a carnivalesque couple made up of *men*—for, despite Osgood's insistence that biology doesn't matter, what appear on the screen are two men. Monroe has relinquished the power she enjoyed as the unruly dumb blonde Lorelei, and Sugar—half of the storybook couple—remains confined to a narrow and pitiful role in the back seat of the boat.

Such a reduction in the figure of the once unruly woman begins with her characterization as a dumb blonde. In this case, however, her dumbness is not an act but real, and it is not the source of her power but the sign of her victimization. Sugar Kane is really Sugar Kovalchik, another woman from the wrong side of the tracks. For her, the all-girl band is a refuge from the "bums" who always leave her holding "the fuzzy end of the lollipop," as well as from her own worst impulses. Life for her has become a matter of "safety first," she says. Like Jerry and Joe, she is escaping danger—but the danger men like them pose to her. As with Billie Dawn, Sugar's drinking is a sign of the pathos of her life, and while all the other women drink, Sugar is the one who gets caught. She blames herself—her "dumbness"—for her troubles, and she is proven right when her instincts draw her once again to a saxophone player, even though he is in disguise. Her dumbness, moreover, has none of Lorelei's ambiguity. It is consistent with her total transparency. She presents herself entirely as she is, with no self-consciousness. While Sugar makes a stab at gold digging—she knows a millionaire would be a good catch—it would be beyond her to play up her dumbness to her own advantage. Her dumbness makes her an innocent victim, rather than allowing her to take advantage of those who would victimize her.

This dumbness is further heightened by her role as butt of a long-running joke in the film. Jokes often depend on a disparity of knowledge between those who share it and those who are its victims. In *Some Like It Hot*, this joke draws on the conventional structure of the cinematic apparatus, which—like the joke (and narrative, as well)—is organized around gender. *Some Like It Hot* stages a voyeuristic joke by keeping the knowledge of Jerry and Joe's sexual identity from the women on the screen but not from the spectator, who is thus allowed to share Jerry and Joe's pleasure in their illicit visual access to the women's bodies. The rhymed shots that introduce "Josephine" and "Geraldine" and Sugar—shots of legs, rear ends, and lingering close-ups of faces—expose the ways cinema exploits women's bodies; however, the film continues to privilege the male perspective by giving point-of-view shots—of Monroe's body—only to the men (Kuhn 67–72).

Joe takes advantage of Sugar by using the conventions of romantic comedy, but in such a way that he, rather than the woman, remains on top. Not only does he disguise himself as the Cary Grant hero, he trips her on the beach like Jean trips Hopsy. His—and the film's—most exploitative moment occurs when he arranges for her to seduce him by playing the role of the "gentle and sweet and helpless" professor-hero. Her efforts to get him to take off his glasses echo Susan's in *Bringing Up Baby*, Sugarpuss's in *Ball of Fire*, and Billie Dawn's in *Born Yesterday*. However, she is not in charge, and the joke is not on the professor but on her, and on her ignorance and trust. The scene's exploitativeness, like that of others in the film, is heightened by Monroe's revealing costumes and by lighting that conceals the line between her dress and her skin, making her appear neither fully dressed nor nude. In the end Sugar redeems Joe, as romantic heroines tend to do, but through no agency of her own. All it takes is an exposure to her innocent sweetness, her vulnerable sexuality, to make a real man out of him; her submissive femininity produces a masculinity that retains the dominance of the gangsters but is also chastened. In the character of Sugar, Monroe loses any trace of transgressive unruliness—of disrupting conventional notions of gender or of challenging masculine authority, or even of claiming any subjectivity. When she walks home from the yacht on Tony Curtis's arm, trailing her silver fox fur beneath the palm trees, she becomes a luminously beautiful—but sadly reduced—image of femininity.

7

Masculinity and Melodrama in Postclassical Romantic Comedy

Norman Jewison's 1987 film *Moonstruck* opens with an enormous moon hanging over the skyline of Manhattan, followed by a montage of shots of the moonlit city, from its bridges festooned with lights to the Metropolitan Opera House to a poster advertising Puccini's opera *La Bohème*. Within moments, the sky brightens and the camera moves closer to the streets awakening with the activity of the day. A truck marked "Metropolitan Opera" moves through the traffic, its path crossed by Loretta Castorini, a superstitious Italian-American widow, walking to her job at a funeral parlor. The film concludes in the interior space of the Castorini home, where Loretta, her mother Rose, and the renewed and expanded clan are seated around a kitchen table. Panning across the grandfather's rowdy pack of dogs as it retreats into the parlor, the camera passes over a series of family portraits and rests finally on those of an aged couple, the matri-arch and patriarch of the extended family gathered nearby. These two scenes establish *Moonstruck*'s thematic and formal tensions. Repeatedly moving between darkness and daylight, images of death and those of life, the film shifts from the pathos of melodrama—most strongly represented by the story-within-the-story of the opera—to the irony and humor of romantic comedy. The film's musical score reinforces these tensions by playing the soaring melodies of Puccini against the corny but charming sounds of Dean Martin singing "When the moon hits your eye like a big pizza pie, that's *amore*."

Moonstruck's interplay of romantic comedy and melodrama does not finally give equal weight to the two genres, however. After all, it is Dean Martin's voice that closes the film as well as opens it and Puccini's arias that are modulated into the schmaltzy pop style of "That's *Amore*." In the same way, romantic comedy mirrors, transforms, and eventually contains the melodramatic themes and motifs of *La Bohème*. The film moves from the dying Mimi, the doomed bride-to-be in the opera, to the comic "re-birth" of the film's heroine Loretta; from one mother on her deathbed in Palermo to another in her kitchen in Brooklyn, drinking to her family; from Loretta's tears as opera spectator to the smiles and laughter of the film spectator; and from the opera's glorification of a romantic love based on woman's loneliness and pain to an alternative which refuses to make a woman's heterosexuality contingent upon her separation from other women, especially her mother. Dramatizing the tensions between roman-tic comedy and melodrama, testing the values of one against the other, *Moonstruck* argues finally for comedy.

Moonstruck's easy mix of melodrama and romantic comedy should come as no surprise given the structural similarities between the two forms. Melodrama and romantic comedy, after all, are the primary genres for telling fictional stories of women's lives. What is more surprising is the increased use of melodrama in recent romantic comedy to tell the stories of *men's* lives. Whereas the classical romantic comedy typically combined skepticism with sentiment in its attitude toward romantic love, the post-classical comedy, beginning in the 1960s, is both more skeptical about love and more sentimental about its victims. It also privileges the subjectivity of its male hero over that of the female. As a result, the unruly woman who resisted his desire in the comedies of the classical period is now viewed with more suspicion, and the formerly chastised male hero is sen-timentalized for his sufferings in love. *Moonstruck*, as I will show, is an important exception that testifies not only to the endurance and adapta-bility of romantic comedy but to its continuing feminist potential. More typically, the postclassical comedy appropriates female suffering, and the feminized genre of melodrama, in the service of a beleaguered masculinity. It asks us to empathize with heroes such as the insomniac widower played by Tom Hanks in Nora Ephron's 1993 hit *Sleepless in Seattle*, who broadcasts the story of his grief on a radio talk show and causes thousands of women across the nation starved for such a sensitive man to weep and fall in love with him.

A glance back to the 1950s shows that these changes were already being anticipated in the period's melodramatic and comedic genres. While "male weepies" by Douglas Sirk, Nicholas Ray, and Elia Kazan explored Oedipal anxieties between fathers and sons with spectacular excess, sex comedies with dumb blondes narrowed the scope of heterosexual desire to male seduction, curbed the power of the unruly woman, and signaled the weakening of gender inversion as a structuring principle of romantic comedy. *Some Like It Hot* (1959) suggested how easily a male hero—and even more, a pair of male heroes—could take over the space of female desire and unruliness, leaving the once unruly woman passive and victimized. By the 1960s, the encroachment of the male hero into the place of the unruly woman became even more pronounced. This symbolic mustering of masculine power occurred at a time of wide-ranging challenges to the nation's traditional structures of authority. The civil rights movement, the revival of feminism sparked by the publication of Betty Friedan's *The Feminine Mystique* in 1963, the Vietnam War, the pill, the rise of the counterculture, the mobilization of the gay rights movement after the 1969 raid on the Stonewall Bar, the wave of assassinations, Watergate, and, finally, inflation all rattled the nation's institutions of racial and sexual privilege.

With the distribution of power between the sexes openly contested, the figure of the woman on top—even in such a limited and anachronistic form as the dumb blonde—became too threatening to stand as a comedic figure of mutual liberation and play. Gender inversion, once a means of negotiating other social anxieties, became the source of a major anxiety in its own right. Thus, as we saw in Chapter 2, sympathetic representations of female unruliness were exiled from cinema to the more domesticated medium of television, where unruly sitcom matriarchs from Lucille Ball and Gracie Allen to Roseanne Arnold replaced the unruly brides of romantic film comedy. On the big screen the heterosexual couple of romantic comedy took a back seat to the male couple of the buddy film. If Miss Piggy kept alive a tradition of comic female unruliness in film, that may have been only because she is a puppet who got her start in television and who appears in works aimed at audiences of children or families.

By the late 1980s and early 1990s, the woman on top has become a figure more likely to be portrayed as a lunatic than as a figure of play, and gender inversion more likely to be found in thrillers and horror films, such as *Fatal Attraction* (1987), *Basic Instinct* (1992), and *Misery* (1990), than in romantic comedies. *Misery*, for example, creates its female lead—the fat, pig-loving Annie (Kathy Bates)—out of fundamental signifiers of female unruliness, but by also depicting her as insane it shows her connection with the demonic to be evil and dangerous. Reversing the conventional gender positions of the slasher film, *Misery* mobilizes fears about an endangered masculinity to horrific effect by having Annie imprison and torture Sam (another man of letters who, this time, writes romance novels) after she discovers that he has killed off her favorite fictional heroine. This cautionary tale about the dangers of female desire, and feminine texts, allows its male hero to kill Annie and write the "serious" novel he has wanted to all along, but it also leaves him haunted and crippled for life.

 Melodramatized Men

Still, if the unruly woman no longer plays the role she once did in romantic comedy, the genre itself has hardly disappeared. The direction it would take in postclassical cinema can be seen in two popular and critically acclaimed films of the 1960s—*The Apartment* (1960), which Billy Wilder directed one year after *Some Like It Hot*, and *The Graduate*, directed by Mike Nichols in 1967. Both films retain structural elements of romantic comedy, primarily a narrative drive to bring together the couple, but with a decided shift of emphasis and tone.

In *The Apartment*, a dark rewriting of the sex comedy, the Swinging Bachelor becomes the troubled Organization Man; Jack Lemmon leaves behind the unruly drag queen he played in *Some Like It Hot* for the character of C. C. Baxter, a passive and suffering insurance clerk who chooses to sleep on the street rather than to deny his superiors the use his apartment for illicit sex. Here, male incompetence, played for comedy in the classical films, becomes a source of pathos. While not flinching from the moral shortcomings of its hero, *The Apartment* ties those shortcomings to his victimization by a corporate world that is not only dehumanizing but specifically emasculating. Anonymous men in suits appear in long shot working at endless rows of desks, an image more commonly associated with women's office work than with men's. To succeed as a man, which means to rise up the corporate ladder, Baxter must subject himself to intimate—that is, feminizing—invasions of his private space and life.

In *The Apartment*, women are not the causes of men's suffering but suffer along with them. That is not true of *The Graduate*, however, which projects its fears about an endangered masculinity onto women. Dustin Hoffman plays Benjamin, a new Harvard graduate bored by and alienated from his well-off parents and their social circle. His perspective dominates the film both narratively and cinematically. One scene, in which he appears dressed in a wet suit, comically literalizes his alienation with subjective wide-angle shots that show the grotesqueness of the world that entraps him. At the same time, unable to combine female power and virtue in one woman, the film fractures its romantic female lead into two: the sexual, predatory, and seductive Mrs. Robinson (Anne Bancroft), who embodies the cynicism and power of the older generation; and her virginal daughter, Elaine (Katharine Ross), a student at Berkeley. By photographing Elaine on campus against the backdrop of the counterculture, the film underscores her position as the right comedic choice, aligned with youth, liberation, and the future.

The film's misogyny is evident in its use of Mrs. Robinson, a phallic mother, as the patriarchal blocking figure who must be defeated before the proper couple can be united. In the first part of the film, her sexual power over Benjamin is played for comedy and she is treated sympathetically, but as the film progresses she becomes increasingly monstrous. Moreover, the film relegates the story of the bride to its second half, and even there limits her agency and presence. *The Graduate* concludes with the couple together at last on a bus, after a runaway-bride sequence that alludes to the film's generic antecedents. The last close-up of the couple, however, exploits the possibilities of wide-screen composition to show the distance between them. In an extraordinarily long take of nearly forty seconds, the camera lingers on their faces as the emotion drains from them, allowing us to ponder the unease of this "happy ending," which acknowledges the governing tension between comedy and melodrama.

Such a foreboding conclusion casts doubt not only on the future of this couple but, prophetically, on *all* couples and the utopian possibilities classical romantic comedy once projected in them. In this way *The Graduate* anticipates what Frank Krutnik has called the "nervous romance," a variation of postclassical romantic comedy which he identifies with such late-1970s films as *Annie Hall* (1977), *Manhattan* (1979), and *Starting Over* (1979).[1] According to Krutnik, the nervous romance pushes toward a melodramatic conclusion, mixing nostalgia for a time of "simpler" romance with a wariness about the possibilities of the heterosexual couple. This wariness is still evident fifteen years later in *Sleepless in Seattle*, which defers not only sexual intimacy between the couple, as in the classical comedies, but virtually any contact at all until the last moments of the film.

Perhaps no figure stands as a more telling example of the infusion of male melodrama into romantic comedy than Woody Allen. If certain elements of Allen's persona (he is intellectual, introspective, Jewish, East Coast, urban) have limited the scope of his popularity, the essence of that persona still taps into broader cultural anxieties about romance and masculinity itself; the neuroses he has examined so relentlessly in his work, from *Annie Hall* and *Manhattan* through *Husbands and Wives* (1992), merely exaggerate more commonly held fears about the impact on men of changes in the status of women. In 1992–1993, Allen's relation to a melodramatized masculinity spilled over from cinema to personal life, when his affair with a stepdaughter was made public and he was accused of incest. During a lengthy and angry battle in the media and courts with his long-term lover Mia Farrow, he presented himself as an innocent victim of a woman driven mad by jealousy.[2]

At first glance, Allen's feminized persona appears to represent just the kind of liberation from a repressive masculinity classical romantic comedy valued. However, the melodramatized male raises troubling issues regarding gender, especially when that characterization resists a comedic framework or critique that might ironize it, as typically occurred in the classical comedies (and in more recent ones, such as *Moonstruck*, that recall the earlier ones). As Juliana Schiesari argues in her study of the historical gendering of melancholy, the melodramatized male, or what she describes as "*homo melancholicus*, the melancholic *man*," stands both in reaction to and in complicity with patriarchy.[3] He appropriates a suffering or loss more commonly associated with the feminine, then recuperates that loss into a "privileged position within literary, philosophical and artistic canons" (11). Whereas in a woman melancholy is coded as *disabling* and pathological, in men it "enables" the transformation of apparent loss into male power "in the guise of moral conscience, artistic creativity, or heightened sensitivity" (14). The apparent feminization of the sensitive male does not undo sexual difference, then, but reauthorizes male power by denying women "the very specificity of their being" (31). In other words, his sensitivity more often reflects an attentiveness to his own needs than to those of women.

Such a male appropriation of femininity, feminized genres, and feminism itself (evident in *Kramer vs. Kramer* [1979], for example) has become especially pernicious in the late 1980s and early 1990s, a period that has been described as postfeminist, as if gender inequity had finally been eradicated. Tania Modleski analyzes this phenomenon in *Feminism Without Women*, where she cites Stanley Cavell as an example of a critic who appears to engage positively with feminist concerns but in fact does just the opposite. Cavell's work on melodrama, she writes, is motivated by the desire to "'preserve' philosophy as he knows it" by assimilating the issues raised by melodrama and feminism into the "feminine" mind of a male philosopher: "In poetically invoking the male philosopher's 'melancholy inexpressiveness,' Cavell solicits our recognition of the male as the superior candidate for our feeling of pathos, the melodramatic sentiment par excellence" (9).

Like Cavell, Woody Allen and the other melodramatized males of the postclassical romantic comedy use their feminization to prop up their own authority, which they then invoke to "instruct" women about relationships, romance, and femininity itself. Woody Allen's feminization is different from that of the male leads in *Bringing Up Baby*, *Ball of Fire*, and *The Lady Eve*, for it occurs at the expense of women; the subjectivity of his male heroes monopolizes his films. In Rob Reiner's *When Harry Met Sally . . .* (1989), something of a remake of Woody Allen's *Annie Hall*, it is Harry (Billy Crystal), not Sally (Meg Ryan), whose thoughts are shared with the audience through the film's only voice-over. Moreover, while popularizing sympathetic representations of Jewish culture, Allen (and Crystal) limit that sympathy to men; it is not Jewish women who are shown to be the object of the Jewish man's desire, but Gentiles, played by Diane Keaton, Mariel Hemingway, Mia Farrow, Meg Ryan.

In these films as well as others, such as *Broadcast News* (1987), *Green Card* (1990), and *Frankie and Johnny* (1991), men educate women, not the reverse. Compare, for example, Hopsy's sermons to the Lady Eve about the nature of love and forgiveness, or, in *It Happened One Night*, Peter's speeches about what he is looking for in a woman, with similar examples from postclassical romantic comedies. The earlier professor-hero is treated with affection, but with irony as well, for his presumptuousness and naiveté. In contrast, little irony surrounds the melodramatized male. If he suffers, we understand and sympathize, for he is not neurotic, merely sensitive. If she suffers, she is simply neurotic—like the hard-driven TV producer in *Broadcast News*, or the order-obsessed woman who loves her garden in *Green Card*, or the alienated waitress in *Frankie and Johnny*. Each of these heroines resists her male suitor less out of her inherent independence or recognition of his need to change than out of something wounded or undeveloped in *her*—qualities which allow the hero to demonstrate his greater wisdom, charm, or sensitivity.

Pretty Woman (Garry Marshall 1990) presents an especially instructive example of the influence of melodrama on the postclassical romantic comedy, not only because of the film's enormous popularity (the only movie to exceed its box office that year was *Ghost*, which goes to extraordinary lengths to melodramatize its male hero), but because it so faithfully adheres to the conventions of classical romantic comedy, yet to such different ends.

One of the factors that has undoubtedly influenced the shape of post-classical romantic comedy and films such as *Pretty Woman* has been the erosion of an overt discourse on social class in postwar America. Films such as *It Happened One Night* and *My Man Godfrey* (1936) used the couple to mediate class conflict, and class to fuel narrative conflict, by exaggerating the obstacles between the heterosexual couple and heightening the stakes in their conflict. Made at the end of a decade in which government policy fostered runaway corporate greed and widened the gap between rich and poor, *Pretty Woman* displays a preoccupation with money unusual in the postclassical romantic comedy. Indeed, the increasing feminization of poverty gives added weight to the film's use of the Cinderella fairy tale. *Pretty Woman*'s attention to money is evident from its opening montage of shots of money changing hands—first, plastic "gold" coins in a magic act at an upper-class party, then real money in a drug transaction on the street. By returning to the class issues that initially shaped the genre during the Depression, the film accomplishes much of the ideological work of the earlier films, using the couple to cover up class differences. At the same time, however, the film's use of melodrama limits its exploitation of the genre's potential regarding gender.

Throughout, *Pretty Woman* displays an awareness of its relation to classical romantic comedy. A shot of Carole Lombard's star on Hollywood Boulevard brings to mind her performances in such romantic comedies as *Twentieth Century* (1934) and *Nothing Sacred* (1937), while Ralph Bellamy's name on the credits recalls his perennial role in the earlier films as doltish rival to the romantic male lead. *Pretty Woman*, like its antecedents, derives both comedy and conflict from the wide social and temperamental gap between its romantic leads. Richard Gere plays Edward, an enormously wealthy corporate tycoon who, like the professor-heroes, hides his real emotional needs behind an obsession with work. Julia Roberts plays Vivian, a small-town girl turned small-time prostitute. While vastly separated by wealth, Edward and Vivian share similar attitudes toward money: neither jokes about it and both "screw people" for it. After a chance meeting, Edward hires Vivian to attend social events with him for a week because his lawyer has warned him that he needs to convey a friendlier image. By the end of the week, Vivian has shed her trampy-looking appearance to become an elegant companion for Edward, Edward has decided that he will no longer break apart vulnerable companies but will rebuild them, and the two have fallen in love. Vivian won't settle for anything less than marriage. Edward resists at first but finally overcomes his fear in a romantic, last-minute "rescue" of Vivian, about to leave town for a new life without him.

Vivian's occupation as a prostitute recalls and updates Mae West's Diamond Lil and the other unruly outlaws and showgirls of the classical films. Flamboyant and uninhibited, she makes a spectacle of herself throughout the film, first by flaunting her streetwalker's style in the lobby of Edward's ritzy hotel, then by modeling the stunning new wardrobe she's bought with Edward's money. As a hooker, she displays expansive body language, swinging her arms and playfully punching people. She laughs loudly at an episode of *I Love Lucy*, and later we see her watching the happy ending of an Audrey Hepburn film, allusions (like the one to Lombard) that link her with performative and narrative elements of female unruliness.

In several ways, the film's characterization of Edward is also consistent with gender inversion. He is stiff, subdued, serious. He can't drive a stick shift, she can. He's afraid of heights—most significantly, of course, emotional ones. Yet the film does not ironize his character or poke fun at the stereotypes of masculinity he embodies. Instead, by taking him, his pain, and his power so seriously, it melodramatizes him. We learn that Edward's ambition is fueled by anger at his wealthy father, who abandoned him as a child: the first company Edward took over was his father's. In one scene, Edward's inarticulable grief spills out in a lonely piano performance in the hotel's nearly deserted dining room. Later, he tells Vivian that he was so emotionally crippled by his father that he needed ten thousand dollars' worth of therapy before he could express his anger. Even then, he could not bring himself to be with his father when he died only a month or so earlier.

The film's most significant use of melodrama is not its sentimentalized treatment of Edward's pain, however, but its substitution of moral judgments for comedic ones. The flaws in Edward's masculinity—his obsession with a cruel and sterile kind of work—express themselves through something that is not foolish but powerful, dangerous, and therefore evil. By associating those flaws with aspects of capitalism gone wrong—aspects readily correctible with romantic love—the film affirms that capitalism itself is ultimately right. *Pretty Woman* distinguishes between two kinds of capitalism: the bad, destructive kind that only "makes money"—plastic coins—and the good kind that "makes *things*." Edward has made his fortune the evil 1980s way, by preying on weak companies. Yet the film foists those evils onto its most odious characters, Edward's father and his unregenerate lawyer, Phil. Phil's status as a melodramatic villain rather than a comedic buffoon is confirmed when he humiliates Vivian and then nearly rapes her. Edward, on the other hand, becomes the capitalist with a human face, and a handsome one at that. When he decides to go into partnership with the righteous but vulnerable shipbuilder played by Bellamy (to build destroyers, in an odd irony), he gains a new, good father.

By setting its Cinderella story against the backdrop of a melodrama of good and evil businessmen, *Pretty Woman* conveys overwhelmingly reassuring messages about class. First, Vivian's transformation shows that the signs of class—upper or lower—are as easily taken up or discarded as a borrowed credit card. After one week with Edward's card, Vivian seems born to wear the casual upper-class attire of designer blazer and jeans we see her in at the end of the film.[4] And Edward's transformation shows that, after one week with the right woman, even the most heartless of businessmen can be redeemed. Yet unlike *The Apartment*, which leaves its modest couple together but unemployed, Edward's reform exacts no financial cost. *Pretty Woman* diverges from the classical comedies in that it unabashedly trumpets the pleasures of being rich as ends in themselves. For example, the lovers travel by private jet to see a performance of *La Traviata*, an opera about a love affair between a courtesan and an aristocrat. The film borrows one scene from the sequence directly from *Moonstruck*, when the performance moves Vivian (in a gown even more brilliantly red than Loretta's) to tears. Yet, while opera is infused formally and thematically throughout *Moonstruck* to reveal the lovers' capacity for passion and to comment on the forms that passion takes, in *Pretty Woman* the trip to the opera provides an opportunity to display how elegantly Vivian wears jewels, how readily she acquires the taste of high culture, and how extravagantly but tastefully Edward spends his money. With its loving depictions of the life Edward can provide Vivian, *Pretty Woman* eroticizes money more than true love.

When Edward tells Vivian at the end of the film that he is the prince rescuing the princess, she immediately replies that she is rescuing him right back. This exchange suggests a redistribution of power between the sexes. However, Edward's masculine authority remains intact. The film affirms a masculinity defined as the ability to make money, and in *Pretty Woman*, money can be evil, but never foolish. The same is true of masculinity. Edward becomes a "nurturing" businessman, but the film has too much respect for his economic prowess, and for the masculinity so closely bound to it, to allow him to play the fool.

 Moonstruck *Again*

Moonstruck offers a very different account of the dilemma of the "post-feminist" man. Like much postclassical romantic comedy, the film inter-

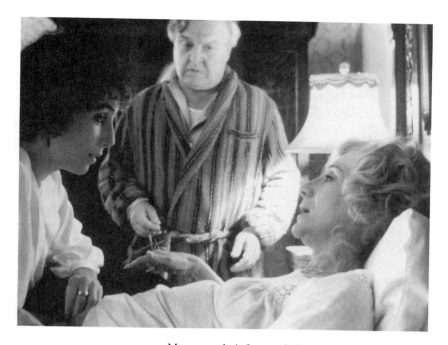

Moonstruck infuses melodrama into romantic comedy
by the attention it gives to its mother–daughter plot.
Here, the philandering Cosmo (Vincent Gardinia) is
framed by his daughter, Loretta (Cher), and his wife,
Rose (Olympia Dukakis). He is confined to the background and excluded from their intimacy.

mingles melodrama and romantic comedy. However, it remains faithful to
melodrama's orientation toward the feminine and to romantic comedy's
affinity for gender inversion. Thus, while allowing its male characters to
make abundant use of melodrama, it insistently challenges their appropriation of the genre, most effectively by turning it into comedy. In addition,
the film extends both genres past the limits each imposes on the telling of
women's stories. Like *Stella Dallas*, *Moonstruck* encompasses the familiar
scripts of love, motherhood, and loneliness. Unlike *Stella Dallas*, though,
it concludes as a comedy—but one significantly altered by its engagement
with melodrama.

Moonstruck centers on the lives of Rose Castorini (Olympia Dukakis)
and her widowed 37-year-old daughter Loretta (Cher). Both are at turning
points in their relationships with men. Cosmo, Rose's husband and Loretta's father, has become depressed and taken a mistress. Loretta has decided to marry again, years after the death of her first husband. Her fiancé,

Johnny, is a safe and infantile man. Almost as soon as he proposes and she accepts, she meets and falls in love with his estranged brother, Ronny, a tempestuous baker played by Nicholas Cage. She tries to halt the affair but accepts Ronny's plea that she go to the opera with him. After seeing *La Bohème*, her resistance to Ronny begins to fade. A third couple, Aunt Rita and Uncle Raymond, happily married for many decades, watches on the sidelines of the story as the other two couples work out their difficulties. By the morning after the opera, Ronny and Johnny are reconciled. So are Cosmo and Rose. Loretta and Ronny agree to marry, and they all raise a toast to the family.

The film introduces the theme of gender inversion in an early scene when Johnny and Loretta witness Perry, a middle-aged professor, being humiliated in a restaurant by his date, a young female student. Johnny giggles, then tells Loretta that a man who cannot control his woman is funny. The remark signals Johnny's lack of self-awareness, but more importantly it establishes a model of love—based on male dominance—that the film will eventually reject. It is important to note from the start that the film's play with genre and gender inversion depends largely on its use of ethnicity. Cosmo has made enough money in his plumbing business to set up his family in a comfortable style of living. Yet, as Italian-Americans, the Castorinis are not the stereotypical upper-middle-class American family. *Moonstruck* suggests that WASP culture may no longer provide as safe a place for comedic scenarios of gender inversion as it did during the classical period. Male weakness and foolishness and female power appear less threatening in the carnivalesque space of Italian-American, Irish-American, Jewish, or African-American culture. Narratives set in WASP culture more often require that male angst such as Cosmo's or Ronny's be played straight instead of as melodrama-turned-comedy. Perry, the WASP professor, is guilty of the same errors and self-pity as Cosmo, but he is granted somewhat more self-awareness and, thus, dignity.

Despite the immediate presence of melodrama in the film, *Moonstruck* is above all a comedy, and its generic tensions must be seen in that light. As in most comedies, the film's conflicts, choices, and dilemmas are organized along the lines of "life" and "death" and the values it associates with each. As a *romantic* comedy, its conflict centers on the couple, on getting the right lovers together. Here, there are two love triangles. Loretta must reject Johnny for Ronny, and Cosmo must choose Rose over his mistress, Mona. Examining throughout how men and women deal with life's inevitable pain, from aging, broken hearts, and broken dreams to mortality, the film ties the avoidance of pain to the avoidance of life.

Repeated images of death appear throughout the film. Loretta works in a funeral home and, in a muted evocation of the grotesque, speaks her first words of the film in a wry exchange with her boss about a corpse. She is living a kind of death-in-life as a widow which her marriage to Johnny would continue. Since losing her husband, she has not fallen in love again, and she is determined to remain emotionally "dead." Johnny, a "big baby" in her father's words, poses no threat to her. Meanwhile, Ronny first appears in the inferno of his bakery, where, covered with sweat and grime, he stokes the fires in the ovens. When he tells Loretta his life story, he proclaims, "I have no life. My brother took my life." Later, when he sweeps Loretta into his arms and off to bed, she tells him, "I was dead," and he answers, "I was dead, too."

Moonstruck does not really target Cosmo's philandering, or Ronny's anger at his brother, or Loretta's denial of her sexuality, so much as the fear, self-pity, or self-absorption that causes each of these characters to withdraw from the values the film associates with being alive. And in *Moonstruck*, it is men more than women who are especially vulnerable to such fear and misguided in their response to it. The Cammareri brothers, Johnny and Ronny, respond by retreating from romantic passion. Johnny becomes the film's buffoon, losing his luggage at every turn and remaining so attached to his mother that he cannot marry as long as she is alive. With Loretta, he plays the child and she the mother. She tells him what to eat, what to wear, and even how to propose to her. Ronny, like Loretta, was once moonstruck and hurt, and so he hides in his bakery. But while Loretta takes a pragmatic approach to her problems, Ronny turns his into the stuff of high tragedy. When Ronny tells Loretta why he won't attend her wedding, he rages, turning over tables like a villainous romantic male hero of melodrama, while an adoring female employee weeps, saying, "He's the most tormented man I know. I'm in love with him." By playing the scene as exaggerated melodrama, the film shows the tropes of fated romantic love—taken seriously in *La Bohème*—to be extremely funny, especially when they privilege the suffering male.

A similar fear of life leads the film's older male characters, Cosmo and the professor, *toward* relationships with women, but relationships based on self-delusion. Cosmo's fear has caused him to turn away from Rose. He can't sleep because "it's too much like death." Although he has plenty of money, he refuses to pay for Loretta's wedding, believing, as Rose says, that if he holds onto his money, he'll never die. He clings to his despair up to the moment before he surrenders to Rose and gloomily tells her: "Man understands one day that his life is built on nothing, and that's a bad, crazy day." Likewise, Perry has become "dead" in his work and feels alive again only when he sees himself anew in the eyes of young female students. Twice before meeting Rose at the neighborhood restaurant, he has had dinner with different female students. Each encounter ends with the student throwing her drink at him and walking out. When he claims not to understand why, Rose points out the obvious. He is too old for these women.

In contrast to the men, *Moonstruck*'s women have a clearer sense of who they are. Loretta is a paradigmatic woman on top, enhanced by the strong unruly offscreen presence Cher brings to the part. Loretta challenges the authority of her father and the other men in her life. Her choice of Johnny for a husband goes against her father's wishes, as does her insistence that he pay for her wedding. She dominates Johnny, and she initiates her romance with Ronny. She seeks him out, lures him from his cave, feeds him raw meat to restore his strength. Because this is a mainstream romantic comedy, Loretta's unruliness is sufficiently softened to make her acceptable as part of an idealized but conventional romantic couple. But once Ronny decides that they ought to stay together, she holds on to her own autonomy as long as possible. In doing so, she follows the same course as the unruly virgins who preceded her in the classical romantic comedies.

Gender inversion appears even more significantly in the film's attention to mothers. Typically, the mother has no place in romantic comedy, and as a rule, Hollywood has had little use for white-haired female characters like Rose (not to mention old lovers like Aunt Rita and Uncle Raymond). But mother figures, both good and bad, are plentiful in this film. Ronny and Johnny's mother is a bad mother, strong enough to rise from her deathbed—another of the film's comic treatments of death—to keep Johnny from marrying. Her fierce will is foreshadowed by the passion of the angry old woman at the airport, cursing the sister who stole the man she loved decades ago. By showing Johnny's failure to separate from his mother as comic, the film reverses the Oedipal logic of traditional romantic comedy by suggesting that it is sons, not daughters, who should leave their mothers; women should not have to mother husbands as well as sons. It is right for Ronny to leave his mother and make his home in Rose's house, as he shows when he eats her oatmeal with gusto.

Rose, of course, is a good mother, and while the name of Cosmo, the patriarch, means "world," the *social* cosmos or community the Castorini family represents is organized around Rose. The prominence of her story and her intimacy with Loretta displace romantic comedy's traditional focus on the isolated heterosexual couple by extending gender inversion into a larger communal context. Throughout the film, Loretta and Rose confide in each other, and their paths often cross. The film conveys their bond by intercutting scenes of each gazing at the moon the night Loretta first sleeps with Ronny. Rose's deadpan wisdom and clear-eyed perceptiveness contrast with the melodramatic suffering of the film's male figures. When Loretta tells her she loves Ronny, Rose says, "Oh God, that's too bad." Her sense of her own identity, as well, contrasts with the self-delusions of the men. When the professor tries to extend the simple dinner they shared to a sexual liaison, she declines without hesitation: "I can't invite you in because I'm married, because I know who I am."

One question puzzles Rose, however, and she seeks its answer throughout the film: Why do men chase women? The answer finally comes from Johnny, who confirms Rose's own intuition: Men chase women because they are afraid of death. Rose uses that answer to bring Cosmo back to his senses and the plot to its resolution. In a showdown in front of the family, she tells him to stop seeing his mistress, Mona: "No matter what you do, you're going to die, just like everyone else." Without a clear-eyed perception of that fact, people lose their bearings, hiding from life rather than accepting it in its totality and meeting it head-on with a gaze as sober and direct as those of the old matriarch and patriarch in the family portrait gallery.

No character can reach such an understanding without acknowledging the forces the film associates with the moon, and hanging over the film like the moon over the city is a sense of the mythic, the magic, the miraculous, conveyed through Loretta's superstition, the talk of "bad blood," the curse of the old woman at the airport, the "miraculous" cure of Johnny's dying mother. Indeed, recent postclassical romantic comedy seems to require overt allusions to some external frame of reference, whether "magic" and "signs" or opera and old movies, to make believable its claims for the fantasy of romantic love.[5] Loretta believes that the death of her first husband resulted from her failure to invoke the right charms—such as a proper proposal, a ring, a church wedding, a gown. The film's most obvious visual and thematic motif, of course, is the moon itself, although other examples of celestial and sylvan imagery abound. The moon, a traditional symbol of the feminine, "brings the woman to the man," the grandfather says. The moon that shines so brightly for Loretta and Ronny is the same moon Raymond thought Cosmo conjured up many years ago when he first gazed at Rose's window with a love he has now forgotten. On the night Loretta and Ronny first make love, "Cosmo's moon" awakens Uncle Raymond and Aunt Rita and rekindles their desire for each other. Its effects linger into the next day when Uncle Raymond, feeling like Orlando Furioso (a figure from Italian romance), greets Loretta by singing, "Hey there, you with the stars in your eyes." Cosmo gives Mona a bracelet with charms of stars and moons. When Ronny compares "storybook" love to the perfection of "stars and snowflakes," his figure of speech is visually repeated in Mona's rhinestone earrings, the crystal chandeliers of the Metropolitan Opera, even the bags of "Sunburst Flour" piled next to Ronny in his dungeon bakery.

The moon also stands for madness ("lunacy"), and so the motif of the wolf, the masculine counterpart to the film's lunar imagery, is a reminder that to be moonstruck—to give oneself over to forces that suspend reason—is also to court danger. In the Sweetheart Wines and Liquors Store, where Loretta stops to buy champagne, a wife chides her husband for how he looked at an attractive young woman ("like a wolf"). When Loretta tells Ronny his story, just as he will do for her later, she calls him a wolf who cut off his hand to save himself from the wrong love. The wolf appears more comically as the grandfather's disorderly pack of small dogs, who howl at the moon on his command. The old grandfather seems to have a special connection with this imagery of magic and romance, and a special love for the moon. If Johnny is the film's buffoon, the grandfather is its wise but puzzled fool, observing its action with the same balance of engagement and detachment the film asks of its viewers, and it is his attitude for which the film ultimately argues.

At one point, the grandfather follows his dogs past a "No Dogs Allowed" sign into a cemetery. This gentle act of transgression, of mixing death and life, is followed by another when the dogs dig up flowers and defecate on the new grave of his friend Alphonsa. For the grandfather, this is no sacrilege. Alphonsa is dead, and the dogs are alive. Whereas Cosmo surrounds death with an aura of self-pity and melodrama, the grandfather takes the attitude of the carnivalesque, which confronts death's inevitability as a fact of life. Standing over the grave, he remarks about how many flowers Alphonsa had received and how beautiful the moon was the night before. He reserves his worry for threats to the living—for how his son Cosmo endangers the family by refusing to pay for Loretta's wedding.

As the grandfather knows, the moon and what it stands for are real. To be moonstruck is to acknowledge the wolf within, to give it its place, to grant that howling at the moon is the foundation of social institutions. When Uncle Raymond saw "Cosmo's moon" for the first time, he says, "I was scared—like it was going to crush the house." Raymond acknowledges that the passion represented by the moon can indeed destroy the house, the family, when it is unacknowledged or misguided, or when the commitments that it leads to are forgotten. And the moon does not always shine. That is clear from the stories of the two old couples in the film. But because the film is a comedy, the moon will, and does, shine again. Rose counters Cosmo's self-pitying speech with "Your life is *not* built on nothing. *Te amo.*" In other words, the love that binds a family together is not "nothing" but in fact is all that there *is*. At last, Cosmo sees his error and replies that he loves her too. He puts down his arms and lifts his glass—"*A la famiglia.*" Rather than "crushing the house," the moon that makes one moonstruck is the very cornerstone of the family, and the family the very bulwark of social life.

Melodrama with its heightened emotion is the generic equivalent of being moonstruck, and the film argues that it too must be granted its place in the more utopian narratives of comedy. Ronny displays his suitability to be the film's romantic hero with his feeling for opera, and for *La Bohème* in particular. While within the film *La Bohème* occupies the position of high art, historically it represents Giacomo Puccini's efforts in the late nineteenth and early twentieth centuries to popularize opera by using characters who are ordinary people rather than aristocrats or mythic heroes—in effect, to feminize it by turning it from tragedy to melodrama. *La Bohème*, which he composed in 1896, tells the story of the poor seamstress Mimi, who experiences a brief period of ecstasy with an artist lover and his bohemian friends before they quarrel and separate and she dies of tuberculosis. The opera, like *Moonstruck*, also plays with its opposing genre in a comic subplot about the unruly Musetta, an outrageous flirt. While Musetta is spared Mimi's heartache and death, she also does not experience the intensity of Mimi's passion and takes second place musically and dramatically to her. It is Mimi's fate that typifies the suffering, passivity, and self-denial of the melodramatic heroine. Romantic love consumes her and leads to glorious unhappiness.[6] The opera's music literally orchestrates the pathos of her story and the emotions of the spectator. "That was so awful. Beautiful. Sad," Loretta says. "She died."

From its earliest moments, the film doubles the comedic couple of Loretta and Ronny with the melodramatic couple of Mimi and Rudolpho. This doubling occurs in part through a series of shots that place the lovers in the snow—first in an advertising poster for the opera, then at the opera itself, and finally on the street before Ronny's apartment. For Mimi and Rudolpho, the snow contrasts the warmth of their love with the coldness of Mimi's impending death. For Ronny and Loretta, the cold is the threat of lovelessness or emotional death that hangs over them both. Loretta shows her awakening feeling with the tears she sheds at the opera when Mimi takes Rudolpho's extended hand, and she in turn takes Ronny's. Later, she takes Ronny's hand once again when the two replay the opera scene on the street. The street scene is the turning point of the film, the culmination of the awakening intimated earlier when Loretta went into the Cinderella Beauty Shop and emerged a "new woman." Here, however, unlike in *Pretty Woman*, it is love, not money, that transforms the princess. When she dyes her hair, makes up her face, and exchanges her drab clothes and boots for a crimson dress and high heels, she re-creates herself as spectacle not to objectify herself or advertise her social position, but to signal her refusal of a premature death.

In a speech to Loretta on the street, Ronny connects being moonstruck with being alive:

> *Love isn't what they told you it is. Love don't make things nice. It ruins everything. It breaks your heart, it makes things a mess. But we're not here to make things perfect. The snowflakes are perfect. The stars are perfect. Not us. Not us. We are here to ruin ourselves, and break our hearts, and love the wrong people, and die. The storybooks are bullshit. Now come up stairs and get in my bed.*

Ronny is arguing for the position of comedy, for an acceptance of the totality of life and the imperfection of experience. "Storybook" love, like that of Mimi and Rudolpho, conceals its pain by romanticizing it into an image of perfection. In "real life," love, like all things, is imperfect and often ordinary. People grow old, or quarrel over trivial things, or become depressed about dying. And so, Ronny says, give yourself over to the moon when it casts its spell on you.

Moonstruck's intermingling of melodrama and comedy comes close to having it both ways. Along with the intensity represented by Mimi and Rudolpho's love, the film retains those elements of melodrama that are most positive from a feminist point of view—the presence of the mother and the connection among women, the recognition of masculine "villainy" and guilt, and the acknowledgment of women's suffering. Despite Ronny's melodramatic speeches, the film resists the temptation to sentimentalize him or any of its male characters. By the end, Ronny has become a full-fledged romantic hero—but not until he has shown himself to be as much a fool as Cosmo, Johnny, and the professor. The very rhyming of his name with his brother's shows that, at least initially, the two have more than a little in common. As a result, the film succeeds in exploiting comedy's double allegiance to anarchy and order, its centrifugal assault on authority and its centripetal drive toward community. It also retains the tonal balance between sentiment and skepticism about romantic love so characteristic of the comedies of the classical period but so often lost in the nervous romance.

Moonstruck insists that dogs will howl at the moon, but it also rejects the melodramatic fate of Mimi, who enacts the tropes of a suffering femininity. If Loretta finally submits to the same lunacy as Mimi when she agrees to "ruin" herself with Ronny, she differs from Mimi in one critical way: while Mimi lives and dies only to give Rudolpho a reason to sing, Loretta remains a woman on top; while Mimi wastes away in isolation, Loretta will draw strength from the company of her mother and a community that extends beyond the individual couple. The comedic crystallization of a new society doesn't occur until Cosmo capitulates to Rose, and Loretta doesn't have to give up her mother to get her man. By giving centrality and weight to its women, *Moonstruck* not only demonstrates the flexibility of a popular and enduring narrative form but takes a step toward more fully realizing its potential to foster new and more inclusive images of community.

It is true that Loretta and Rose represent considerably subdued versions of the unruly women I examined in Part One of this book—the laughing murderers of *A Question of Silence*, Miss Piggy and the sorority of swine, Mrs. Noah, and the Domestic Goddess, Roseanne Arnold. It should also be no surprise that some of the boldest appropriations of the comedic forms that have been the subject of this book can be found in the margins of our culture rather than in the mainstream, where women are confined to the discourses of heterosexuality, romantic love, and the family. For example, *A Question of Silence*, which was produced in the Netherlands and has had a limited circulation in this country, places the issues of women's rage and laughter within the context of radical feminism. Other examples of experimental film and video use comedy in compelling (and often extremely funny) ways to convey the voices of lesbians, women of color, and others excluded from mainstream media. Works by Cecelia Condit, Ayoka Chenzira, and Ann Alter, among others, push at the limits of female unruliness—to make visible and laughable the tropes of femininity affirmed by melodrama, to redefine the terms on which women look and can be seen, to convey anger, create pleasure, and forge bonds of solidarity among women.[7]

This transformative potential, as we have seen, is illuminated by the social and literary traditions of the carnivalesque. Extending Mikhail Bakhtin's class-based analysis to gender, Natalie Davis defined the topos of the unruly woman, or the woman on top, as a figure of female transgression that is both threatening and vulnerable. The unruly woman shares the multivalence Mary Douglas has identified with dirt, Victor Turner with liminality, and other anthropologists with creatures of the threshold, such as the pig. While vast differences separate the cultures Bakhtin and Davis studied from our own, comedic forms are highly conventionalized and the tropes of unruliness—including fatness, rebelliousness, and a sharp tongue—persist into contemporary culture. Today, Miss Piggy, for example, recalls the husband-thrashing Mrs. Noah in her aggressiveness, Ursula the Pig Woman in her hedonism and gross corporeality, and Mae West in her parodic performance of femininity.

These traits converge even more dramatically in the figure of comedian Roseanne Arnold, whose impact on contemporary culture testifies to the continued vitality of the woman on top as a site of insurgency, a place for contesting and recoding dominant notions of "woman." Arnold violates multiple taboos through her body's fatness and looseness, her speech, her jokes, and her spectacle making. Most important, in her public appearances—in interviews, standup comedy, talk shows, her autobiography, her sitcom—she presents herself as author and subject: author of a "self" who reclaims her experience by recoding the terms (such as "Domestic Goddess") the culture imposes on her; and subject of an angry laughter at the inequities of class and gender in U.S. culture. The extreme ambivalence she provokes has caused her to be the object of vicious verbal attacks, but has also placed her sitcom at the top of the ratings for much of its first six seasons.

Arnold exercises the power that she does in part because she works outside the structures of narrative that shape the Hollywood film, where a woman who lays claim to her desire is likely to be mocked in misogynist forms of comedy or pitied in melodrama, which blames her attachment to other women—her refusal to sever the mother-daughter bond—for her failure to achieve her proper place in patriarchy. Narrative, however, also contains liminal moments that correspond to the carnivalesque, especially in the critically overlooked and undervalued genres of laughter. This tension can be seen in romantic comedy. On the one hand, the genre expresses an impulse central to many comedic forms—the impulse toward social integration and renewal—by narrating the story of the woman's successful accommodation to heterosexuality and her acceptance of her proper place in the patriarchy. On the other hand, however, romantic comedy also expresses comedy's antiauthoritarian impulse, especially when it employs the structure of gender inversion. Many of the films I have examined in Part Two of this book illustrate romantic comedy's feminist potential in their promise of a restructured sexuality as the basis for community.

That potential emerged in a strain of romantic comedy produced between the early 1930s and 1940s. Early in this period, the swaggering performance of unruly burlesque queens and vaudeville stars such as Mae West gave way to narratives requiring more demure brides, such as Claudette Colbert in *It Happened One Night*. This shift did not exact as big a cost as might first appear, however. *Sylvia Scarlett* showed that the character of the female virgin required by the plot of New Comedy possesses considerable strengths—in her deferral of "fertility, humility, community," her resistance to the social claims of a mature heterosexuality, and her efforts to prolong that liminal period when, like Ellie in *It Happened One Night*, she belongs briefly to no man. With Katharine Hepburn, the virgin acquired an androgyny that heightened the heroine's power to destabilize the social and sexual norms of gender.

By *Bringing Up Baby* and *The Lady Eve*, the virgin as woman on top dominated her professor-hero, shook the structures of patriarchy, and brought about the birth of a new man who found his virility in part through his recovered femininity. These films depict the uncanny and ambivalent power of the female gaze to look on the castrated man and restore his potency. Even as the dumb blonde, like Billie Dawn in *Born Yesterday*, the unruly woman retained some power to deflate masculine pretensions. The extent of the unruly woman's domestication in postwar America, however, can be seen by contrasting the blonde sex queen who ushered in this era with the one who concluded it—the autonomous Mae West and the vulnerable Marilyn Monroe. Finally, the unruly woman was driven out of film into the new medium of television, where she resurfaced as the unruly matriarch of the domestic situation comedy, typified by Lucille Ball. Today, as Roseanne Arnold's career suggests, the unruly woman continues to find a more tolerant home on television than in film.

In the postclassical period, romantic comedy has remained a popular film genre, but one changed by persistent anxieties over changes in the status of women. The nervous romance reflects a cultural wariness about the possibilities of the heterosexual couple, expressed in an appropriation of melodrama to portray the victimization of men, not women. However, melodrama has also been used to mock the self-indulgent male and to challenge a notion of femininity based on victimization and suffering. *Moonstruck* employs melodrama to assert the validity of the fantasy of romance and family it proposes, yet its comic framework prevents any sentimentalizing of that fantasy, much as Muggsy's wisecrack undercuts the utopian ending of *The Lady Eve*.[8]

In the broadest sense, romantic comedy's message about finding life in social connection and embracing its totality is entirely conventional. Indeed, like all mainstream narrative forms, the genre is inherently conservative, depoliticizing women's oppression and class conflict. If the dumb blonde is susceptible to hostile readings, so too is the spoiled heiress, as suggested by the critical tendency not to see past Ellie Andrews's "brattiness" in *It Happened One Night*, or the hostility that has accompanied our culture's widespread admiration for Katharine Hepburn. However, romantic comedy also gives expression to the contradictory nature of women's desires concerning romantic love and the relations between the sexes, reminding us of the doubleness of all cultural forms, the intermingling of the ideological and the utopian within them. The very conventionality of its message suggests that it endures in part because it speaks to powerful needs to believe in the utopian possibilities condensed on the image of the couple—the wish for friendship between women and men, for moments of joy in relationships constrained by unequal social power. The same can be said for the domestic sitcom, which addresses similar contradictions within family life—the wish to believe in the family as a refuge from the alienation and injustices of the outside world, rather than as deeply implicated in producing them.

From *It Happened One Night* to *Moonstruck* to *Roseanne*, these comedic forms hold out the promise of dissolving the barriers between the public and private, work and play, the social and the sexual. Rooted in traditional forms that attempt to reconcile the two, they give much-needed occasions for laughter along the way toward new forms that might more fully express our desires. They also remind us of the potential for openness in the most highly conventionalized forms, and for seriousness in the most lighthearted.

fterword
Shape-Shifting

In real life, women are exceptionally courageous, defiant, and strong, exceptionally, or you couldn't live one day in this country.

—ROSEANNE ARNOLD (INTERVIEW)

Near the end of her autobiography, Roseanne Arnold describes her affection for New Orleans, which she sees as a city of darkness and which is the only U.S. city, in fact, where a vestige of carnival survives: "Everything dark is quick and unsure and can shape-shift," she writes (*Roseanne* 195). Darkness possesses the same creative potential as margins, dirt, dream work, and joke work. Tidiness and light banish that potential. Just as the history of romantic comedy tracks a kind of narrative shape-shifting in the direction of melodrama, a longer look at Arnold's career shows that her use of the semiotics of unruliness has been anything but static, and in fact might be seen as moving in a similar direction. While maintaining a profile that remains as prominent as ever, Arnold has reinvented her persona by altering both the literal contours of her body and the narrative in which it is understood. Before concluding, I would like to take a brief look at that reinvention and the questions it raises about time, change, and the limits of female unruliness in contemporary popular culture.

Throughout this study I have argued that the comedic tradition of female unruliness must be seen in relation to melodrama and the cultural preference for women's tears over their laughter. While Arnold has continued to define herself in terms of comedy, she too has been subject to the desire to see "deviant" women as victims rather than rebels. In September 1991 Arnold publicly disclosed her childhood experiences of incest and abuse.[1] Some commentators greeted the news with skepticism and accused her of simply seeking publicity. Others used it to cast subtle doubts on all charges of incest (see Darnton). But soon they were following the lead of the largely female audience of the daytime talk shows who, without skipping a beat, supported Arnold's movement from comedy into the melodramatic discourse of confession, therapy, and recovery. When she made her first extended appearance after the announcement, on *The Sally Jesse Raphael Show*, and recounted her story with obvious pain, tears streamed down the faces of many members of the studio audience. Soon she was being widely praised for her courage. And soon publications that had previously ignored or disdained her were publishing pieces full of respect for the realism and gutsiness of her sitcom (see Wolcott; Cole). Arnold had triggered a dramatic shift in her place in the culture, reversing the hostility and derision that had culminated just over a year earlier when her rendition of the national anthem provided a frightening reminder of the dangers to which transgressive women are always vulnerable.

The media's softening toward her might be explained by the genuine sympathy her account of her suffering aroused, or by her legal victory over the tabloids, or by the evolving polish and subtlety of her series. I believe, however, that Arnold's incest disclosures fractured the comedic framework of her earlier persona. Earlier, in her autobiography, comedy acts, and interviews, Arnold had alluded to episodes in her childhood that seemed unconventional, and often bizarre. In retrospect, clues were already present, although curiously unexplained, as when she wrote, in her autobiography, of her sisters calling her from Salt Lake City, "locked in their rooms from fear of violence."[2] By imposing a comedic narrative on such incidents, however, the book helped construct a persona that avoided pathos while retaining the power of the grotesque. In contrast, the new disclosures allowed her persona to be understood in the less unsettling, more familiar and reassuring terms of melodrama—a melodrama of outraged parents, siblings in denial, lie-detector tests, and lawsuits.

Arnold had finally provided an *explanation* for her out-of-bounds behavior—and one that was ideologically acceptable. To insist, as she previously had done, that a woman could be fat by choice, angry at men, immune to social control, and sane at the same time defies ideology. Incest provided not only an explanation for her deviance, but one which opened the door to recuperating her as a tough, scrappy survivor. A cultural consensus exists on incest and child abuse. We do little to prevent or respond to these crimes, but we insist that they horrify us. A culture that ignores or represses the facts of incest and child abuse would still rather tie a woman's anger and deviance to the personal abuse she suffered in the privacy of her home than to the structural abuses that produce (or at least tolerate) incest and child abuse in the first place.

Arnold has used her sitcom, in its most recent seasons, to elaborate on this explanation. For the first three seasons, "Roseanne Conner" appeared to draw primarily on Roseanne Arnold's well-publicized accounts of her experiences as an adult—as wife, mother, homemaker, factory worker, "woman." Since then, the show increasingly has tackled subjects relevant to Arnold's newly recovered memories of her childhood—subjects that even Arnold has been hard-pressed to treat as comedy rather than melodrama. For example, in a two-part episode on domestic violence, Roseanne discovers that Jackie's boyfriend has been beating her, and helps her confront the abuse they both suffered as children. In another episode, Roseanne buries her father and, over his coffin, expresses her extreme ambivalence toward him. In yet another, she changes her mind about refusing to let Darlene's boyfriend move in with the Conners after she sees his mother treat him with shocking cruelty.

If all of this has helped produce a kind of shape-shifting in Arnold's persona, that shape-shifting has been literal as well. Her reidentification of herself as an incest survivor (which followed by a few months her name change from Barr to Arnold) coincided with her appearance in a "new" body, trimmed by sixty pounds and toned by workouts. Later, she displayed that body in glamorous photo spreads in women's magazines, documenting her makeover with sexy poses and high-fashion makeup and hair. This glamour was not new for her and she had put it on quite successfully when she was fat—as the International Goddess and in Annie Leibovitz's December 1990 photo essay in *Vanity Fair*, which juxtaposes shots of the Arnolds mud wrestling with others of them dressed in formal attire. What *was* new was seeing such glamour as part of the "real Roseanne." Later in 1992, cosmetics gave way to cosmetic surgery—breast reduction, fat removal, a nose job.

Overall, Arnold's metamorphosis poses challenging questions about the signifiers of unruliness once so unambiguously inscribed on her body. First, her bodily changes might be viewed as consistent with the melodramatization I have just described. Before, Arnold had cultivated a coding of her body as a grotesque monument to self-indulgence rather than self-denial, a material testimony to her rebellious immunity to social control, her refusal to diet, work out, make up, and shut up. At least initially, she explained the new body by reinterpreting the former one (and the transgressive behavior that accompanied it) as symptoms of the pain of her childhood abuse and the addictions which that abuse drove her to. Explicitly connecting her new body to its newly recovered history, she said her repressed memories enabled her to understand, and thus overcome, her addictions to alcohol, nicotine, and food. Despite her scrupulous use of the word *survivor*, the formerly fat body became the body of a victim, the body of melodrama, "a prison of flesh." ("Only in the last two years have I realized the consequences of keeping our [family's] secret. I have lived the majority of my life in a flesh prison that I was trying to blow up, break out of, whittle away" [Barr, "I Am an Incest Survivor" 87].) [3]

Arnold went to considerable lengths to place her breast-reduction surgery in the same therapeutic framework of health and recovery, describing it in an episode of her sitcom as a means of relieving back pain. However, the cosmetic surgeries that followed seem to suggest how closely "health" and "recovery" in our culture are also tied to pathology—to accepting crippling ideologies of gender, class, and ethnicity. Just as Arnold's slimmer body suggests a repudiation of her former "poor white trash" body, so the new nose (and her silence about it) might be seen as an evasion of her Jewishness (McLeland). [4] By displacing onto the old "unhealthy" body the pain required to shape the new one, Arnold covers up the connection between the scars of the scalpel and those of an ever-present regulatory discourse directed toward women about the normal, the healthy, and the beautiful. [5]

However, I believe that it is too easy to see the new Roseanne only in this light. First, to do so is to risk replicating patriarchy's judgment of women according to their "face" (or body) value. [6] Arnold, of course, has invited such judgment from the outset, since she built her career on a foundation of body politics. But while we are apt to remember and applaud her vindication of fatness, it is perhaps more important to remember that that vindication was rooted in a refusal to accept other people's evaluations of her on the basis of her body. Women rarely choose to be fat, ungainly, or out of step in other ways with cultural standards of beauty; and their relations to their bodies, and their feelings and choices about their appearance, are rarely simple or easy. Just as feminism has advanced beyond its once categorical dismissal of pornography toward a more complex understanding of sexual fantasy, so we must keep in mind that women use the resources available to them to create their identities out of deeply internalized images and contradictory desires.

Moreover, if Arnold's transgressive power appears to have diminished, perhaps that may arise from the nature of transgression itself in contemporary popular culture—from a kind of half-life that follows from familiarity and limits the potential of any single figure to break cultural boundaries. Transgression, like spectacle, possesses what might be called an "inexhaustible compulsion to excess,"[7] a need to "up the ante" and outdo itself as each boundary is overstepped. At the same time, transgression is not absolute and static, but relational and historically contingent. While the boundaries in a culture are never stable, one person's potential to test them resides not in the individual alone but in the intersection between that individual and a particular historical moment. The history of rock and roll, for example, is also the history of successive violations of taboo, beginning only a few decades ago with acts that once were shocking but now seem quite tame. As Arnold's image rapidly became familiar, that familiarity began to mute its danger and to draw it from the margin toward the center. Consider Madonna, recently sniped at as the "hardest working sex symbol in the history of show business" for her performance in *Body of Evidence* (1992). She now appears stymied by the challenge of exceeding not only the persona she created, but a "brilliant appropriation" of it by actress Sharon Stone in *Basic Instinct* (1992), an imitation that exceeded the original (Rafferty).[8]

I would prefer to view the new Roseanne—who seems such a radical departure from the old one—in the context of continuity rather than rupture, as one more manifestation of a capacity for shape-shifting and an affinity for darkness, dirt, and liminality that were always already there. While Arnold has based her claims for authority on the identity between her self and her act, the very excessiveness of that self/act has kept its boundaries fluid and unstable. Her power, I believe, has been enhanced by that undecidability, that continuing difficulty in determining just how to read her. (Did she really mean to sing the anthem as she did? What exactly did she mean by the homophobic remarks she made in a fax war with several TV critics in 1992?) One of the most intriguing phenomena about Arnold is the drive she elicits to "place" her. However, I believe we must resist the temptation for closure, for a critical practice that would subject her to a logic of either/or. Why not both/and?

This "both/and" is evident in the fact that Arnold has hardly abandoned comedy, her original and defining performance mode, even as she has become a familiar and generally well-behaved presence in mainstream culture. Nor has she moderated the rage she expresses through comedy. Her third HBO special, "Roseanne Arnold" (June 1992), is even angrier than the previous two, and her most savagely and explicitly political to date. Using bitter and scarcely veiled allusions to her own childhood as a basis for wider social commentary, she covers topics ranging from how girls are taught passivity to how emotional violence within the family produces eating disorders. As quoted in a 1992 article headlined "The New Roseanne," she made her boldest challenge to women yet: "Be as threatening, big, looming, loud-mouthed, as you can possibly dig down into your gut to be" (Van Buskirk 32). Most important was her role as producer of *The Jackie Thomas Show*, a star-vehicle for her husband, Tom Arnold, which aired in 1992–1993 immediately after *Roseanne*. Arnold used the highly self-reflexive show to re-create her own televisual history, but with ironic gender substitutions and inversions. In this case it is "Jackie Thomas," not Roseanne Arnold, who stands as a larger-than-life example of out-of-bounds white trash. Jackie terrorizes his staff and bosses, breaks rules, and simply does not fit into the Hollywood scene. Yet to the frustration of everyone around him he remains untouchable because his show, like Roseanne Arnold's, is so successful. With promotions and cross-show appearances linking *The Jackie Thomas Show* with *Roseanne*, Tom Arnold made no effort to conceal the fact that his show owed its existence to his wife's clout and that the power before it on the evening lineup was also the power behind it.

Roseanne Arnold's new body, as well, benefits from an inclusive interpretation, a feminist critique that would also accommodate the more ambiguous cases of Michael Jackson and the early 1990s wave of piercing, tattooing, and other forms of mutilation as ways of laying claim to one's body. Consider the example of Orlan, a French multimedia-and-performance artist who is rebuilding her face in a series of seven public performance/surgeries, each designed to replicate a single idealized feature from art (the forehead of Leonardo's *Mona Lisa*; the mouth of Boucher's *Europa*; the chin of Botticelli's *Venus*) (Rose).[9] Like Orlan's, Arnold's new body might be seen as another variation of masquerade, or "putting on the feminine." Moreover, much as that body is now perceived as new, how different is it really from the old one? Even as it moves—or appears to move—toward the classical or bourgeois, that very fluidity and changeability keep it tethered to the grotesque, in the category Mary Douglas has described as "danger" rather than "purity."

If anything, Arnold's current persona is even more marked by contradiction and undecidability than ever. When she describes cosmetic surgery as her "latest addiction" and cracks jokes about losing weight the easy way because she can afford to, she once again catches us off guard. These jokes are unsettling, foregrounding issues of power, image, and identity. But—like the best jokes—they are powerful *because* they are unsettling. At this point, it is hard to imagine Arnold outdoing her most outrageous joke, her performance of the national anthem. Yet rather than assuming, just yet, that she has exhausted her potential for disruption, I would rather watch for less dramatic but perhaps more provocative acts of unruliness—for example, exploiting the potential of melodrama, as she has in the fifth and the sixth seasons of her sitcom, to deepen her critique of the family; or preserving in other ways that sense of indeterminacy and instability, even as she shape-shifts into a figure that seems more familiar.

Early in her career, Arnold chose to take her message—which originated in the margins of feminist, avant-garde, and gay comedy clubs—to a popular audience, and since then she has continually negotiated the space between the two, driving an insistent wedge into the mass media to accommodate her unruly presence and so changing its contours as she has changed her own. For that reason she remains a compelling example of the disruptive potential of the unruly woman in the 1990s. Her ready and successful adaptation of the sitcom confirms the power of familiar narrative forms, such as romantic comedy, as well as their adaptability. She has used her version of the sitcom to place in the public consciousness a woman's perspective on motherhood—a perspective as underrepresented in the avant-garde as in the mainstream—and her career testifies to the political power of women's laughter to "bring down the house."[10]

That defiant laughter at authorities inside and outside the house recalls the laughter of Medusa and the Dutch killers, and of Mrs. Noah, Ursula the Pig Woman, and Miss Piggy. Lingering past the "privileged time of carnival and stage play," in Natalie Davis's words, it "widens behavioral options" for women. Just as Arnold moves between mainstream and margin, so she exerts her authorship on both sides of the camera. Her performance in front of the camera, marked so strongly with her presence behind it, is a reminder of the authorship inherent in the performances of other women—from Mae West to Cher—who, by making unruly spectacles of themselves, have also made a difference.

otes

Introduction: Feminist Film Theory and the Question of Laughter

1. The term *patriarchy* has come under attack as a universalizing concept that threatens to obscure the various ways sexual asymmetry exists in different cultural contexts (for instance, Butler 35). With this caution in mind, I will retain the term to refer to the general organization of societies around such asymmetry, or, more emphatically, around women's oppression.

2. The women are Christine, a housewife and mother; Ann, a waitress; and Andrea, a secretary. All three have silently endured humiliation in their jobs and private lives because they are women. Their lives converge one day in a dress shop, where they participate in the murder of a patronizing male shopkeeper. A

fourth woman, Janine, is a psychiatrist recruited by the court to help prosecute them, but her investigation is hampered by Christine's refusal to speak. Janine comes to understand the motive behind the crime in part through her awakening awareness of her husband's oppressive behavior toward her. When the women in the courtroom see that her explanation is entirely beyond the grasp of the court, they break out in laughter. The prisoners are led away, and Janine leaves the courtroom. Instead of joining her waiting husband, she turns to the women who left the building with her.

Although now a feminist classic, the film has generally not been well received by male viewers. As Jeanette Murphy notes, male reviewers have been mostly hostile, some saying it lacked humor but was technically excellent, others the reverse (105); and conversations between men and women after screenings of the film have often been heated.

3. This book began as a response to Russo's powerful and original essay, and I would like to acknowledge here my debt to her.

4. "Genres of laughter" is Laura Mulvey's term (in her essay "Changes: Thoughts on Myth, Narrative and Historical Experience") for the forms of narrative and performance associated with carnival.

5. Those exceptions, in addition to Russo, include Patricia Mellencamp and Lucy Fischer. For recent work on film comedy, also see Curry, Henry Jenkins, Mirza, Roberts, and Robertson. On television comedy, see Jeremy Butler, Desjardins, and McPherson.

6. Nearly sixty feminist scholars contributed to a discussion of these issues in a double issue of *Camera Obscura* (20–21) in 1989.

7. Mary Russo 213. I will return in a later chapter to Douglas's *Purity and Danger*. Throughout this book, I generally use the term *comedy* in relation to narrative forms; *carnival* to discuss semiotics and social practices; *parody* to describe forms of representation that imitate other forms, usually to comic effect; and *irony* to describe a technique in which a representation's literal and implied meanings differ. I use *joke* in Freud's sense to describe a discursive structure or interaction, and *masquerade* to describe a woman's parodic "putting on" of femininity.

8. The terms *woman*, *female*, *femininity*, and *the feminine* (perhaps even more than *patriarchy*) pose a dilemma for a feminism increasingly aware of the dangers of imposing a single name on a multiplicity of experiences. As Judith Butler argues, "woman" and "female" are unfixed and relational, "troubled" concepts rather than "natural" and "inevitable" (x). Yet abandoning a politics of identity also has its dangers, including a loss of focus and an inability to name our common experiences. Especially in an age that has been characterized as postfeminist, I believe these terms retain a

strategic importance, provided they are used with an awareness that their value lies in just that rather than in any unchanging categories they appear to define.

Doane's work, like that of most feminist film theorists largely dependent on psychoanalysis, emphasizes the processes of spectatorship and the more general category of "the feminine." This approach differs from more sociologically oriented criticism, which concerns the themes and content of texts and the experiences of particular "women" as "audiences." Both terminologies, I believe, have their place. I find *women* preferable in discussing the social context of texts because it is a reminder of the grounding of the symbolic in the material and of the abstract in the particular. At the same time, those experiences cannot be talked about without a degree of generalization. And so the *feminine* is useful in discussing texts themselves and the universalized qualities many of them ascribe to "women."

9. Recent feminist work on masquerade generally begins with Joan Rivière's 1929 essay, which argues from a psychoanalytic framework that women who wish for masculinity may "put on" the feminine as a defensive reaction to avert anxiety and appease men whom they have offended by usurping their privilege. Luce Irigaray uses the term *mimesis* for the same strategy, although she views it more positively as a means of taking control of one's representation within discourse. She reserves *masquerade* for the false position of a woman who experiences desire only as male desire for her. See also Johnston, "Femininity and the Masquerade: *Anne of the Indies*"; Doane, "Film and Masquerade" and "Masquerade Reconsidered"; and Heath. I agree with Pat Mellencamp's assertion that "another interpretation of masquerade as a possibility for feminism rather than a disguise, lure or mark of envious lack is necessary" (*Indiscretions* 132).

10. The joke requires a joke-maker, a laugher (both presumed male), and a butt—quintessentially, an absent woman; classical cinema also assumes a bonding between men, established by a relay of looks, and the absence of a looking female. The photograph's terms of address implicate the viewer in a particular way—positioning *him* (and the viewer is assumed to be male) to share a laugh with the photographer at the woman's blindness to her own surroundings.

11. Here and throughout this book I draw on Teresa de Lauretis's analysis of the Oedipal structure of narrative in "Desire in Narrative," an essay in *Alice Doesn't* (103–157).

12. See "In the Name of Feminist Film Criticism." An example of such a film is Jacques Rivette's *Celine and Julie Go Boating* (1974), which was almost universally denounced by male critics for its "silliness" but has become a favorite of feminists. Pitting a new kind of comedy against the

genre of melodrama, the film suggests a seemingly unending capacity for prolonging the middle section of narrative with its invention, liminality, and play. See also Lesage's "*Celine and Julie Go Boating*: Subversive Fantasy."

13. Rich warns against an overemphasis on form or "signifying practices" in judging a film's feminist potential. Her call for "a bit of phenomenology" about the existence and experience of the female spectator remains as cogent today as when she made it in 1978. Comedy's potential for feminism has long been recognized as well by Patricia Mellencamp, whose persuasive and witty work on the subject began with articles on the Marx Brothers ("Jokes and Their Relation to the Marx Brothers"), Lucille Ball, and Gracie Allen and has continued through her recent books on the avant-garde, television, and the discourses of scandal.

14. Medusa retains even greater currency in the avant-garde. Her story is rewritten, feminized, and conflated with that of Eve in Monique Wittig's *Les Guérillères* (see Suleiman 132). Her face appears on the cover of a recent book about female performance artists (Juno and Vale, *Angry Women*). Suleiman describes the laughing Medusa as a "trope for women's autonomous subjectivity and for the necessary irreverence of women's writing—and rewriting" (168).

15. De Lauretis makes a provocative move in this direction when, in the context of a "politics of the unconscious," she rewrites the Medusa story so that Medusa is not sleeping but is awake when Perseus slays her (*Alice Doesn't* 134–136). By doing so, she points to the fact that our culture demands that women be "asleep" whenever it asks us to identify with the images of dead women it parades before us and when it privileges "aesthetic" standards at the expense of any other kind of identification. I take a similar position in relation to high cultural modes of criticism in "Romanticism, Sexuality, and the Canon."

16. As Jane Root explains, that choice was consistent with the group's decision to market *A Question of Silence* as a feminist film rather than an art film. Art films tend to downplay humor in order "to sell more intellectually 'important' activities" (218). See also Jeanette Murphy.

17. Other more realistic explorations of female revenge include Nelly Kaplan's *A Very Curious Girl* (1969) (also known as *Pirate Jenny's Revenge* in reference to Brecht's *Three Penny Opera*) and Karen Arthur's *Lady Beware* (1987).

18. In some ways, the film does resemble a feminist rewriting of the classic tragedy of Oedipus, redeeming "woman" from the role of the mysterious animal/human Sphinx, literally on the margins of the polis, or from

that of the mother/wife Jocasta. Janine has agency, and like Oedipus, she seeks to solve a mystery, to find out who *she* is, to answer a riddle about the "why" of the crime. Whereas Oedipus unwittingly murders his father, Janine takes part in a sustained assault on the patriarchy that only begins with the murder of the shopkeeper. Just as Oedipus compounds patricide with incest when he marries his mother, so Janine turns from her husband to a forbidden union with the women who awaken her feminist consciousness. Her heroism occurs, not through hubris or the principle of individuation, like that of Oedipus, but through joining a community of women in which "Honor thy mother/sister" replaces the law of the father.

19. For a similar argument, see Lucy Fischer's *Shot/Countershot*, where she describes the film as a "grand cinematic 'joke'" (300).

20. According to Kaja Silverman (131–149), this taped laughter disrupts the synchronization between the female voice and female body that confines female subjectivity as it is represented in mainstream cinema.

21. Black feminism has made a similar critique of middle-class white feminism. See especially Hurtado, who argues for the importance of the differences between white women and women of color in their relation to white men, the holders of power in our society. See also Collins; Bobo and Seiter; and Gaines.

22. See Jaggar on liberal feminism and radical feminism, the primary feminisms the film considers.

23. By *intertextuality*, I refer to Bakhtin's notion, developed in *The Dialogic Imagination* and elsewhere in his writings, that languages (or signs, such as the tropes of female unruliness which I will examine in this book) must be understood discursively, in terms of their usage within a social context, and that those uses are always implicated in prior or simultaneous uses. For a discussion of Bakhtin's thinking about intertextuality, genre, and the history of literature, see Todorov 60–93.

1. Pig Ladies, Big Ladies, and Ladies with Big Mouths: Feminism and the Carnivalesque

1. The Muppets include Miss Piggy, Kermit the Frog, Scooter, the Great Gonzo, Fozzie Bear, and Animal. They have appeared in several groupings on different shows: *The Muppet Show*, a weekly comedy show; *Sesame Street*, the acclaimed PBS children's program; *Muppet Babies*, a Saturday-morning cartoon show; and a number of feature-length films and television specials. They also appear on a range of Muppet products. Kermit is the only regular Muppet character who appears on *Sesame Street* as

well. The *Sesame Street* puppets also include Cookie Monster, Big Bird, Bert and Ernie, and Grover. *The Muppet Show* has been called one of the first "truly global television programs" and at the peak of its popularity, in the late 1970s, was seen weekly by 250 million viewers in over one hundred countries (Owen 32). Jim Henson provided the voice of Kermit until his death in 1990, when he was replaced by Steve Whitmire.

2. Miss Piggy provokes one of their battles by telling the tabloids—falsely—that they are married. Unruly women, from Zsa Zsa Gabor to Roseanne Arnold, have a special relationship with the tabloids, which exploit the excesses of their public personae but also contribute to their identity as unruly women.

3. That framework is based on the notion of sexual inversion, which I will discuss in more detail later in this chapter. I substitute *gender inversion* for *sexual inversion*, to avoid any ambiguity that might arise from the latter's associations with homosexuality in psychoanalytic discourse. While the list that follows is my own, it is largely indebted to Davis, as is this entire study. Like Mary Russo's, her work has made immeasurable contributions to my own.

4. Bakhtin's work was suppressed in the Soviet Union for decades, in part because *Rabelais and His World*, a study of transgressive social practices in medieval and Renaissance Europe, was also a veiled critique of Stalinism. In the 1960s, *Rabelais and His World* was translated and became available in the West. Until fairly recently, it remained on the outskirts of Western Marxist discourse.

5. To say this is not, of course, to deny Bakhtin's general value to feminist scholarship, as Russo and Davis indicate. Julia Kristeva, whose work in linguistics and on abjection is clearly indebted to Bakhtin, has gone so far as to suggest that dialogism may well supplant binarism as the "basis for our time's intellectual structure" (*Desire in Language* 89). Dialogism also contains a theory of the subject that differs from Lacan's and is more consistent with feminist critiques of psychoanalysis by Nancy Chodorow and Jessica Benjamin. Feminist media scholars who have been influenced by Bakhtin include Patricia Mellencamp, Barbara Creed, and Virginia Wright Wexman.

6. To cite another instance: whereas Bakhtin uses the comic litany of phrases in praise of Gargantua's "mighty cod" (418) as an example of the exuberance of carnivalesque speech, the womb does not fare so well, and, to my knowledge, there is no comparable hymn to it, either in Rabelais or Bakhtin.

7. The following historical account of the unruly woman is largely indebted to Davis.

8. See Willeford for a more detailed account of the fool in general, and Mother Folly in particular (177). Mother Folly survives today in the modern circus clown mother, usually a transvestite man pushing a buggy full of identical babies.

9. See Grotjahn (45) on Sarah and, more generally, on the contrast between ancient Greek culture and the Judeo-Christian tradition regarding laughter. Unlike the Homeric tradition, the Bible provides scant evidence of laughter by either sex. The Judeo-Christian tradition's characteristic sobriety and seriousness may be due to its roots in law and the vulnerability of law to laughter.

10. Women have traditionally and misogynistically been associated with a love of talk. Despite sanctions on public speech by women, in the private sphere of women's culture talk has had deep and positive significance. See the etymology and history of the words *gossip* (Lippard 37) and *flibbertigibbet*. See also Rysman.

11. Other complications muddy these ambivalences. For example, the female mouth is castigated not only for "producing" too much (bodily fatness or speech) but for "consuming" too much, in the familiar identification of women with consumption. In addition, the fat woman is associated with a male fear of reincorporation into the maternal body. I will return to the social meanings of fatness in the next chapter.

12. Karyn Kay's "*Part-Time Work of a Domestic Slave . . .*" first alerted me to the connections between medieval drama, especially the Mrs. Noah figure, and the screwball comedy film. In medieval Europe, mystery plays were based loosely on Biblical stories, embellished with material that was often rollicking and bawdy. This theater was both sacred and profane, meant to instruct and entertain. Local citizens, as well as professional troupes of itinerant players, took part in the plays, adding their own jokes.

13. Medieval scholars have identified a variety of sources for the Mrs. Noah character. Some are from popular culture, where she is linked to Eve and tempted by the devil (Mill). Others are from literary culture: Latin satire, sermons, comic poems, and fabliaux where the tradition of misogyny was overwhelmingly prevalent (Woolf 138–139). One particularly vivid source is the account of women in Andreas Capellanus's widely read *Art of Courtly Love*.

14. Parker explains that this sisterhood includes three Greek female figures associated with delay and often confused or conflated: Circe, who turns Odysseus's men into swine by her spells; Penelope, who is courted by suitors described as "swinelike" (and puts off their proposals by her weaving); and Calypso, who delays Odysseus on his voyage home. In Greek culture, prostitutes were called "pig merchants," and "porcus" was

a nursery word used by nurses to describe the genitals of little girls (Stallybrass and White 45). In Italian culture, to call someone's mother a pig ("porca madonna") is an extreme insult.

15. The account of the pig that follows is largely drawn from Stallybrass and White, who also note how the persecution of the Jewish people is linked to their traditional association with the pig. For a materialist anthropological account of the pig, see Harris. For the pig's place in mythology, see Campbell.

16. As de Lauretis notes, in mythology "the limen, frontier between desert and city, threshold to the inner recesses of the cave or maze," is the realm of monsters who become metaphors for the symbolic boundary between nature and culture (*Alice Doesn't* 109).

17. This resemblence works to comical effect in Luis Buñuel's film *The Obscure Object of Desire* (1977). A woman on a busy city street carries what appears to be a baby wrapped in swaddling but is actually a pig. Modern circus acts also make use of the resemblence of human babies to little pigs (see Stallybrass and White 58). The pig acquired its present connotations in industrialized Western nations from the experiences of an earlier, rural culture which lived more closely with it.

18. Societies try to contain that power by ritually framing it. When they do so, the "abomination" can become the source of tremendous power because it mediates between two spheres. That is what happens in the sacrament of communion, which ritually frames an abomination—the consumption of human flesh—in order to redefine it as an act which mediates between the human and the divine. When accepted authorities perform such an act, they deepen the legitimate, external power that their cultures already endow them with. In the hands of the marginalized, on the other hand, such power is considered unconscious, uncontrolled, and dangerous.

19. The marginalization of all women is enforced by pollution taboos on the aspects of their bodies which Bakhtin most associates with the grotesque—menstruation, childbirth, lactation, those processes that confound the border between inside and out.

20. Critiquing what she calls the "banality" of much current work in cultural studies, Meaghan Morris discusses the potential naiveté of searching for "lost origins" and "ideal models." Charging that cultural studies has lost its critical edge and is over-optimistic about popular culture, she argues for a path somewhere between the "cheerleaders" and the "prophets of doom." That strikes me as a wise course to follow.

21. Such a usurpation of women's procreative powers by men has been described as "the Bachelor Machine" (see Russell; Penley). This usurpa-

tion is consistent with the bourgeois devaluing of the "lower" bodily stratum in favor of the upper; however, it vastly predates capitalist society. In Freud's view, civilization made an enormous stride with the replacement of matrilineage with patrilineage because determining a child's mother is a simple matter of visual perception, but establishing paternity depends on a "higher," more abstract form of knowledge. The replacement of the chthonic matriarchal goddesses, associated with the lower earth, with patriarchal gods associated with the sky represents a similar advance. Sky gods such as Jehovah could create life out of breath or the Word, or, like Zeus, out of their heads.

22. Bataille does little to counter cultural associations of women with sex, irrationality, and negativity. Like Freud, he allows women no place for desire or, in his terms, "sovereignty"—because they are already in the realm of "continuity." His work is peppered with misogynistic descriptions of women and signs of a revulsion at the body. His statement, "No one doubts the ugliness of the sexual act" (*Death and Sensuality* 145), too easily becomes: "For a man, there's nothing more depressing than an ugly woman, for then the ugliness of the organs and the sexual act cannot show up in contrast" (145).

23. Turner sees other forms of liminality evolving out of the historic shift from the communal to the individual and idiosyncratic. He calls these forms "liminoid." Exemplified by the theater of Brecht, Artaud, and Pinter, liminoid forms address a more fragmentary audience than liminal ones do and tend to subvert more than invert, often through "rational critique of the established order—from various structural perspectives" (54).

24. See, for example, Schechter's study of the Russian clown Vladimir Durov, who was arrested in 1907 for an act that exploited the semiotic status of the pig to satirize the kaiser and the German attraction to militarism.

25. Bourdieu's description of modern popular entertainment—formerly the circus and melodrama, today "messy" popular sports (wrestling as opposed to polo) and the "big feature film"—also recalls Bakhtin on the carnivalesque (34). For critiques of Fiske's work in particular and cultural studies in general, see Budd, Entman, and Steinman; O'Shea; and Morris.

2. Roseanne: The Unruly Woman
as Domestic Goddess

1. I interviewed Roseanne Arnold on June 20, 1991. Earlier in her career, Arnold was known as Roseanne Barr. She took the name of her husband, Tom Arnold, in 1991, when they renewed their wedding vows and

he converted to Judaism. These comments came in response to my question about whether she had had any new thoughts, almost a year later, about the national-anthem incident.

2. As Arnold herself noted, the reaction to her performance, not the performance itself, carried the more alarming message. As for Bush, she says, he "should have been paying attention to Kuwait" (quoted in Hirschberg 224).

3. Later that year, the incident appeared in an episode of the courtroom drama series, *L.A. Law*, where it was rewritten as a conflict between a sympathetically portrayed, heavy black male blues singer and a team owner, whose stuffiness was shown to be un-American.

4. In May 1991 ABC also canceled the Saturday-morning show *New Kids on the Block*, a favorite of girls, and Saturday morning TV became exclusively boy oriented. Network executives noted that only girls were watching *New Kids on the Block* and that while girls will watch shows with male heroes, boys won't watch shows with female heroes.

5. In July 1991, she beat four male competitors—Dan Quayle, Saddam Hussein, U.S. Senator Jesse Helms, and developer Donald Trump—to win the first annual "Sitting Duck" award given by the National Society of Newspaper Columnists ("People" 2A).

6. After being deluged with letters from her readers, Maynard later acknowledged that she had felt threatened by a woman who discarded so many of the super-woman expectations that she had placed on herself. Subsequently Maynard described the breakup of her own marriage and ended her column. Arnold has criticized the middle-class biases of popular U.S. feminism: "I feel bad when I read *Ms.* magazine and they have a whole article about, like Tracey Ullman and Carol Burnett and Bette Midler, and don't mention me—I mean, as a woman who did the first show about how women really live. And then I go, it's classism. It's even more insidious than any sort of sexism . . . Because I'm of a working-class background. I mean, I get every kind of ism that there is. And they're all ugly" (quoted in Hirschberg 231).

7. Marcia Millman writes that fat people arouse "horror, loathing, speculation, repugnance, and avoidance" (71). In the working class, fatness becomes a sign of a failure to achieve upward mobility. She also notes that some men hold a secret attraction to fat women.

8. Her sense of herself as an artist helps explain her attitude toward the reactions her work provokes: "Being an artist, it's not my responsibility, and I can't care about how I'm understood because it's up to everybody to understand me. In the end, the way that people understand or get me or see me says more about them than it does about me" (Arnold,

Interview). As for the literal authorship of her work, Arnold says the Domestic Goddess character is her creation, although her sister Geraldine claims some credit and has sued her over this issue. *Roseanne* is written largely by staff writers, whose work Arnold oversees. An example of her own writing on the show is the speech of encouragement and celebration Roseanne makes to Darlene about her first period.

9. See, for example, "Roseanne Goes Nuts!" in the *National Enquirer* (April 9, 1989) and "My Insane Year" in *People* (October 9, 1989). On the Oprah Winfrey show, she described how her madness muffled the voices of others and created a space of silence where she could listen only to her self. For more on this topic, see Barr, *Roseanne* 83.

10. Other studies confirm this scenario. As Mary Douglas suggests, people tend to direct jokes "downward," toward groups that are lower in social power (*Implicit Meanings* 95). Or, as lesbian comedian Kate Clinton writes, "Male penile humor—the ultimate in stand-up comedy—is based on the hierarchical power structure of the put-down" (quoted in Pershing 224). Studies of the socialization of women (McGhee) show that in mixed company, women look to men for permission to laugh. Girls learn early in their lives that their role is not to "make" jokes themselves, to be comic artists, but to smile or laugh at the jokes men make, often at women's expense. Joke making is considered unfeminine.

11. Mabley, who had spent most of her career on stage in the segregated circuits of the South, was discovered by white audiences when the changing racial climate of the 1960s allowed her to perform on nationally televised popular comedy and variety television shows. Like Tucker, she used the "mother" image in her routine to control her relationship with her audience (see Elsie Williams). And like Arnold, she traced her inspiration to her grandmother.

12. Lily Tomlin and Whoopi Goldberg, for example, are virtuoso performers who slip in and out of multiple roles, but both tend to retain a distinct "self" apart from the characters they play. Neither has launched a film career on the basis of a persona. Goldberg's film career has also been hampered by Hollywood's reluctance to cast a black woman in traditional romantic roles, as well as by the shortage of strong alternative roles for women. After her highly acclaimed performance in Steven Spielberg's *The Color Purple* (1985), she won an Oscar for her comic performance as a con-artist medium in *Ghost* (1990). She played her first role as a romantic lead in the 1993 film *Made in America*, opposite Ted Danson, after *Sarafina* and the hit *Sister Act* in 1992.

13. Bill Pentland, Arnold's husband at the time, plays her husband in the frame story; Tom Arnold, her friend (and future husband) plays the

fictional husband and fantasy lover; and two sets of actors play her real children.

14. She explains: "I was just making fun of the whole idea of celebrity. It's really ridiculous how people exploit it. It's just so funny to me, so I decided to become that. What if me, my regular character that everybody knows, now is a diva? Because that's what happens to people. Often they come from working-class families and backgrounds or from poor backgrounds and then they come out here and they make some money and all of a sudden, their lineage is of English royalty. It's all part of the aspiration to be rich and WASP" (Arnold, Interview). One might argue that Arnold does precisely this herself. While she spends her money ostentatiously, however, she makes no effort to conceal her class background in doing so.

15. Arnold says: "First you're domesticated like all women are. And then, once you step outside the house, you belong to the world. The Domestic Goddess is a huge star, so she belongs to the world. So it's still like a Goddess, but now it's an International Goddess rather than just a Domestic Goddess. Which I think pretty much patterns the last thirty years of the women's movement, too" (Arnold, Interview).

16. Interestingly, Whoopi Goldberg in *her* second HBO special also dropped the characters she played in her earlier specials (such as the philosopher-junkie Fontaine) for the direct address of a standup monologue. Filming the special in south central Los Angeles, she assumed an angrier voice and made more topical political and social commentary than in her earlier specials.

17. See Ellis for an analysis of differences between TV and cinema. Feminist critics interested in television's relation to everyday life within the home have produced much important work on TV. See, for example, Seiter; Modleski, *Loving With a Vengeance*; Ang; and Spigal and Mann.

18. See Joyrich on postmodernism, Lipsitz on the sitcom family, and Mann on early TV's parodies of Hollywood melodrama and romance. See also Mellencamp's *High Anxiety*. Mellencamp describes TV as part of a shift in subjectivity from the one represented by film (which centers on male desire, sex, and scopophilia) to another centering on female desire, money, and "epistemophilia," or the wish to know.

19. Barbara Ehrenreich first used the term "proletarian feminism" to describe Arnold's position (quoted in O'Connor).

20. Arnold adds that Matt Williams, the producer at the time, wanted to base the show on castration jokes and center it on the point of view of the little boy, DJ (Jerome 85–86). Elsewhere, Arnold describes an incident when male writers didn't understand a script written by a woman, Safford

Vela, in which 15-year-old Becky stops talking to her mother for two weeks. The male writers thought that the character would have to be on drugs or having trouble with a boyfriend to stop talking. They missed the fact that she stopped talking "because she's 15" (quoted in Klaus 100).

21. See Wexman for a Bakhtinian analysis of the carnivalesque fat man Jackie Gleason. Like Arnold, Gleason was snubbed by the Emmies; he did not receive an honorary award even after his death. And like *All in the Family*, *M*A*S*H* eventually tempers the clownishness of its main female character, turning Hot Lips into Margaret.

22. *Roseanne*'s attention to homosexuality has continued into its fifth and sixth seasons, with regular appearances by Sandra Bernhard as Nancy, a family friend who comes out as a lesbian.

23. The law is a common motif for patriarchy in feminist work (e.g., *A Question of Silence*) and provides a familiar site for female disruption in mainstream work (e.g., the 1953 film *Gentlemen Prefer Blondes*). Note also how Leona Helmsley, Zsa Zsa Gabor, Imelda Marcos, and Tammy Faye Bakker have all been recently involved in highly publicized trials.

24. As Phyllis Chesler might have testified, women's space in contemporary American culture is so freely violated that many women surrender their "privacy, life space, sanity and selves . . . in order not to commit violence" (quoted in Henley 39). Here, a "room of her own," to borrow from Virginia Woolf, becomes a bathroom.

3. Narrative, Comedy, and Melodrama

1. Genre bears a privileged place in materialist cultural criticism because it represents the intersection between the individual and the social. As Thomas Schatz has argued (in *Hollywood Genres* and "The Structural Influence"), audiences participate actively and collectively, although indirectly, in the production of film genres by choosing to patronize some films and not others. Genre study, however, can easily lapse into a formalist typology when it fails to retain its analysis of, in Fredric Jameson's words, a genre's social "conditions of possibility."

2. Some strains of cultural criticism, such as Jameson's, envision the practice of theory itself as a tragic quest for a failed community. For recent examples of scholarly work on tragedy, see Kintz, *The Subject's Tragedy*; Zeitlin; and Winkler.

3. See Gledhill's anthology *Home Is Where the Heart Is* for an excellent selection of studies on melodrama. Melodrama's formal antecedents, along with a critical tendency to disparage plays that don't follow the

rules of tragedy, can be traced as far back as Greek drama, when Aristophanes mocked the tragedies of Euripides, which share many qualities of melodrama.

4. When sexual love plays an important part in a tragedy, it is often subsumed into the hero's quest for the "extraordinary" limits of experience, which in turn masks the supreme egotism of the death wish. In the context of sexual love, that quest becomes the *Liebestod* of Tristan and Isolde (Cook 479). The more a tragedy emphasizes sexual love, the more likely it is to be critically disparaged as melodrama. Thus, among Shakespeare's tragedies, *Romeo and Juliet*, *Antony and Cleopatra*, and *Othello* are often considered the least "tragic."

5. The most important of those exceptions is Carl Dreyer's film *The Passion of Joan of Arc* (1928). I am grateful to Robin Blaetz for introducing me to the concept of "explanation by emplotment" and providing me with the example of Joan of Arc.

6. Olympia Dukakis was nominated for her performance as Rose in *Moonstruck*. I discuss *It Happened One Night* in Chapter 4, *Born Yesterday* in Chapter 6, and *Moonstruck* in Chapter 7. Mary Pickford won an Oscar for her performance in *Coquette* (1929); Diane Keaton for *Annie Hall* (1977); Julie Andrews for the musical *Mary Poppins* (1964); and Jessica Tandy for *Driving Miss Daisy* (1989).

7. Stanley Solomon's *Beyond Formula: American Film Genres* includes the musical but not comedy among the six genres it studies. Stuart Kaminsky, in *American Film Genres*, does include a chapter on comedy, but after two pages on the "man versus woman" type, he devotes the rest of the chapter to comedies in what he describes as "the mode of the individual." When Ryan and Kellner argue that the Left should abandon its "dour" and "purist" approach for a more serious engagement in popular forms, they also betray a subtle uneasiness about comedy: "Effective work has to be undertaken in other cinematic arenas like fantasy, melodrama and even comedy" (286). See Woodward (71–72) for a similar argument about the lack of critical attention to film comedy.

8. Andrew Horton describes this kind of comedy as "pre-Oedipal," which he distinguishes from "Oedipal" comedy, a kind of comedy that, like romantic comedy, moves toward accommodation (10–12). Dana Polan notes a similar tension in screwball comedy, which, he writes, "would seem an eminently dialectical genre" because it combines one notion of comedy as "aspiration" with another of comedy as "materialization" ("The Light Side of Genius" 136).

9. In film, this kind of comedy is variously called structural comedy (Mast), situation comedy (Seidman), Oedipal comedy (Horton), man ver-

sus woman comedy, couples comedy, crazy comedy (Wollen), screwball comedy, or romantic comedy. I prefer romantic comedy because the genre, especially in its cinematic forms, is deeply dependent on the thematics of romantic love. I will have more to say about this category later, in this chapter and in those following.

10. This canon also includes, among others, Mack Sennett, Fatty Arbuckle, Harold Lloyd, Harry Langdon, Laurel and Hardy, the Three Stooges, the Marx Brothers, W. C. Fields, Jerry Lewis and Dean Martin, Bob Hope and Bing Crosby, Peter Sellers, Dudley Moore, Mel Brooks, Monty Python, Cheech and Chong, Woody Allen, Robin Williams, Dan Aykroyd, the Belushi brothers, Chevy Chase, Steve Martin, Eddie Murphy, and Danny DeVito.

11. Most studies of comedian comedy, such as Seidman's, note the hero's "sexual confusion" but give scant attention to larger issues of gender. Krutnik acknowledges the misogyny and latent homosexuality in the male comedy team, but does not develop his suggestive remark that the "sexual specificity" of comedian comedy is "most blatantly indicated by the veritable absence of *female* comedians" ("The Clown-Prints of Comedy" 57). Work is only now being done to recover women's contributions to film comedy, especially during the silent and early sound period (e.g., those of Mabel Normand, Marie Dressler, ZaSu Pitts, Thelma Todd, Patsy Kelly, and others). For an example of such scholarship, see Henry Jenkins's *What Made Pistachio Nuts?*

12. Those romantic subplots, of course, exist in nearly all mainstream Hollywood films. Bordwell, Staiger, and Thompson found that romance figured in at least one story line in ninety-five out of the one hundred films they surveyed in their study of classical Hollywood cinema (16).

13. In U.S. popular culture, the glorification of youth usually affirms the freedom of the male youth (e.g., Huck Finn and Tom Sawyer) from the domestic confines imposed by home and mother, who becomes a repressive guardian of morality, whether in comedy (W. C. Fields) or melodrama (D. W. Griffith's hostility to the "Uplifters" in *Intolerance* [1916]).

14. Frye writes: "Comedy ranges from the most savage irony to the most dreamy wish-fulfillment romance, but its structural patterns and characterizations are much the same throughout the range" (*Anatomy* 177). Comedy has been "remarkably tenacious in its structural principles and character types" (163)—the braggart soldier of Aristophanes and Menander resurfacing in Chaplin's Great Dictator, for example. "The audiences of vaudeville, comic strips and television programs still laugh at the same jokes that were declared to be outworn at the opening of *The Frogs*" (163).

15. While the essential structure of the New Comedy plot that underlies

most romantic comedies has endured since the days of early Greek and Roman drama, various ideologies, including Christianity and Courtly Love, have been layered onto it in succeeding centuries and altered the meaning of the couple's union. In the twentieth century, with the increased idealization and fusion of marriage and romantic love, the union of the couple has come to signify the satisfaction of all personal desire. I argue here not for a reconsideration of the institution of romantic love but for a look at other tensions and possibilities that coexist with it in its narrative representations.

16. The stronger the presence of women in a romantic comedy, the more a film is likely to problematize the heterosexual couple. This will become clearer in Chapter 7, when I discuss *Moonstruck*, but it is also suggested by the "working girl" comedies of the early 1930s. These films suggest that when a woman marries, she gives up a female-centered world of community and support provided by roommates, sisters, and girlfriends.

17. Much of my thinking about mothers in melodrama and romantic comedy is derived from Naomi Scheman's "Missing Mothers/Desiring Daughters," a response to Stanley Cavell's analysis of melodrama and what he calls the "comedies of remarriage." I am grateful to Leland Poague for directing me to this article.

4. Romantic Comedy and the Unruly Virgin in Classical Hollywood Cinema

1. Grant began his career with a series of successful appearances opposite other flamboyant women: Thelma Todd in *This is the Night* (1932); Tallulah Bankhead in *The Devil and the Deep* (1932); and Marlene Dietrich in *Blonde Venus* (1933). The Motion Picture Production Code, written in 1930, grew out the Hays Office, which was founded in the 1920s to encourage self-regulation in the film industry. The Code went into strict effect in 1934, under the Production Code Administration headed by Joseph Breen. The Legion of Decency was also established that year.

2. It is commonly agreed that Hollywood produced its most outstanding sound comedies during the 1930s and 1940s. Beyond that, there is less certainty over just how to categorize and understand this group of films, most of them loosely sharing a comic plot about the difficulties in bringing a couple together. "Screwball" identifies these films in terms of "crazy" characters, especially "zany" women. Stanley Cavell (in *Pursuits of Happiness*) finds them most clearly defined by the couple's progess from initial loss to rediscovery, a pattern exemplified by what he calls the "comedy of remarriage." For Thomas Schatz (in *Hollywood Genres*), they are most

noteworthy for their negotiation of class issues. For my purposes, as I explained in the preceding chapter, Frye's structural notion of comedy is most helpful. I use "romantic comedy" to describe a film that centers thematically on romantic love (or the relation between the sexes) and is loosely structured by the plot of New Comedy.

3. The term *chastisement* is Andrew Britton's, and it effectively describes the experience of the male hero in romantic comedies structured by gender inversion. Wes Gehring's definition of screwball comedy asserts that the male hero is a "frustrated" anti-hero who suffers at the hands of the female heroine. His view of the importance of gender inversion in this genre thus comes close to my own.

4. Studlar criticizes Laura Mulvey for overlooking in her early work the pre-Oedipal, masochistic desire to give oneself over to the power of the female/mother figure and for emphasizing, exclusively, the sadistic drive of scopophilia to strengthen the political power of her argument—its extension to relations of power under patriarchy. Studlar's analysis is primarily based on Dietrich but also draws on West.

5. See "The Leg Business" 44, and *Horrible Prettiness*. Allen links burlesque with such traditions of carnival as the Feast of Fools. He argues that burlesque's play with gender helped refigure femininity outside a sentimentalized notion of the bourgeois family and that, in fact, its transgressive gender inversions extended to class. Unlike vaudeville, which was aligned with a middle-class family audience, burlesque offered both a comic inversion of the bourgeois world and a vulgar "other" against which the bourgeoisie defined itself.

6. Quoted in Seidman (71). However, West's persona obviously meant other things as well to audiences at the time. For example, her reassuring speech to the fallen woman takes on special significance at a time when unemployment was increasing the ranks of prostitution. See Curry.

7. See Studlar; Kaplan (49–59); and also Johnston ("Women's Cinema as Counter-Cinema"), who is sympathetic toward stylized rather than "realistic" representations of femininity in cinema but also suspicious of the image of the fetishized woman, such as West.

8. It is worth remembering here that most narrative endings are problematic from a feminist point of view, and that a feminist criticism that is unwilling to bracket the conventional ending, at least temporarily, in order to consider what precedes it will be a discouraging project.

9. Capra is closely identified with the screwball comedy in part because of *It Happened One Night* but also because of a series of other films he directed during the 1930s and early 1940s, including *Mr. Deeds Goes to Town* (1936), *Mr. Smith Goes to Washington* (1939), and *Meet John Doe* (1941).

These films diverge from the romantic comedies of sexual inversion primarily in their shift of interest from the couple to social issues centering on the male hero.

10. See Shumway, who disputes Stanley Cavell's argument that these films enlighten us about marriage and connects Cavell's failure to address the cultural work of the films with his neglect of feminism.

11. Bordwell, Staiger, and Thompson (108–112, 325–326). While this consolidation was a decade-long process, it was fairly pronounced by the early 1930s at the major studios and on "high-end" star-genre formulations, such as the films discussed here. Haskell argues that the "equality" of the couple was well suited to classical style and editing, the use of symmetrical two-shot compositions, and the contributions of women scriptwriters; and that by defining the couple in terms of mutuality and equality, this genre provided a space for women with heightened aspirations toward social equality to meet men as equals, if only on the terrain of romance (9, 194).

12. According to Naomi Scheman, this absence undermines the feminist potential of these films, and she argues on this basis against Cavell's claims for them.

13. As Brian Henderson argues, romantic comedy's deferral of sexual consummation depends on a belief that the self can be most fully realized through a "sexual dialectic," an engagement with a sexual "other," and therefore requires that sexual consummation be deferred while that relationship is established.

14. British feminism has taken up at length the issue of gender as the paradigmatic barrier (male/female) or difference. See Coward. In such films as *Broadcast News* (1987), *Green Card* (1990), and *Pretty Woman* (1990), a woman's virginity is not important, but the sense of what her proper relation to a man should be remains remarkably unchanged.

15. Cavell begins to approach the issues a feminist analysis of romantic comedy might raise when he suggests in "Psychoanalysis and Cinema" and "Ugly Duckling" that the repressions of romantic comedy surface in melodrama. But his analysis of melodrama is similarly limited by his failure to situate his own work in relation to feminism and film theory. (See, especially, "Ugly Duckling" 217–218.) This failure is even more serious, given the extensive engagement of feminist film theory with melodrama. See Cavell's response to Tania Modleski in "Postcript."

16. Huston argues that because masculine power is often the power to take life, as in the hunt or war, it is antithetical to the mother's power to give life. The virgin is allowed to enter a holy realm apart from or beyond

nature because she has not yet become visibly subject, like the mother, to the laws of nature in the cycles of pregnancy, childbirth, and lactation. Once the hymen has been pierced, once the virgin has succumbed to this first wound, all other wounds become possible. The deflowered female body is "irremediably permeable, irreversibly vulnerable" (129).

17. This label became attached to her in 1937–1938, after *A Woman Rebels* (1936) flopped, but it stuck even after the critical and popular successes of *Bringing Up Baby* and *Holiday*, both in 1938. Hepburn's earlier roles included Mary in *Mary of Scotland* (1936), an aviatrix in *Christopher Strong* (1933), and a tomboy faith healer in *Spitfire* (1934). See Bell-Metereau (especially pp. 109–115) for more on male impersonation.

18. In her essay "It's Different for Girls," Williamson (*Consuming Passions*) analyzes an ad depicting a woman in a bathing suit water-skiing. The woman, actually a man who has had a sex-change operation, retains the long, lean lines of his masculine frame. "The 'silliest,' least valued shape for either men *or* women is 'womanly,'" she writes (50). From this perspective, anorexia is an "unfunny parody" of the cult of the boyish figure. I would argue, following Williamson, that this context gives a disturbing cast to the current fashion of muscular, trained women's bodies, such as Madonna's, Sigourney Weaver's in *Alien* (1979) and *Aliens* (1986), and Linda Hamilton's in *Terminator 2* (1991).

19. Kuhn argues that the drive to fix gender is an effort to fix subjectivity; to be ungendered is to be inhuman. Cross-dressing helps denaturalize sexual difference, but often it simply reaffirms sexual difference. Its uses in comedy, she argues, tend to be limited; because the spectator is let in on the secret, he or she is not "challenged." It is often more effective in the thriller.

20. See Willeford on the tradition of the fool, a figure he describes as hermaphroditic and mother-bound. He writes: "From his position on the fringes of the social world and of the human image, the fool mocks the conventional relations of man to woman and keeps visibly alive the sexual morass from which the form of marriage emerges or upon which it is imposed" (175). From a psychoanalytic perspective, Sylvia's ease in masquerading as a boy might be explained by the "lack of conviction" women have upon entering heterosexuality without the threat of castration, and their reluctance to surrender their connection with the mother.

21. *Wisecracks*, Gail Singer's 1992 documentary on female comedians, includes a performance by The Clichettes, who in effect do just that, and to hilarious effect. The Clichettes lip-sync standard ballads of machismo and male angst and parody male body language wearing a variety of male

costumes and body suits. In one number, they strip down to their boxer shorts, revealing large patches of chest hair stuck on their breasts. Kalli Paakspuu and Daria Stermac also use this group's work in their film *I Need a Man Like You . . . To Make My Dreams Come True.*

5. Professor-Heroes and Brides on Top

1. My debt to Andrew Britton in this reading of *Bringing Up Baby* will be evident to anyone who knows his article "Cary Grant: Comedy and Male Desire." Also see Cohan.

2. Some other films with professor-heroes are *Vivacious Lady* (1938); *Good Girls Go to Paris* (1939); *The Doctor Takes a Wife* (1940); *The Feminine Touch* (1941); *The Major and the Minor* (1942); and *The Talk of the Town* (1942). After *Bringing Up Baby* (1938) and *Ball of Fire* (1941), Hawks returns to the character type in *Monkey Business* (1952). Jerry Lewis uses it as the basis for *The Nutty Professor* (1963).

3. According to John Boswell, the term *gay* was associated with sexual license long before its current usage in reference to homosexuality. Earlier in this century, he writes, "it was common in the English homosexual subculture as a sort of password or code. . . . Its first public use in the United States outside of pornographic fiction appears to have been in the 1939 [*sic*] movie *Bringing Up Baby*" (43n). Grant's British origins and the sexual fluidity of his star image would seem to bear out Boswell's assertion about the double entendre in the film.

4. In addition to *Bringing Up Baby* and *Ball of Fire*, Hawks's other comedies include *Twentieth Century* (1934), *His Girl Friday* (1941), *I Was a Male War Bride* (1949), and *Monkey Business* (1952). In Chapter 6 I discuss his 1953 film *Gentlemen Prefer Blondes*.

5. Freud describes the uncanny as "that class of the terrifying which leads back to something long known to us, once very familiar" ("The Uncanny" 218–219). It is "nothing new or foreign, but something familiar and old-established in the mind that has been estranged only by the process of repression" (243). Inevitably that something is castration, the mother's wounded body.

6. Kris notes that the intimate relation between fear and laughter can be seen in the changing effects gargoyles produced, from terror to laughter and finally to amusement. It can also be seen in the etymology of the French word *drôle*, which meant *dread* before its current meaning of *comic*.

7. Nancy Huston makes this point when she discusses the rites prohibiting mothers (marked with the female power to create life) from hunting or otherwise engaging in the power to take life away (designated as male).

8. In *His Girl Friday* (1940), Hawks recaptures much of the tone of *Bringing Up Baby* but goes even farther than he does in *Ball of Fire* to restore the power of the male hero. That can be explained in part by his use of the masculine newspaper setting rather than the feminized enclave of professors in *Ball of Fire*. In his later films, *I Was a Male War Bride* (1949) and *Gentlemen Prefer Blondes* (1953), he returns to scenarios of gender inversion similar to that of *Bringing Up Baby*. *I Was a Male War Bride* poses the greatest test for Grant in retaining his masculine appeal, as Hawks loses the sense of romance that *Bringing Up Baby* and the earlier comedies of inversion preserve. *Monkey Business* (1952), in which Grant plays an absent-minded scientist, replays the theme of gender inversion but with a 1950s spin that includes the introduction of a dumb blonde.

9. See Krutnik, especially 70–71, n4. For an analysis of the social and cinematic history of 1940s, see also Polan, *Power and Paranoia*.

10. Noah berates his sons for looking at him when he slept naked, but tradition holds that the sons castrated him. Freud says the "evil eye" reflects a fear that something fragile we possess is the object of another person's envy. That envy "betrays itself in a look even though it is not put into words" ("The Uncanny" 242).

6. Dumb Blondes

1. For an excellent social history of the period, see May. See also French for the impact of these changes on film.

2. Other, less outrageously sexual stars of the decade were marked by a cool blondness, a "plastic vapidity, a sameness, a blandness," in Marjorie Rosen's words (315).

3. It is likely that new readings of Doris Day's star persona may emerge when her work is reexamined from the perspective of gay and lesbian film theory. She was reputed to be a lesbian or bisexual, and *Calamity Jane* (1953), for example, lends itself to lesbian readings. My thanks to Lesli Larson, and to Meryem Ersoz, for this insight and for introducing me to this film.

4. My reading of Monroe's star image is largely indebted to Dyer's *Heavenly Bodies*.

5. For a critical feminist reading, see Turim. For a positive feminist reading, see Arbuthnot and Seneca. Robin Wood includes the film as one of the director's "failures and marginal works" in the appendix to his book on Hawks (*Howard Hawks* 170–172). (He also describes the "brittle, petty humour" of Anita Loos's 1925 book as "incompatible with Hawks' robust and generous comic sense" [171].)

6. See MacKinnon for an argument about how patriarchy eroticizes women's submission. This argument is the basis of her more controversial case against pornography.

7. Films centered on such a couple are rare, and they are more often shaped into melodrama than comedy, because of the dominant assumption that women who are not identified by their relationship with a man can only be unhappy. See, for example, Bergman's *Persona* (1966). The handful of mainstream lesbian films in the 1980s shows the beginning of a change (*Personal Best* [1982], *Desert Hearts* [1985]). Yet the controversial ending of *Thelma and Louise* (1991) shows the enormous pressure to emplot in melodrama the stories of strong women strongly identified with women.

8. The film's treatment of homosexuality has been read with varying degrees of sympathy. See Tyler (*Screening the Sexes*); Vito Russo; and Bell-Metereau.

7. Masculinity and Melodrama in Postclassical Romantic Comedy

1. *Semi-Tough* (1977) raised similar questions about romantic comedy for Brian Henderson in the late 1970s. For a similar argument to mine, see Krutnik's "The Faint Aroma of Performing Seals," which also provides an overview of the history of romantic comedy. See also Neale and Krutnik; Lapsley and Westlake; and especially Neale, who distinguishes between the nervous romance and what he identifies as the "new romance," which, he argues, is marked by a nostalgia for romantic love.

2. The affair echoed the May–December romances Allen has examined in such films as *Manhattan* and *Husbands and Wives* (1993). Allen's presentation of himself as the victim of a jealous, spurned woman calls to mind the Senate hearings in 1991 about Clarence Thomas's appointment to the Supreme Court. Thomas similarly cast himself in the mode of melodrama when Anita Hill charged him with sexual harassment. He defended himself indignantly, accused her of causing him to suffer unjustly, and his supporters tried to discredit her by painting her as a woman who would stop at nothing to punish an innocent man who had rejected her.

3. Citing the witchcraft trials of the seventeenth century, Schiesari argues that "sensitive manhood" has increased as a popular style of masculinity during periods defined by "the brutal suppression of any or all forms of femininity understood as excessive or threatening" (21).

4. It is important that the myth invoked is that of Cinderella, not Pygmalion, which forms the basis of the musical *My Fair Lady* (1964). In

contrast to *Pretty Woman*, *My Fair Lady* details the laborious and painful efforts required to conceal the signs of the romantic heroine's working-class background. Even in *Born Yesterday*, Billie must work hard to pass herself off as middle class.

5. *L.A. Story* (1991) uses a magic freeway sign. In *Sleepless in Seattle* (1993), characters find echoes of the movie *An Affair to Remember* (1957) in their own lives and interpret them as "signs." The film also makes heavy use of love ballads from the past. Neale has noted that recent romantic comedies often use "signs and values of 'old-fashioned romance'" to create a sense of the possibility of romance today (295–296).

6. Sally Potter's film *Thriller* (1979) retells the story of *La Bohème* from the point of view of Mimi, who asks why her death is necessary for the hero to achieve his heroism.

7. Some examples include *Hairpiece* (1985) by Chenzira; *Possibly in Michigan* (1983) by Condit; *See Dick Run* (1987) by Alter; Joan Braderman's *Joan Does Dynasty* (1986); *I Need a Man Like You . . . to Make My Dreams Come True* (1986) by Kalli Paakspuu and Daria Stermac; and *We're Talking Vulva* (1990) by Shawna Dempsey and Tracy Traeger.

8. *Moonstruck* is not unique in playing comedy against melodrama or in giving comedy the last word (a pattern that can be found in Shakespeare's *As You Like It* and *Much Ado About Nothing*). Indeed, many more explicitly feminist texts invite us to look at melodrama through the lens of comedy. Jacques Rivette's *Celine and Julie Go Boating* (1974), Joan Braderman's videotape *Joan Does Dynasty* (1986), and Allison Anders's *Gas Food Lodging* (1992), for example, use comedy to denaturalize not only melodrama but the "romance" in romantic comedy. Unlike *Moonstruck*, which remains faithful to the ideology of heterosexuality that defines both romantic comedy and melodrama, these works, and others like them, posit to varying degrees other forms of family and community where passion, play, and love can thrive, especially among women.

Afterword: Shape-Shifting

1. In making this announcement, she joined former Miss America Marilyn Van Derbur Atler, Oprah Winfrey, and LaToya Jackson, all of whom had recently made public their own experiences of childhood abuse. She explained that she had repressed these memories until two years earlier, when they were brought to her consciousness by her husband's therapy.

2. Barr, *Roseanne* 163. Arnold does not give any further details about

what her sisters were fleeing. She goes on to write that they joined her in Denver, where "we began to tell the truth to each other. We began to heal. We began to come out of denial." As I mentioned earlier, the book, like all autobiographies, is best understood as partial. Likewise, it is not the truth of the charges against her family I wish to examine or the psychological processes of repression and denial, but the ongoing evolution of her persona and the effect such revelations have had on it.

3. "I tortured my body, smoking five packs a day and indulging in drug, alcohol and food abuse that had me weighing either 100 lbs. or 200 lbs.," she said in "I Am an Incest Survivor."

4. Arnold's identity as a Jew has been an important part of her persona in all contexts except her most visible one, her sitcom. One might also note Cher's plastic surgery to alter her more "exotic" looks.

5. This discourse has produced the new phenomenon of "scalpel slaves," a pejorative term plastic surgeons use for women who seek repeated cosmetic surgeries. This phenomenon is, of course, class based, and repeated cosmetic surgery is available only to those women with the means to pay for it. See Balsamo. Other women describe silicone implants as necessary to succeed in modeling careers.

6. Such a judgment also replicates white feminism's gaps in theorizing the bourgeois family—gaps the new religious right has only too readily moved in to fill. See Kintz's "Sacred Representations."

7. The term is Forest Pyle's, who discusses the relation between spectacle and cinema in "One Bad Movie Too Many."

8. Arnold's experience of incest may help explain her wariness about a style of female performance she identifies with Madonna, her contemporary rival in unruliness. Madonna has been widely praised for treating religion, race, and sexuality in ways that are not only clever but "sex- and fantasy-positive." However, Arnold argues that Madonna's play with our culture's images of femininity comes dangerously close to perpetuating their most destructive aspects, especially by eroticizing victimization. Madonna's appropriation of Marilyn Monroe's image does not succeed in rewriting that image into one that is more empowering for women, she says. Men simply like her too much: "It's so 'Daddy's girl' shit. It's so rape victim and molestation victim, just all victim. . . . They always give her kudos because she has a brain, in the end. They think she has a brain because she's making a lot of money" (Arnold, Interview).

9. With thanks to Peggy Zeglin Brand for directing me to Rose's article. Fay Weldon's novel *The Life and Loves of a She-Devil* takes the theme of cosmetic surgery to grotesque limits. The book was made into a mini-

series for British television and a film (*She-Devil* [1989]) directed by Susan Seidelman and starring Roseanne Arnold and Meryl Streep.

10. The term is Regina Barreca's, a literary critic who argues wide-rangingly for the subversive power of women's laughter (in "Bringing Down the House"). For a study of women's humor in American culture, see Walker.

orks Cited

Allen, Robert C. *Horrible Prettiness: Burlesque and American Culture.* Chapel Hill: University of North Carolina Press, 1991.

———. "The Leg Business: Transgression and Containment in American Burlesque." *Camera Obscura* 23 (1990): 43–70.

Altman, Rick. *The American Film Musical.* Bloomington: Indiana University Press, 1987.

Andelin, Helen. *Fascinating Womanhood.* Santa Barbara, Calif.: Pacific Press, 1965.

Ang, Ien. *Watching Dallas: Soap Opera and the Melodramatic Imagination.* Translated by Della Couling. New York: Methuen, 1985.

Arbuthnot, Lucie, and Gail Seneca. "Pre-text and Text in *Gentlemen Prefer Blondes.*" In *Film Reader* 5, pp. 13–23. Evanston, Ill.: Northwestern University Press, 1982.

Armstrong, Nancy. "The Critic and Whore of Culture: Theory in Postmodern Culture." Unpublished essay, 1989.

Arnold, Roseanne. Interview with Kathleen Rowe. June 20, 1991.

———. See also Barr, Roseanne.

Bakhtin, Mikhail. *The Dialogic Imagination*. Edited by Michael Holquist. Translated by Caryl Emerson and Michael Holquist. Austin: University of Texas Press, 1981.

———. *Rabelais and His World*. Translated by Helene Iswolsky. Bloomington: Indiana University Press, 1984.

Balsamo, Anne. "On the Cutting Edge: Cosmetic Surgery and the Technological Production of the Gendered Body." *Camera Obscura* 28 (1992): 207–238.

Bamber, Linda. *Comic Women, Tragic Men: A Study of Gender and Genre in Shakespeare*. Stanford, Calif.: Stanford University Press, 1982.

Barber, C. L. *Shakespeare's Festive Comedy: A Study of Dramatic Form and Its Relation to Social Custom*. Princeton, N.J.: Princeton University Press, 1959.

Barr, Roseanne. "I Am an Incest Survivor: A Star Cries Incest." *People* October 7, 1991: 84–88.

———. *Roseanne: My Life as a Woman*. New York: Harper and Row, 1989.

———. See also Arnold, Roseanne.

———. "What Am I, a Zoo?" *New York Times* (national ed.), July 31, 1989: I15.

Barreca, Regina. "Bringing Down the House." *Ms.* March/April 1992: 767–777.

———, ed. *Last Laughs: Perspectives on Women and Comedy*. New York: Gordon and Breach, 1988.

Bataille, Georges. *Death and Sensuality: A Study in Eroticism and Taboo*. Translated by Mary Dalwood. New York: Walker Press, 1962.

———. *Literature and Evil*. Translated by Alastair Hamilton. New York: Marion Boyars, 1985.

Baudrillard, Jean. "The Ecstasy of Communication." Translated by John Johnston. In *The Anti-Aesthetic: Essays on Postmodern Culture*, edited by Hal Foster, pp. 126–134. Port Townsend, Wash.: Bay Press, 1983.

Bell-Metereau, Rebecca. *Hollywood Androgyny*. New York: Columbia University Press, 1985.

Benjamin, Jessica. "A Desire of One's Own: Psychoanalytic Feminism and Intersubjective Space." In *Feminist Studies, Critical Studies*, edited by Teresa de Lauretis, pp. 78–101. Bloomington: Indiana University Press, 1986.

Berger, John. *Ways of Seeing*. New York: British Broadcasting Corporation and Penguin Books, 1972.

Bergson, Henri. "Laughter." In *Comedy*, edited by Wylie Sypher, pp. 61–190. Baltimore: The Johns Hopkins University Press, 1956.

Bergstrom, Janet, and Mary Ann Doane. "The Female Spectator: Contexts and Directions." In "The Spectatrix," edited by Janet Bergstrom and Mary Ann Doane. Special issue of *Camera Obscura* 20–21 (1989): 5–27.

Bernardoni, James. *George Cukor: A Critical Study and Filmography*. Jefferson, North Carolina: McFarland, 1985.

Bevington, David, ed. *Medieval Drama*. Boston: Houghton Mifflin, 1975.

Blaetz, Robin. "Explanation by Emplotment: Joan of Arc and the Romance." Paper presented at the Society for Cinema Studies Conference, Washington, D.C., 1990.

Bobo, Jacqueline, and Ellen Seiter. "Black Feminism and Media Criticism: *The Women of Brewster Place*." *Screen* 32 (1991): 286–302.

Bordwell, David, Janet Staiger, and Kristin Thompson. *The Classical Hollywood Cinema*. New York: Columbia University Press, 1985.

Boswell, John. *Christianity, Social Tolerance, and Homosexuality*. Chicago: University of Chicago Press, 1981.

Bourdieu, Pierre. *Distinction: A Social Critique of the Judgement of Taste*. Translated by Richard Nice. Cambridge, Mass.: Harvard University Press, 1984.

Britton, Andrew. "Cary Grant: Comedy and Male Desire." *CineAction!* 3–4 (1986): 37–51.

Budd, Mike, Robert M. Entman, and Clay Steinman. "The Affirmative Character of US Cultural Studies." *Critical Studies in Mass Communication* 7 (1990): 169–184.

Butler, Jeremy G. "Redesigning Discourse: Feminism, The Sitcom, and Designing Women." *Journal of Film and Video* 45.1 (1993): 13–26.

Butler, Judith. *Gender Trouble: Feminism and the Subversion of Identity*. New York: Routledge, 1990.

Campbell, Joseph. *The Mythic Image*. Princeton, N.J.: Princeton University Press, 1974.

Capellanus, Andreas. *The Art of Courtly Love*. Translated by John J. Parry. Edited by Frederick W. Locke. New York: Frederick Ungar, 1957.

Carpenter, Lynette. "Guilty Pleasures." *Ms.* May/June 1991. 74–76.

Cavell, Stanley. "Postscript (1989): To Whom It May Concern." *Critical Inquiry* 16 (1989–1990): 248–289.

———. "Psychoanalysis and Cinema: The Melodrama of the Unknown Woman." In *Images in Our Souls: Cavell, Psychoanalysis and Cinema*, edited by Joseph H. Smith and William Kerrigan. Baltimore: Johns Hopkins University Press, 1987. 11–43.

———. *Pursuits of Happiness: The Hollywood Comedy of Remarriage*. Cambridge, Mass.: Harvard University Press, 1981.

———. "Ugly Duckling, Funny Butterfly: Bette Davis and *Now Voyager*." *Critical Inquiry* 16 (1989–1990): 213–247.

Chodorow, Nancy. *The Reproduction of Mothering: Psychoanalysis and the Sociology of Gender*. Berkeley: University of California Press, 1978.

Cixous, Hélène. "The Laugh of the Medusa." Translated by Keith Cohen and Paula Cohen. In *New French Feminisms*, edited by Elaine Marks and Isabelle de Courtivron, pp. 245–264. Brighton: Harvester, 1980. Originally published as "Le Rire de la Méduse." *L'Arc* 61 (1975): 39–54.

Cohan, Steven. "Cary Grant in the Fifties: Indiscretions of the Bachelor's Masquerade." *Screen* 33.4 (1992): 394–413.

Cole, Lewis. "Roseanne." *The Nation* June 21, 1993. 878–880.

Collins, Patricia Hill. "Learning from the Outsider Within." *Social Problems* 33 (1986): 514–532.

————. "The Social Construction of Black Feminist Thought." *Signs* 14 (1989): 745–773.

Cook, Albert. "The Nature of Comedy and Tragedy." In *Theories of Comedy*, edited by Paul Lauter, pp. 475–496. New York, Doubleday, 1964.

Coward, Rosalind, ed. *Female Desire: Women's Sexuality Today.* London: Paladin, 1984.

Creed, Barbara. "From Here to Modernity: Feminism and Postmodernism." *Screen* 28.1 (1987): 47–67.

Curry, Ramona. "Mae West as Censored Commodity: The Case of *Klondike Annie*." *Cinema Journal* 31.1 (1991): 57–84.

————. "Power and Allure: The Mediation of Sexual Difference in the Star Image of Mae West." Dissertation, Northwestern University, 1990.

Darnton, Nina. "Surviving Incest: Can Memories be Trusted?" and "The Pain of the Last Taboo." *Newsweek* October 7, 1991: 70–72.

Davis, Natalie Zemon. *Society and Culture in Early Modern France.* Stanford, Calif.: Stanford University Press, 1975.

Desjardins, Mary. "Lucy and Ricky and Fred and Ethel 'Crossing Wavelengths.'" Paper presented at the Console-ing Passions Conference, 1993.

de Lauretis, Teresa. *Alice Doesn't: Feminism, Semiotics, Cinema.* Bloomington: Indiana University Press, 1984.

————. *Technologies of Gender: Essays on Theory, Film and Fiction.* Bloomington: Indiana University Press, 1987.

Doane, Mary Ann. *The Desire to Desire: The Woman's Film of the 1940s.* Bloomington: Indiana University Press, 1987.

————. "Film and Masquerade: Theorising the Female Spectator." *Screen* 23.3–4 (1982): 74–88.

————. "Masquerade Reconsidered: Further Thoughts on the Female Spectator." *Discourse* 11.1. (1988–1989): 42–54.

Doty, Alexander. "The Cabinet of Lucy Ricardo: Lucille Ball's Star Image." *Cinema Journal* 29.4 (1990): 3–22.

Douglas, Mary. *Implicit Meanings: Essays in Anthropology.* Boston: Routledge & Kegan Paul, 1975.

————. *Purity and Danger: An Analysis of the Concepts of Pollution and Taboo.* 1966. Reprint ed., New York: Ark, 1988.

Dyer, Richard. *Heavenly Bodies: Film Stars and Society.* New York: St. Martin's Press, 1986.

————. *Stars.* London: British Film Institute, 1979.

Eckert, Charles. "The Anatomy of a Proletarian Film: Warner's *Marked Woman*." In *Movies and Methods II*, edited by Bill Nichols, pp. 407–425. Berkeley: University of California Press, 1985.

Ellis, John. *Visible Fictions: Cinema, Television, Video.* Boston: Routledge & Kegan Paul, 1982.

Erasmus, Desiderius. *The Praise of Folly.* Translated by John Wilson. Ann Arbor: University of Michigan Press, 1971.

Feuer, Jane. *The Hollywood Musical*. Bloomington: Indiana University Press, 1982.

Firestone, Shulamith. *The Dialectic of Sex: The Case for Feminist Revolution*. New York: Bantam, 1970.

Fischer, Lucy. *Shot/Countershot*. Princeton, N.J.: Princeton University Press, 1989.

———. "Sometimes I Feel Like a Motherless Child: Comedy and Matricide." In *Comedy/Cinema/Theory*, edited by Andrew Horton, pp. 60–78. Berkeley: University of California Press, 1991.

Fiske, John. *Understanding Popular Culture*. Boston: Unwin Hyman, 1989.

Foucault, Michel. *Discipline and Punish: The Birth of the Prison*. Translated by Alan Sheridan. New York: Random House, 1979.

French, Brandon. *On the Verge of Revolt: Women in American Films of the Fifties*. New York: Frederick Ungar, 1978.

Freud, Sigmund. *Jokes and Their Relation to the Unconscious*. Translated by James Strachey. New York: W. W. Norton, 1960.

———. *Moses and Monotheism*. In *The Standard Edition of the Complete Psychological Works of Sigmund Freud*, edited and translated by James Strachey et al. 24 vols. 23: 3–137. London: Hogarth Press, 1966–1974.

———. "The Uncanny." In *The Standard Edition of the Complete Psychological Works of Sigmund Freud*, edited and translated by James Strachey et al. 24 vols. 17: 217–256. London: Hogarth Press, 1966–1974.

Frye, Northrop. *Anatomy of Criticism: Four Essays*. Princeton, N.J.: Princeton University Press, 1957.

———. "The Argument of Comedy." In *English Institute Essays, 1948*, edited by D. A. Robertson, Jr., pp. 58–74. New York: Columbia University Press, 1949.

Gaines, Jane. "White Privilege and Looking Relations—Race and Gender in Feminist Film Theory." *Screen* 29.4 (1988): 12–27.

Gehring, Wes D. *Screwball Comedy: A Genre of Madcap Romance*. Contributions to the Study of Popular Culture 13. New York: Greenwood Press, 1986.

Georgatos, Dennis. "When the Fat Lady Sings . . . Some San Diego Padre Fans Are Glad When It's Over." *Eugene* [Oregon] *Register-Guard* July 27, 1991: A1, A4.

Gledhill, Christine. "The Melodramatic Field: An Investigation." In *Home is Where the Heart Is: Studies in Melodrama and the Woman's Film*, edited by Christine Gledhill, pp. 5–42. London: British Film Institute, 1987.

———, ed. *Home Is Where the Heart Is: Studies in Melodrama and the Woman's Film*. London: British Film Institute, 1987.

Goffman, Erving. *Frame Analysis: An Essay on the Organization of Experience*. Boston: Northeastern University Press, 1986.

Grotjahn, Martin. *Beyond Laughter: Humor and the Subconscious*. New York: McGraw-Hill, 1966.

Harris, Marvin. *Cows, Pigs, Wars and Witches: The Riddles of Culture*. New York: Random House, 1974.

Harvey, James. *Romantic Comedy in Hollywood*. New York: Alfred A. Knopf, 1987.

Harvey, Stephen. "Salute to Judy Holliday." *New York Times* October 17, 1982: B1, B28.

Haskell, Molly. *From Reverence to Rape: The Treatment of Women in the Movies.* New York: Holt, Rinehart and Winston, 1974.

Heath, Stephen. "Joan Rivière and the Masquerade." In *Formations of Fantasy*, edited by Victor Burgin, James Donald, and Cora Kaplan, pp. 45–61. New York: Methuen, 1986.

Heilbrun, Carolyn G. *Writing a Woman's Life.* New York: Ballantine, 1988.

Henderson, Brian. "Romantic Comedy Today: Semi-Tough or Impossible?" *Film Quarterly* 31.4 (1978): 11–22.

Henley, Nancy M. *Body Politics: Power, Sex and Non-Verbal Communication.* Englewood Cliffs, N.J.: Prentice-Hall, 1977.

Hicks, Jack. "No Holds Barred." *TV Guide* January 28, 1989: 2–5.

Hirschberg, Lynn. "Don't Hate Me Because I'm Beautiful." *Vanity Fair* December 1990: 182–186+.

Hodge, Robert, and David Tripp. *Children and Television: A Semiotic Approach.* Stanford, Calif.: Stanford University Press, 1986.

Holland, Norman N. *Laughing: A Psychology of Humor.* Ithaca, N.Y.: Cornell University Press, 1982.

Horton, Andrew, ed. *Comedy/Cinema/Theory.* Berkeley: University of California Press, 1991.

Hurtado, Aida. "Relating to Privilege: Seduction and Rejection in the Subordination of White Women and Women of Color." *Signs* 14 (1989): 833–855.

Huston, Nancy. "The Matrix of War: Mothers and Heroes." In *The Female Body in Western Culture*, edited by Susan Suleiman, pp. 119–136. Cambridge, Mass.: Harvard University Press, 1986.

Irigaray, Luce. *This Sex Which Is Not One.* Translated by Catherine Porter. Ithaca, N.Y.: Cornell University Press, 1985.

Jaggar, Alison. *Feminist Politics and Human Nature.* Sussex: Rowman & Allanheld, 1983.

Jameson, Fredric. *The Political Unconscious: Narrative as a Socially Symbolic Act.* Ithaca, N.Y.: Cornell University Press, 1981.

Jenkins, Henry. "'Don't Become Too Intimate With That Terrible Woman!' Gender and Performance in Early Sound Comedy." Unpublished paper. A shorter version was published as "'Don't Become Too Intimate With That Terrible Woman': Unruly Wives, Female Comic Performance and *So Long Letty*." *Camera Obscura* 25–26 (January/May 1991): 202–223.

———. *What Made Pistachio Nuts? Early Sound Comedy and the Vaudeville Aesthetic.* New York: Columbia University Press, 1992.

Jenkins, Linda. "Locating the Language of Gender Experience. *Women and Performance: A Journal of Feminist Theory* 2 (1984): 5–20.

Jerome, Jim. "Roseanne Unchained." *People* October 9, 1989: 84–98.

Johnston, Claire. "Femininity and the Masquerade: *Anne of the Indies*." In *Psycho-*

analysis and Cinema, edited by E. Ann Kaplan, pp. 64–72. New York: Routledge, 1990.

———. "Women's Cinema as Counter-Cinema." In *Movies and Methods*, edited by Bill Nichols, pp. 208–217. Berkeley: University of California Press, 1976.

Jonson, Ben. *Bartholomew Fair*. Edited by E. A. Horsman. The Revels Plays. Cambridge, Mass.: Harvard University Press, 1962.

Joyrich, Lynne. "All that Television Allows: TV Melodrama, Postmodernism, and Consumer Culture." In *Private Screenings*, edited by Lynn Spigal and Denise Mann, pp. 227–252. Minneapolis: University of Minnesota Press, 1992.

Juno, Andrea, and V. Vale, eds. *Angry Women*. San Francisco: Re/search Publications, 1991.

Kaminsky, Stuart. *American Film Genres*. 2nd ed. Chicago: Nelson Hall, 1985.

Kaplan, E. Ann. *Women and Film: Both Sides of the Camera*. London: Methuen, 1983.

Katz, Ephraim. *The Film Encyclopedia*. New York: Harper and Row, 1979.

Kay, Karyn. "*Part-Time Work of a Domestic Slave*, or Putting the Screws to Screwball Comedy." In *Women and the Cinema: A Critical Anthology*, edited by Karyn Kay and Gerald Peary, pp. 311–323. New York: E. P. Dutton, 1977.

Kellner, Doug. *Television and the Crisis of Democracy*. Interventions: Theory and Contemporary Politics. Boulder, Colo.: Westview Press, 1990.

Kinder, Marsha. *Playing With Power in Movies, Television and Video Games: From Muppet Babies to Teenage Mutant Ninja Turtles*. Berkeley: University of California Press, 1991.

Kintz, Linda. "Gendering the Critique of Representation: Fascism, the Purified Body, and Theater in Adorno, Artaud and Maria Irene Formes." *Rethinking Marxism*, Fall 1991: 83–110.

———. "Sacred Representations: Gender and the Religious Right." Paper presented at the Center for the Study of Women in Society, University of Oregon, 1993.

———. *The Subject's Tragedy: Political Poetics, Feminist Theory, and Drama*. Ann Arbor: University of Michigan Press, 1992.

Klaus, Barbara. "The War of the Roseanne." *New York Magazine* October 22, 1990: 92–108.

Kris, Ernst. "Ego Development and the Comic." In *Theories of Comedy*, edited by Paul Lauter, pp. 446–447. New York, Doubleday, 1964.

Kristeva, Julia. *Desire in Language: A Semiotic Approach to Literature and Art*. Edited by Leon S. Roudiez. Translated by Thomas Gora, Alice Jardine, and Leon S. Roudiez. New York: Columbia University Press, 1977.

Krutnik, Frank. "The Clown-Prints of Comedy." *Screen* 25.4–5 (1984): 50–59.

———. "The Faint Aroma of Performing Seals: The 'Nervous' Romance and the Comedy of the Sexes." *Velvet Light Trap* 26 (1990): 57–72.

Kuhn, Annette. *The Power of the Image: Essays on Representation and Sexuality*. Boston: Routledge & Kegan Paul, 1985. 48–73.

Lapsley, Robert, and Michael Westlake. "From *Casablanca* to *Pretty Woman*: The Politics of Romance." *Screen* 33.1 (1992): 27–49.

Lauter, Paul, ed. *Theories of Comedy*. New York: Doubleday, 1964.

Leff, Leonard J. "The Breening of America." *Publication of the Modern Language Association* 106 (1991): 432–445.

Le Roy Ladurie, Emmanuel. *Carnival in Romans*. Translated by Mary Feeney. New York: George Braziller, 1979.

Lesage, Julia. "*Celine and Julie Go Boating*: Subversive Fantasy." *Jump Cut* 24–25 (19): 37–43.

———. "Women's Rage." In *Marxism and the Interpretation of Culture*, edited by Cary Nelson and Lawrence Grossberg. Chicago: University of Illinois Press, 1988. 419–428.

Lippard, Lucy. "Some Propaganda for Propaganda." *Heresies* 3.1 (1980): 35–39.

Lipsitz, George. "The Meaning of Memory: Family, Class, and Ethnicity in Early Network Television Programs." In *Private Screenings*, edited by Lynn Spigal and Denise Mann, pp. 71–110. Minneapolis: University of Minnesota Press, 1992.

Lyotard, Jean François. *The Post-Modern Condition: A Report on Knowledge*. Translated by Geoff Bennington and Brian Massumi. Minneapolis: University of Minnesota Press, 1984.

MacKinnon, Catharine A. *Feminism Unmodified: Discourses on Life and Law*. Cambridge, Mass.: Harvard University Press, 1987.

Mann, Denise. "The Spectacularization of Everyday Life: Recycling Hollywood Stars and Fans in Early Television Variety Shows." In *Private Screenings*, edited by Lynn Spigal and Denise Mann, pp. 41–69. Minneapolis: University of Minnesota Press, 1992.

Marc, David. *Comic Visions: Television Comedy and American Culture*. Boston: Unwin Hyman, 1989.

Mast, Gerald. *The Comic Mask: Comedy and the Movies*. 2nd ed. Chicago: University of Chicago Press, 1979.

May, Elaine Tyler. *Homeward Bound: American Families in the Cold War Era*. New York: Basic Books, 1988.

Maynard, Joyce. "Domestic Affairs." *The Oregonian*. February 11, 1989: C1.

McGhee, Paul E. "The Role of Laughter and Humor in Growing Up Female." In *Becoming Female: Perspectives on Development*, edited by Clair B. Kopp, pp. 183–206. New York: Plenum Press, 1979.

McLeland, Susan. "Reshaping the Grotesque Body: Roseanne, *Roseanne*, Breast Reduction and Rhinoplasty." Paper presented at the Society for Cinema Studies Conference, New Orleans, 1993.

McPherson, Tara. "Disregarding Romance and Forgetting Family: Getting Down and Dirty with the Designing Women." Paper presented at the Society for Cinema Studies Conference, Pittsburgh, 1992.

Medvedev, P. N./Bakhtin, Mikhail. *The Formal Method in Literary Scholarship*. Translated by A. J. Wehrle. Baltimore: Johns Hopkins University Press, 1978.

Mellencamp, Patricia. *High Anxiety: Catastrophe, Scandal, Age & Comedy*. Bloomington: Indiana University Press, 1992.

———. *Indiscretions: Avant-Garde Film, Video, & Feminism*. Bloomington: Indiana University Press, 1990.

———. "Jokes and Their Relation to the Marx Brothers." In *Cinema and Language*, edited by Stephen Heath and Patricia Mellencamp, pp. 63–78. Frederick, Md.: University Publications of America, 1983.

———. "Situation Comedy, Feminism and Freud: Discourses of Gracie and Lucy." In *Studies in Entertainment*, edited by Tania Modleski, pp. 80–95. Bloomington: Indiana University Press, 1986.

Merrill, Lisa. "Feminist Humor: Rebellious and Self-Affirming." In *Last Laughs: Perspectives on Women and Comedy*, edited by Regina Barreca, pp. 271–280. New York: Gordon and Breach, 1988.

Mill, Anna Jean. "Noah's Wife Again." *Publication of the Modern Language Association* 56 (1941): 613–626.

Millman, Marcia. *Such a Pretty Face: Being Fat in America*. New York: W. W. Norton, 1980.

Mirza, Candace. "The Collective Spirit of Revolt: An Historical Reading of *Holiday*." *Wide Angle* 12.3 (July 1990): 98–116.

Miss Piggy's Guide to Life, as Told to Henry Beard. New York: Alfred A. Knopf, 1981.

Mitchell, Elvis. "Smug Trafficking." *The Village Voice* April 25, 1989: 47–48.

Modleski, Tania. *Feminism Without Women: Culture and Criticism in a 'Postfeminist' Age*. New York: Routledge, 1991.

———. *Loving With a Vengeance: Mass-Produced Fantasies for Women*. New York: Methuen, 1982.

———. "The Terror of Pleasure: The Contemporary Horror Film and Postmodern Theory." In *Studies in Entertainment*, edited by Tania Modleski, pp. 155–166. Bloomington: Indiana University Press, 1986.

———. *The Women Who Knew Too Much: Hitchcock and Feminist Theory*. New York: Methuen, 1988.

Morris, Meaghan. "Banality in Cultural Studies." In *Logics of Television*, edited by Patricia Mellencamp, pp. 14–43. Bloomington: Indiana University Press, 1990.

Mulvey, Laura. "Changes: Thoughts on Myth, Narrative and Historical Experience." In *Visual and Other Pleasures*, by Laura Mulvey, pp. 159–176. Bloomington: Indiana University Press, 1989. Originally published in *Discourse* 7 (Fall 1985): 11–30.

———. "Visual Pleasure and Narrative Cinema." In *Visual and Other Pleasures*, by Laura Mulvey, pp. 14–26. Bloomington: Indiana University Press, 1989. Originally published in *Screen* 16 (1975): 6–18.

Murphy, Jeanette. "*A Question of Silence*." In *Films for Women*, edited by Charlotte Brunsdon, pp. 99–108. London: British Film Institute, 1986.

Murphy, Mary, and Frank Swertlow. "The Roseanne Report." *TV Guide* January 4, 1992: 6–13.

Neale, Steve. "The Big Romance or Something Wild?: Romantic Comedy Today." *Screen* 33.3 (1992): 284–299.

Neale, Steve, and Frank Krutnik. *Popular Film and Television Comedy*. New York: Routledge, 1990.

Newcomb, Horace M. "On the Dialogic Aspects of Mass Communication." *Critical Studies of Mass Communication* 1 (1984): 34–50.

O'Connor, John J. "By Any Name, Roseanne is Roseanne is Roseanne." *New York Times* August 18, 1991: B1, B27.

Orbach, Susie. *Fat is a Feminist Issue II*. London: Arrow, 1982.

———. *Hunger Strike: The Anorectic's Struggle as a Metaphor for Our Age*. New York: W. W. Norton, 1986.

O'Shea, Alan. "Television as Culture: Not Just Texts and Readers." *Media, Culture and Society* 11 (1989): 375.

Owen, David. "Looking Out for Kermit." *The New Yorker* 69 (August 16, 1993): 30–43.

Pacteau, Francette. "The Impossible Referent: Representations of the Androgyne." In *Formations of Fantasy*, edited by Victor Burgin, James Donald, and Cora Kaplan, pp. 62–84. New York: Methuen, 1986.

Parker, Patricia. *Literary Fat Ladies: Rhetoric, Gender, Property*. New York: Methuen, 1987.

Penley, Constance. "Feminism, Film Theory and the Bachelor Machine." *m/f* 10 (1985): 39–59.

"People." *Eugene* [Oregon] *Register-Guard* July 1, 1991: A2.

Pershing, Linda. "There's a Joker in the Menstrual Hut: A Performance Analysis of Comedian Kate Clinton." In *Women's Comic Visions*, edited by June Sochen, pp. 193–236. Detroit: Wayne State University Press, 1991.

Polan, Dana. "The Light Side of Genius: Hitchcock's *Mr. and Mrs. Smith* in the Screwball Tradition." In *Comedy/Cinema/Theory*, edited by Andrew Horton. Berkeley: University of California Press, 1991.

———. *Power and Paranoia: History, Narrative, and the American Cinema*. New York: Columbia University Press, 1986.

Pyle, Forest. "One Bad Movie Too Many: Sam Shephard's Visions of Excess." *Velvet Light Trap* 32 (Fall 1993): 13–22.

Rafferty, Terrence. "The Current Cinema: Baser Instincts," *The New Yorker* January 25, 1993: 95–97.

Rhoden, William C. "Sports of the Times: In the Land of the Free." *New York Times* (national ed.), July 31, 1990: B9.

Rich, Adrienne. "Compulsory Heterosexuality and Lesbian Experience." In *Blood, Bread, and Poetry: Selected Prose 1979–1985*, pp. 23–75. New York: W. W. Norton, 1986.

———. *Of Woman Born: Motherhood as Experience and Institution*. New York: W. W. Norton, 1986.

Rich, B. Ruby. "In the Name of Feminist Film Criticism." In *Movies and Methods*

II*, edited by Bill Nichols, pp. 340–358. Berkeley: University of California Press, 1985. (Originally published in *Jump Cut* 19 [1978].)

Rivière, Joan. "Womanliness as Masquerade." In *Formations of Fantasy*, edited by Victor Burgin, James Donald, and Cora Kaplan, pp. 35–44. New York: Methuen, 1986. (Originally published in *The International Journal of Psychoanalysis* 10 [1929].)

Roberts, Shari. "'The Lady in the Tutti-Frutti Hat': Carmen Miranda, a Spectacle of Ethnicity." *Cinema Journal* 32.3 (1993): 3–23.

Robertson, Pamela. "'The Kinda Comedy That Imitates Me': Mae West's Identification With the Feminist Camp." *Cinema Journal* 32.2 (1993): 57–72.

Root, Jane. "Distributing *A Question of Silence*—A Cautionary Tale." In *Films for Women*, edited by Charlotte Brunsdon, pp. 213–223. London: British Film Institute, 1986.

Rose, Barbara. "Is It Art? Orlan and the Transgressive Act." *Art in America* 81.2 (1993): 82–87.

"Roseanne's Shotgun 'Wedding from Hell'; Pregnant Roseanne's Wedding Shambles Goes Off With 101 Hitches." *Star* February 6, 1990: 10–14.

Rosen, Marjorie. *Popcorn Venus*. New York: Avon, 1973.

Rowe, Kathleen K. "Class and Allegory in Jameson's Film Criticism." *Quarterly Review of Film and Video* 12.4 (1991): 1–18.

———. "Romanticism, Sexuality, and the Canon." *Journal of Film and Video* 42.1 (1990): 49–65.

Russell, David J. "Bachelor Machine: Black Maria/False Maria." Paper presented at the Society for Cinema Studies Conference, Iowa City, 1989.

Russo, Mary. "Female Grotesques: Carnival and Theory." In *Feminist Studies, Critical Studies*, edited by Teresa de Lauretis, pp. 213–229. Bloomington: University of Indiana Press, 1986.

Russo, Vito. *The Celluloid Closet: Homosexuality and the Movies*. New York: Harper and Row, 1981.

Ryan, Michael, and Douglas Kellner. *Camera Politica: The Politics and Ideology of Contemporary Hollywood Film*. Bloomington: Indiana University Press, 1988.

Rysman, Alexander. "How the 'Gossip' Became a Woman." *Journal of Communication* 27 (1977): 176–180.

Schatz, Thomas. *Hollywood Genres: Formulas, Filmmaking and the Studio System*. Philadelphia: Temple University Press, 1981.

———. "The Structural Influence: New Directions in Film Genre Study." In *Film Genre Reader*, edited by Barry Keith Grant, pp. 91–101. Austin: University of Texas Press, 1986.

Schechter, Joel. *Durov's Pig: Clowns, Politics and Theatre*. New York: Theatre Communications Group, 1985.

Scheman, Naomi. "Missing Mothers/Desiring Daughters: Framing the Sight of Women." *Critical Inquiry* 15 (1988): 63–89.

Schiesari, Juliana. *The Gendering of Melancholia: Feminism, Psychoanalysis, and the*

Symbolics of Loss in Renaissance Literature. Ithaca, N.Y.: Cornell University Press, 1992.

Seidman, Steve. *Comedian Comedy: A Tradition in Hollywood Film.* Ann Arbor, Mich.: UMI Research Press, 1981.

Seiter, Ellen. "Introduction." In *Remote Control: Television, Audiences and Cultural Power,* edited by Ellen Seiter et al., pp. 1–15. New York: Routledge, 1989.

———, et al. "'Don't Treat Us Like We're So Stupid and Naive': Toward an Ethnography of Soap Opera Viewers." In *Remote Control: Television, Audiences and Cultural Power,* edited by Ellen Seiter et al., pp. 223–247. New York: Routledge, 1989.

Selig, Michael. "*The Nutty Professor*: A 'Problem' in Film Scholarship." *Velvet Light Trap* 26 (1990): 42–56.

Shumway, David. "Screwball Comedies: Constructing Romance, Mystifying Marriage." *Cinema Journal* 30.4 (1991): 7–23.

Silverman, Kaja. "Dis-Embodying the Female Voice." In *Revisions: Essays in Feminist Criticism,* edited by Mary Ann Doane, Patricia Mellencamp, and Linda Williams, pp. 131–149. American Film Institute Monograph Series 3. Frederick, Md.: University Publications of America, 1984.

Solomon, Stanley J. *Beyond Formula: American Film Genres.* New York: Harcourt Brace Jovanovich, 1976.

Spigal, Lynn, and Denise Mann, eds. *Private Screenings: Television and the Female Consumer.* Minneapolis: University of Minnesota Press, 1992.

Stallybrass, Peter, and Allon White. *The Politics and Poetics of Transgression.* Ithaca, N.Y.: Cornell University Press, 1986.

Stam, Robert. "Bakhtin, Eroticism and Cinema." *CineAction!* 9 (1987): 13–20.

———. *Subversive Pleasures.* Baltimore: Johns Hopkins University Press, 1989.

Straayer, Chris. "Redressing the 'Natural': The Temporary Transvestite Film." *Wide Angle* 14.1 (1992): 36–55.

Studlar, Gaylyn. "Masochism, Masquerade, and the Erotic Metamorphosis of Marlene Dietrich." In *Fabrications: Costume and the Female Body,* edited by Jane Gaines and Charlotte Herzog, pp. 229–249. New York: Routledge, 1990.

Suleiman, Susan Rubin. *Subversive Intent: Gender, Politics, and the Avant-Garde.* Cambridge, Mass.: Harvard University Press, 1990.

Thewelheit, Klaus. *Male Fantasies.* Vol. 1. Translated by Stephen Conway. Minneapolis: University of Minnesota Press, 1987.

Thumim, Janet. "The 'Popular,' Cash and Culture in the Postwar British Cinema Industry." *Screen* 32.3 (1991): 245–271.

Todd, Jane Marie. "The Veiled Woman in Freud's 'Das Unheimliche.'" *Signs* 11 (1986): 519–528.

Todorov, Tzvetan. *Mikhail Bakhtin: The Dialogical Principal.* Translated by Wlad Godzich. Minneapolis: University of Minnesota Press, 1984.

Toth, Emily. "Questioning the Quest." (Review of *Writing a Woman's Life,* by Carolyn G. Heilbrun.) *Women's Review of Books* February 1989: 11.

Turim, Maureen. "Gentlemen Consume Blondes." In *Movies and Methods II,* edited by Bill Nichols, pp. 369–378. Berkeley: University of California Press, 1985.

Turner, Victor. "Frame, Flow and Reflection: Ritual and Drama as Public Liminality." In *Performance in Postmodern Culture*, edited by Michel Benamou and Charles Caramello, pp. 33–55. Milwaukee: University of Wisconsin-Milwaukee Press, 1977.

Tyler, Parker. Introduction. In *The Films of Mae West*, by Jon Tuska, pp. 6–16. Secaucus, N.J.: Citadel Press, 1973.

———. *Screening the Sexes: Homosexuality in the Movies*. New York: Holt, Rinehart and Winston, 1972.

Underdown, David E. "The Taming of the Scold: The Enforcement of Patriarchal Authority in Early Modern England." In *Order and Disorder in Early Modern England*, edited by Anthony Fletcher and John Stevenson, pp. 116–136. Cambridge: Cambridge University Press, 1985.

Van Buskirk, Leslie. "The New Roseanne—The Most Powerful Woman in Television"; "Roseanne!" *US* May 1992: 28–36.

Walker, Nancy A. *A Very Serious Thing: Women's Humor and American Culture*. Minneapolis: University of Minnesota Press, 1988.

Waters, Harry F., with Steven Waldman, Daniel Glick, and Kim Fararo. "Rhymes With Rich: A Queen on Trial." *Newsweek* August 21, 1989: 46–51.

Weimann, Robert. *Shakespeare and the Popular Tradition of Theater: Studies in the Social Dimension of Dramatic Form and Function*. Translated by Robert Schwartz. Baltimore: Johns Hopkins University Press, 1978.

West, Mae. *Goodness Had Nothing to Do With It*. New York: Macfadden-Bartell, 1959.

Wexman, Virginia Wright. "Returning from the Moon: Jackie Gleason, the Carnivalesque, and Television Comedy." *Journal of Film and Video* 42.4 (1990): 20–32.

White, E. B., and Katharine S. White. *A Subtreasury of American Humor*. New York: Random House, 1948.

White, Hayden. *Metahistory: The Historical Imagination in Nineteenth-Century Europe*. Baltimore: Johns Hopkins University Press, 1973.

Will, George. "Cities Gleam with Gunfire." Syndicated column in *Eugene* [Oregon] *Register-Guard* August 1, 1990: A15.

Willeford, William. *The Fool and His Scepter: A Study in Clowns and Jesters and Their Audiences*. Chicago: Northwestern University Press, 1969.

Williams, Elsie. "Moms Mabley and the Afro-American Comic Performance." In *Women's Comic Visions*, edited by June Sochen, pp. 158–178. Detroit: Wayne State University Press, 1991.

Williams, Raymond. *Modern Tragedy*. Stanford, Calif.: Stanford University Press, 1966.

Williamson, Judith. *Consuming Passions: Dynamics of Popular Culture*. New York: Marion Boyars, 1986.

Wilt, Judith. "The Laughter of Maidens, the Cackle of Matriarchs: Notes on the

Collision Between Comedy and Feminism." In *Gender and Literary Voice*, edited by Janet Todd, pp. 173–196. New York: Holmes and Meier, 1980.

Winkler, John J. "The Ephebes' Song: *Tragoidia* and *Polis*." *Representations* 11 (1985): 26–61.

Wolcott, James. "On Television: Roseanne Hits Home." *The New Yorker* 26 (October 1992): 123–124.

Wollen, Peter. *Signs and Meaning in the Cinema*. Bloomington: Indiana University Press, 1972.

Wood, Robin. *Howard Hawks*. London: British Film Institute, 1983.

———. "Ideology, Genre, Auteur." *Film Comment* 13.1 (Jan.–Feb. 1977): 46–51.

Woodward, Katherine S. "College Course File: American Film Comedy." *Journal of Film and Video* 42.2 (1990): 71–84.

Woolf, Rosemary. *The English Mystery Plays*. Berkeley: University of California Press, 1972.

Woollacott, Janet. "Fictions and Ideologies: The Case of the Situation Comedy." In *Popular Culture and Social Relations*, edited by Tony Bennett, Colin Mercer, and Janet Woollacott, pp. 196–218. Philadelphia: Open University Press, 1986.

Young, Stark. "What Maisie Knows: Mae West." In *Women and the Cinema*, edited by Karen Kay and Gerald Peary, pp. 90–92. New York: E. P. Dutton, 1977.

Zeitlin, Froma I. "Playing the Other: Theater, Theatricality, and the Feminine in Greek Drama." *Representations* 11 (1985): 63–94.

ndex

Annie Hall, 195, 196, 197, 234n6
Anorexia, 63, 239n18
Anti-intellectualism, 148
Anti-Semitism, 44, 45, 66, 228n15
Apartment, The, 194, 200
Apocalypse Now, 88
Arbuthnot, Lucie, 180
Aristophanes, 148, 234n3, 235n14
Aristotle, 100
Armstrong, Nancy, 45
Arnez, Desi, 77, 81
Arnold, Roseanne, 50–91; abuse experi-
    ences, 20, 54, 66, 214–215, 243–
    244nn1,2,8; and anger, 75–77; as author,
    65–70, 210, 230–231n8; and body, 20, 33,
    36, 37, 54, 59, 60–65, 215–217; career of,
    55–56, 70; and carnivalesque, 32, 60, 85;
    and class, 57, 59, 75, 84, 86, 232n14; and
    dirt/pollution, 64–65; as Diva, 73–75,
    232nn14,15; familiarity of, 217; on femi-
    nism, 230n6; and femininity, 67–68; and
    gender inversion, 55; image changes, 20,
    54, 213–219; Jewish identity of, 66, 216,
    244n4; on Madonna, 244n8; and Mae
    West, 67, 117; and masquerade, 7; and
    media, 56, 57–59, 61, 214, 226n2, 230n5;
    and melodrama, 59, 67; name change, 54,
    56, 215, 229–230n1; national anthem per-
    formance, 3, 32, 50–54, 69, 230nn2,3; and
    prejudice, 19; public ambivalence about,
    10, 56–57, 59–60; "The Roseanne Barr
    Show," 55, 70–73, 231–232n13; and
    speech, 63–64; and stardom, 59–60; and
    television medium, 115, 211; visibility of,
    52–53; as "woman on top," 54–55, 83. *See
    also Roseanne*
Arnold, Tom, 54–55, 56, 73, 218, 231–232n13
Artaud, Antonin, 229n23
Art films, 224n16
Arthur, Jean, 143
Atler, Marilyn Van Derbur, 243n1
Austen, Jane, 134
Auteurism, 101
Avant-garde, 48, 67, 224n14

Backfield in Motion, 56
Bakhtin, Mikhail, 2, 4, 8, 9, 10, 17, 32, 34, 41,
    43–45, 47, 62, 95, 96, 108, 109, 154, 225n23,
    226nn4–6, 228n19
Bakker, Tammy Faye, 33, 58, 233n23
Ball, Lucille, 37, 77, 80, 193, 211
Ball of Fire, 146, 156–161; and *Bringing Up
    Baby*, 151; danger in, 159–160, 174; gender

inversion in, 146, 157; male hero in,
    157–158, 159–160, 190, 197; mother figure
    in, 161, 163; romantic triangle in, 149;
    speech in, 150, 158; unruly woman in, 109,
    119, 156–157, 158–159
Bamber, Linda, 100
Bancroft, Anne, 195
Bankhead, Tallulah, 236n1
Barbara Stanwyck Theatre, The, 156
Barber, C. L., 108
Barr, Geraldine, 231n8
Barr, Roseanne. *See* Arnold, Roseanne
Barreca, Regina, 245n10
Basic Instinct, 194, 217
Bataille, Georges, 43, 46–47, 229n22
Bates, Kathy, 194
Batman, 33
Batman Returns, 33
Baudrillard, Jean, 46, 48
Bellamy, Ralph, 198, 200
Berger, John, 120
Bergman, Ingmar, 242n7
Bergson, Henri, 149
Bergstrom, Janet, 4
Bernardoni, James, 136
Bernhard, Sandra, 233n22
Bevington, David, 38
Bewitched, 81, 89
Bible, 36, 39, 227n9
Big, 103
Big Valley, 156
Bill and Ted's Excellent Adventure, 103
Blonde Venus, 236n1
Body: and carnivalesque, 33–34, 35–38; and
    dirt/pollution, 42, 64–65, 228n19, 229n22;
    and grotesque, 12, 17, 33, 62, 218–219; ma-
    ternal, 33–34, 36, 63, 153, 227n11; Rose-
    anne Arnold's changes, 215–217, 218–
    219; and social control, 61–62; societal
    ideals, 17, 33, 60, 62–63, 64, 65, 142,
    216–217, 239n18; and visibility, 11–12. *See
    also* Fatness
Body of Evidence, 217
Bohème, La, 203, 207, 208, 243n6
Bombeck, Erma, 69, 134
Boosler, Elayne, 70, 72
Bordwell, David, 235n12
Born Yesterday, 100, 171, 172–178, 190,
    243n4; anxiety in, 172–174; class in, 176,
    177; unruly woman in, 109, 136, 175–177,
    211
Boswell, John, 240n3
Bourdieu, Pierre, 47, 64, 229n25

Erasmus, Desiderius, 36, 47
Esquire, 57
Ethnicity. *See* Non-WASP ethnic groups
Euripides, 234n3

Fantasy, 6
Farrow, Mia, 196
Fascism, 45
Fatal Attraction, 98, 194
Father Knows Best, 81
Fatness, 17, 58, 59, 227n11; and carnivalesque, 35–36; and evil, 194; and gender inversion, 27, 29; and power, 37, 49; and social control, 61–63, 64; and speech, 37–38, 62; stigmatization of, 60–61, 62, 76, 230n7; as symptom of victimization, 216, 244n3; and virginity, 134. *See also* Body
Femininity: and body, 34; and composure, 17, 31, 121–122; and cross-dressing, 143, 185; and dirt/pollution, 45; exposure of, 6, 11, 67–68, 180–181; and feminist criticism, 222–223n8; fetishized, 6, 123, 237n7; and heterosexual love, 27, 130, 139–140; loss of ambivalence, 44–46, 228–229n21; male appropriation of, 45–46, 228–229n21; and male hero, 104, 110, 142–143, 196, 197, 211, 242n3; as masquerade, 5–7, 27, 28, 29–30, 117, 119, 182, 183, 218, 222n7, 223n9; and melodrama, 5–6, 11, 96; in 1940s–1950s films, 170; rejection of, 72, 80, 90, 91, 122; and romantic comedy, 96–97; and self-denial, 30; and silence, 125–126; suppression of, 242n3; and violence, 14; and weakness, 138–140. *See also* Gender inversion
Feminism, 75, 89, 244n6; and class/race differences, 15–16, 18, 59, 225n21, 230n6; male appropriation of, 196–197; proletarian, 81, 232n19; and Roseanne Arnold, 66, 81, 232n19; separatist, 16, 112
Feminist criticism, 7, 10, 222–223n8, 237n8; and laughter, 4–5, 43; and psychoanalysis, 4–5, 223nn8,9
Ferris Bueller's Day Off, 103
Fetishism, 6, 123, 155, 237n7
Feuer, Jane, 90
Fields, W. C., 122, 235n14
Film noir, 7, 8, 88, 98, 118
Finley, Karen, 33
Fischer, Lucy, 70, 104, 111
Fiske, John, 48, 57, 62
Fonda, Henry, 161, 162, 167, 181
Fonda, Jane, 65

Fool, 36, 142–143, 206, 239n20
Foucault, Michel, 12, 62, 129
Frankfurt School, 45
Frankie and Johnny, 197
French, Brandon, 170
Freud, Sigmund, 153–154, 229nn21,22, 240n5; on jokes, 6, 68, 69, 102, 105. *See also* Psychoanalysis
Friedan, Betty, 193
Front Page, The, 182
Frye, Northrop, 4, 14, 102, 107–110, 235n14, 237n2

Gable, Clark, 125, 127, 140, 144, 174, 181
Gabor, Zsa Zsa, 58, 226n2, 233n23
Gangster film, 185, 186, 188, 189
Garbo, Greta, 117, 126
Garland, Judy, 74
Gas Food Lodging, 243n8
Gehring, Wes, 237n3
Gender, 26–27; in comedian comedy, 235n11; and cross-dressing, 136, 138; destabilization of, 43, 186–189; Roseanne Arnold's treatment of, 74–75, 85, 86; and subjectivity, 142; in *Sylvia Scarlett*, 137–140. *See also* Cross-dressing; Femininity; Gender inversion
Gender inversion, 35, 55, 118, 210, 218, 241n8; in *Ball of Fire*, 146, 157; and burlesque, 237n5; and chastisement of male hero, 118, 237n3; and ethnicity, 197, 202; and female couple, 181–183; in *It Happened One Night*, 132; and Mae West, 119, 183; and Miss Piggy, 27, 29, 41; in 1940s–1950s films, 170–171, 178, 181–183; in postclassical romantic comedy, 197, 199, 201; and signifiers of unruly woman, 226n3; and speech, 38–39. *See also* Cross-dressing
Genre, 12–13, 71–72, 96, 233n1. *See also* specific genres
Gentlemen Prefer Blondes, 178–183, 233n23; class in, 131, 176; gender inversion in, 171, 181–183, 241n8; genre of, 178, 184; sexuality in, 179–180; unruly woman in, 117, 171, 180–181
Georgatos, Dennis, 51
George Burns and Gracie Allen Show, The, 81
Gere, Richard, 198
Ghost, 197, 231n12
Gilda, 171
Gleason, Jackie, 33, 233n21
Gledhill, Christine, 98, 111
Godard, Jean-Luc, 97–98

189; education of, 131–132, 157, 164; and fear, 203–204, 205; and femininity, 104, 110, 142–143, 196, 197, 211, 242n3; and genres of order, 100; melodramatization of, 194–200, 242n2; and moral righteousness, 175; as pedant, 147, 148, 197, 240n2; and phallus, 149–150, 159–160; restoration of, 156, 157, 193, 241n8; rigidity of, 149, 163–164; and sexuality, 127–128; and tragedy, 97, 98; weakness of, 137–138. *See also* Chastisement of male hero

Male impersonation. *See* Cross-dressing

Manhattan, 195, 196, 242n2

Mann, Denise, 80–81

Mansfield, Jayne, 171

Marc, David, 77

Marcos, Imelda, 58, 233n23

Marginalization. *See* Liminality

Marriage, 79, 114, 125, 126, 135–136, 177–178, 183, 238n10. *See also* Heterosexual love

Married with Children, 33, 59

Marshall, Garry, 197

Martha Raye Show, The, 80

Martin, Dean, 192

Marx, Karl, 108

Marx Brothers, 104, 105–106

Mary of Scotland, 239n17

Mary Poppins, 234n6

Mary Tyler Moore Show, The, 77

Masculinity. *See* Male hero

M*A*S*H, 77, 233n21

Masquerade, 18, 155, 182, 218; femininity as, 5–7, 27, 28, 29–30, 117, 119, 182, 183, 218, 222n7, 223n9. *See also* Cross-dressing

Matriarch, 105–106

May, Elaine, 67

Maynard, Joyce, 59, 230n6

McGhee, Paul E., 231n10

McLeland, Susan, 216

Medieval drama, 36–39, 47–48, 226n12

Medusa, 9–11, 14, 224nn14,15

Medvedev, P. N., 95

Meet John Doe, 237n9

Mellencamp, Patricia, 1, 69, 224n13, 232n18

Melodrama, 4, 13, 224n12, 235n13, 242n7; disdain for, 29–30; femininity in, 5–6, 11, 96; and feminist criticism, 4, 5, 6; formal antecedents of, 233–234n3; and post-classical romantic comedy, 192, 194–200, 201, 208, 211, 243n8; and romantic comedy, 110–114, 167–168, 238n15; and Roseanne Arnold, 59, 67; vs. tragedy, 98–99, 233–234n3; transformation of, 14–15; and

women as objects of laughter, 59; women's anger in, 7, 8

Menander, 235n14

Menstruation, 64–65

Meredith, George, 134

Mère Folle, 36

Merman, Ethel, 106

Merrill, Lisa, 100

Merrill, Robert, 51

Metcalf, Laurie, 83–84

Midler, Bette, 33, 113

Mildred Pierce, 112

Mill, Anna Jean, 227n13

Millman, Marcia, 230n7

Mimesis, 223n9

Miranda, Carmen, 123

Misery, 42, 194

Misogyny, 45, 195, 227n10, 229n22; and body, 34, 63; and comedy, 68, 101, 102, 105–106, 195. *See also* Women as objects of laughter

Miss Piggy: aggressiveness of, 3, 27, 28, 29, 30, 37, 38; antecedents of, 30, 117, 210; body of, 27, 29, 33, 36, 48–49; and gender, 26–27, 29, 41; and liminality, 41

Mitchell, Elvis, 59

Modern Times, 124

Modleski, Tania, 7, 18–19, 63, 196–197

Monkey Business, 171, 241n8

Monroe, Marilyn, 67, 171, 179–180, 244n8; and Mae West, 117, 119, 178, 179, 180, 184, 211

Monty Python, 104, 105

Moonstruck, 10, 100, 108, 200–209, 234n6, 236n16; genre of, 192, 202, 208, 211; opening scenes of, 191–192; resolution in, 161

Morris, Meaghan, 228n20

Mother, 113–114, 204–205, 239n20; absence of, 111, 126, 137, 238n12; body of, 33–34, 36, 63, 153, 227n11; and fear, 153, 240n5; hostility toward, 105–106, 235n13; and male masochism, 120, 237n4; power of, 195, 240n7; and romantic comedy, 111–112, 163, 236n17

Mother Folly, 36, 227n8

Motion Picture Production Code, 116, 128–129, 169–170, 236n1

Mr. Deeds Goes to Town, 237n9

Mr. Smith Goes to Washington, 237n9

Mrs. Noah, 37, 38–39, 47, 227n13

Ms., 230n6

Mulvey, Laura, 8, 25, 107, 237n4

Muppet Movie, The, 27, 28, 29

14, 233n23; marketing of, 13, 224n16; Oedipal paradigm in, 224–225n18